Published by:

National Association for Public Safety

please visit us on the web at:
www.napsusa.org

or contact us at:
hallopeter@sunrise.ch

© Copyright 2016 Sherman D. Manning

ISBN 978-0-9743260-9-2

No part of this book may be reproduced, scanned, or distributed in any printed or electronic form without the author's written permission. This is a non-fiction book and the author is solely responsible for the contents.

Contact the A&M (*Andrist & Manning*) consulting firm at hallopeter@sunrise.ch. See http://gbgod.blogspot.com.

Cover design by A&M Enterprises
Attorney Robert D. Blasier, Robert Shapiro, and O.J. Simpson

# Other Books By Sherman D. Manning

*Reach Beyond The Break and Hold On*

*Dream and Grow Rich*

*Teens Are Dying/Parents Are Crying*

*Blue Eyed Blonde (fiction)*

*Blue Eyed Blonde Book II*

*Kids Killing Kids (KKK)*

*American Dream, A Search For Justice*

*From the Palace to the Prison*

*Creating Monsters*

*Left for Dead*

*Bad Boys*

*Don't Mess With Texas*

*Congressional Terrorists*

*America's Richest Pedophiles*

*Why Republicans Go To Hell*

*Cracking the Code to Criminal Justice in the 21$^{st}$ Century*

*The Obama Project (Why We Can't Fail)*

See your local bookstore, E-Books, Amazon.com, www.NAPSUSA.org, or www.ShermanDManning.com.

# TABLE OF CONTENTS

| | Page |
|---|---|
| About The Author | 4 |
| Strategic Response Team | 7 |
| Joseph Stratton | 10 |
| Attorney Robert Blasier | 13 |
| Alec Loorz | 15 |
| Judge Allison Claire | 24 |
| How To Get Away With Murder | 29 |
| Congressman Elijah Cummings | 30 |
| Robert Shapiro | 37 |
| A Nation of Cowards | 40 |
| Behind the Scenes with F. Lee Bailey | 45 |
| Andy Wu and UC Berkeley | 49 |
| John Grisham | 51 |
| Jacob Paske | 54 |
| The Truth About O.J. Simpson | 57 |
| Long Walk To Freedom | 154 |
| The Sherman D. Manning Speaker's Bureau | 162 |
| Never Quit | 165 |
| The Killers Amongst Us | 166 |
| How You Can Help | 173 |
| Empire: Mass Incarceration | 176 |
| Mass Incarceration: 2016 | 178 |
| The Barack Obama Project | 182 |
| American Crime Stories | 183 |
| Epilogue | 185 |

# About the Author

*Sherman D. Manning* is a professional motivational speaker, author and entrepreneur. He is an expert in criminal justice, prison politics, police brutality, prison guard corruption, free speech, criminal gangs and psychological institutionalization. Prior to his *wrongful* conviction he was mentored (as an ecclesiastical prognosticator) by (civil rights legend) *Rev. Hosea Williams* and Ambassador *Andrew Young*. Rev. Williams stated that, "*Rev. Sherman D. Manning* is the *Martin Luther King Jr.* of the pulpit…He's an eloquent orator."

Harvard Law School graduate *Bob Blasier* states that, "*Sherman* might be the most brilliant client I've had in 44 years as a lawyer. I hope criminal justice and criminal law professors (i.e. Harvard, Columbia, Stanford and Yale etc.) around the world will invite him to lecture at their institutions. I've received more calls (from judges and pastors etc.) regarding *Sherman* than I have of any of my clients (with the exception of *O.J. Simpson*)." Blasier continues, "I hope that *Sherman* and I can promote his book together and perhaps do some interviews together…"

*Sherman* founded G.B.G. (*Gang Bangers* for *God*) and he's also the president of *NAPS*. His consulting company will produce CDs, podcasts and other products for college and law school students and professors. Upon his exit from prison he makes his home in Atlanta, Georgia and Richmond, Virginia (with a satellite office in Zürich Switzerland). To schedule *Sherman* for a lecture, speech, college, association or church event etc. email him at ShermanDManning@Gmail.com.

Rev. Sherman Manning with Rev. Hosea Williams (sitting)

and in a nursing home in Switzerland

Sherman preaching in a church in Atlanta Georgia

Sherman Manning and Peter Andrist

John L. Burton Ex-California Senate President pro Tem

# Strategic Response Team

I was placed in the worst part of the prison at P.V.S.P. after I got out of the hospital. One would think that after a 14 month hospitalization and being near death – prison authorities would have a little mercy. Yet Marion E. Spearman (my black homeboy) and Captain Shannon (also an African American) placed me in a hole within a hole. It was called "the dungeon." It's an enclosed part of the hole in which 13 or 14 cells are partitioned off in concrete. You can't see or hear anyone.

Now I'd been near death and I was recuperating from a deadly disease. And ISIS (aka CCPOA, aka prison authorities) decided that I should be placed in a part of the prison where I could not be heard if I yelled for a nurse. I shall repeat that prison guards are the coldest, most vicious and evil folks I've ever encountered in my lifetime. The guards at P.V.S.P. who guarded me at the hospital tortured me. People such as T. Negrete, D. L. Criner, C.O. Merreilles, etc…

I recall one time I coded and nearly died. And as Dr. Glade Roper (the son of a judge; Roper is an awesome physician) alerted the trauma team that they were losing me I looked at a female guard by the name of Daly. And she was smiling; hoping I'd die. C.O. Merreilles berated and belittled me so badly that one night a black female doctor threatened to have him removed. She told me he was running my blood pressure up and threatening my life. "If I need to call your watch commander and have you personally banned from doing overtime at this hospital I will," she told him. "And I'll call my union," he replied…

I remember wondering "What have I done to those guards? I don't even know them." And I got my answer one night from a black guard from Louisiana. C.O. Linda Forte told me, "Don't you die on me boy. These white folks want your black ass to die because you expose them in your books. Don't give them the satisfaction of seeing you die"… A white nurse on a motor scooter told me, "My name is Mary Bell. I can see you're in a lot of pain. I have a group of women who meet once a week for prayer. We are going to pray for you." I had to fight tears; to juxtapose her love with the hatred of ISIS…

I've been in prison over a decade. And the only time I've been placed in a cell with no water, no mattress, no heat, no toilet paper and no clothing was at P.V.S.P. and it was ordered by Black Atlantan – Marion E. Spearman. I nearly froze to death. And remember I was recuperating from Valley Fever. We talk a lot about race in this country. But the Uncle Tomahawks like Marion, Captain Walker (at P.V.S.P. He was a buddy of Marion's), Sergeant Holloway, etc. have proven to me that anybody can do evil. And there are some Black Hitlers also. Quite frankly I believe that the kind of abuse and human rights violations I've seen in prisons can create terrorists. This kind of abuse can cause persons to rise up against authorities. Because guys like Marion are operating in official capacities as government officials… When I was at the hospital near death, C.O. Tasi placed me in five point restraints on orders from Marion E. Spearman…

I want to form a *Strategic Response Team*. When people are abused by police officers or prison guards etc. SRT can help them. I need *you* (the reader) to help us form this team…

*Cell extractions* are supposed to be for emergencies only. These are done to forcefully remove an inmate from a cell in an emergency, i.e. if an inmate refuses to exit his cell but is threatening to kill himself. Eight guards will put on helmets, pads and boots. And they will pepper-spray the inmate. And then rush in with a shield and throw him to the floor. Then cuff him and drag him out. You'll hear them yelling, "Quit resisting" over and over. They do this to justify beating the inmate. But cell extractions are dangerous and violent. And they are only authorized for emergency only.

…At P.V.S.P. I had a rules hearing and was found guilty of calling Spearman an "Uncle Tom." The Lieutenant said, "You will lose your T.V. for 30 days." When I was in the cell a guard came to the door to get the T.V. and I refused to give it to him. Marion E. Spearman ordered a cell extraction. I asked him, "How many inmates have been extracted to get a T.V.?" He replied, "You're gonna be the first one." As a Valley Fever patient they're not to use pepper-spray on me. They indeed attacked, pepper-sprayed and extracted me to get a T.V. It was clearly not an "emergency."

…But David said to Saul, "Your servant used to keep his father's sheep, and when a lion or a bear came and took a lamb out of the flock, I went out after it and struck it and delivered the lamb from its mouth; and when it arose against me, I caught it by its beard, and struck and killed it. Your servant has killed both lion and bear… The Lord who delivered me from the paw of the lion and from the paw of the bear, He will deliver me from the hand of the Philistine…" And Saul said to David, "Go and the Lord be with you!" (I Samuel 17:34-37).

Everything that David went through in his life *prepared* him to slay the giant Goliath. In retrospect you may ought to go back and *kiss* the bear and the lion because they prepared "you" for the next… I'm convinced that everything "you" have gone through in your life was preparation for your destination. David was not a trained soldier. But he used what he learned by kicking a lion and a bear's butt to defeat a giant.

We know that Joseph spent 13½ years in a prison for a sex crime. And every minute, hour, day, week, month and year he spent in that prison prepared him to become the Prince of Egypt. From a prisoner to a prince? Mr. Mandela spent 27 years in prison and when he got out he…the prison prepared Mr. Mandela for the presidency. From a prisoner to a president? If I read Mr. Mandela's story in a fiction tome I'd say it's too unrealistic… Ipso Facto, I've come to believe that everything we go through is preparation. Not one thing we have gone through was by accident. Sometimes we act like we think God is making this up as He goes. But God has considered our future as He has our past. And everything we did not get. The stuff we wanted and missed. The people who hurt us and mistreated us. It is all the lion and the bear that has prepared us to kick Goliath's ass. So…

I look back on how they tortured me. I think about how ISIS (The CCPOA, J. Stratton, R. Wenker, Bunnell, etc.) are treating me right now. I look at my prison and I now know that God is preparing me for something. Maybe (seriously) I'll be hosting "virtual" criminal justice classes on the internet. Perhaps I'll establish a US Commission on Criminal Justice for the president. I'll lecture at Stanford, Harvard, UC Berkeley, Morehouse, Emory, Clark Atlanta and Yale etc. about torture, abuse and human rights violations in jail.

But God did not let me be put in a "dungeon" by a black man for nothing. Maybe God is getting me ready to lecture on the evils of black-on-black crime. Perhaps I need to give seminars on gangs. The most powerful gang in California is *ISIS*. Our *ISIS* is the *CCPOA*. If the DEA knew how many prison gangs run drugs, cell phones and porn etc. into prisons etc. they'd forget about the Mexican Mafia. The Bloods and the Crips pale in comparison to the Green Wall. And the twin demon gang is the *Thin Blue Line*: LAPD. The most well armed gang/militia in the state? The LAPD! You saw them murder Christopher Dorner for crossing them. You saw them shoot up a truck (with two women in it) just because it was the same color as the truck driven by Dorner.

America has a violence problem. As our militarized police departments perpetuate that violence when they (routinely) murder citizens on the streets. And…the torture I've gone through prepared me to tell my readers that we must organize a Strategic Response Team… And I don't want to put it all out there on paper. Let's do it… I want Ben (24 from Waverly, IA), Cody and Hayden Voss (from Big Brother 2014) etc. on the team… Readers need to reach Jais Malcolm, Vincent Thompson, Nick Prugo, Jesus Ayala (in Colusa), Nick Ecker, Nick Topete, Nick Pelham, Mark Kashirets, Zack Everhart, Teddy Coffee, Casey Askew, Emilio Pech, Will Rains, Attorney Mike Rains, Paola Najera, Kristen Wagaman, Kenan Gebiz, Josh Lyle, Keenan Harris, Jose Sangria, Caleb Light, Caleb Lamb, Lil Kano, Jacob Faulkenber, Kent Boyd, Aaron Kelly and Cody Baetge forthwith. Tell them I want them on my team. Call *Miranda's Thrift Shop* and tell *Esteban* Miranda I need him. I need Leila Knox, Ben Pavone and Joshua Scannell.

We must respond to the crisis caused by ISIS… Deadly guards (i.e. Mike Jiminez, J. Stratton, M. Bunnell etc.) create monsters… And the monsters will come home to roost. How many men who are going to Syria to team with ISIS were in prison?... Read this book and learn *The Truth About O. J.* (and *No J*) Simpson… Sherman D. Manning January 2015

# Joseph Stratton

    He is mentioned in various parts of this book. He's a functionally illiterate, corrupted duplicitous and wicked prison guard. He's willing to break any rule, break laws and commit crimes to punish the people whom he dislikes. People like Joe fill the ranks of the "Green Wall" (aka CCPOA or 723) throughout the California prison system. And they are propped up by a judicial system which covers for them. C.D.C. makes it almost impossible for an inmate to get a lawsuit into court. And on the rare occasion that an inmate gets his case into court the guards own the court. I talk about that in this book…

    At this very moment (in November and December of 2014 etc.) I'm placed in another "box." I've had an ultimatum forced upon me. "Accept a celly or get transferred," per Stratton. And whatever celly I have (when you read this) is a celly at risk. If anyone in the prison system deserves, requires and needs single cell status it is me. But the fact of the matter is they have their fingers crossed. It took me a long time to realize that A. W. Ross Meier, Mike Jimenez, Marion Spearman etc. these guys want me to get attacked, beat or murdered by a celly. That is why (as you read this) I have a celly…

    Stratton placed inmate Garcia into the cell with inmate David Hernandez in 2012. Several guards told Stratton that Garcia had a history of in-cell assaults and Hernandez was an old man with a cane. Stratton said, "Well good; maybe he'll kill him." A week after Stratton put Garcia in the cell he attacked Hernandez in his sleep and nearly killed him. If my celly and I had not been awake (at 1:30 a.m.) so I could kick the door and get the guards etc. David might be dead. When they responded it took them an hour and many minutes to finally drag David out of the cell. He could have bled to death…

    Stratton wants my current celly to attack me. And… My ultimatum is to "accept" him or go to Ad-Seg and if I go to Ad-Seg I'll be transferred (by Meiers) with deliberate speed. Readers ought to call State Senators (in California) and ask them to clean up corrections. As long as the Joseph Stratton types are able to run prisons with no oversight etc. they'll continue to produce killers. We have folks like Lieutenant Kukrall and Mike Jiminez etc. running the nation's largest prison system and these guys are racist backwoods hillbillies. And these are the guys who would assassinate President Obama if they could get a chance. I'm in a system which suffers from systemic and institutional racism… Jimmy Kimmel doesn't fare much better. Jimmy has absolutely no (zero) blacks working for him. And C.D.C. has very few working for them. I saw 43 C.D.C. cadets yesterday. 37 were white, 4 Mexican and 2 were black. C.D.C. doubles as "Ferguson, Missouri"…

    I laugh when I see the backwoods hillbilly guards announce that they are Republicans. These guys earn $60 grand per year. A lot of them earn $100 grand per year but they work 70 – 80 hours per week to do so. But they don't understand politics. I can count prison guards who are functionally literate on one hand and have fingers remaining. They're not well informed. I talked to a guard the other day who had no idea that Colorado has legalized recreational marijuana use. Same guard said, "I've never heard the term" no pun intended. "Wow!" But he is "conservative in my politics, my religion and in my sexuality." If I told him he'd get better tax cuts under a Democratic regime because he's not wealthy he'd faint. If I told him he's part of the 47% Mitt Romney spoke of he'd be heartbroken. If I told him he is what Paul Ryan called a "taker" he'd be lost…

But Republicans like Ted Cruz (and Cruz will try to run for President in 2016. Although – since he was born in Canada he can't run. See my book "*Don't Mess With Texas*" for more on Cruz) and Paul Ryan consistently re-tweak their "words" to try to convince the ill-informed. I'm amazed when I see Republican analysts give big speeches about how they need to change "how" they "say" things. But Paul Ryan and company never say "perhaps we need to change our position on immigration, voting rights and on guns etc…"

…I need you readers to be gladiators (aka "Shermanators") for me and contact these people whom I can't reach. Please find Teddy Coffee, Emilo Pech, Max Hodges, Casey Askew, Paola Najera, Dave Jessop, Kristen Wagaman, Kenan Gebiz, Josh Lyle, Matt Prokop, Bobby Mitchell, Jr. (in N. Chelmsford, MA), Tiffany Lapham, Alex Karlsen, Jonathan Godinez, Daniel Swain, Oswaldo Hernandez, Steven Schultz, Stephen Wilheim, Ryan (the barista at Pete's Coffee House who was on Jimmy Kimmel), Zach Murray, Joshua James, John Joshua Daniel, Tyson Lee Hull Jr., Jordan Bianco, Dillon Banionis, Daniel Coverston, Jack Dale, Matt Clunie, Raider Runner, Chris Austad, Dylan Heath, Andrew Jerbrink, Jeff Gerber, Nick Simmons, Peter Nowalk, Shane Bruce, Daniel Jensen, Michael Hernbroth, Matt Holbrook, Brittney Cooper, Bryan Butler, Tyler Fehr, Ryan Fehr, Bradley Raiford, *Brooks Randolph*, *Phong Vo*, M. Hiscel, David Pate, Max Steele, Tyler Batterson (Ottumua, Iowa), Rev. Willis Johnson, Cameron Polom, Dan Childs (at ABC) and Collin Finnerty. Contact them and tell them they are in this book. They should email me asap… Jais Malcolm, Nick Prugo, Nick Pelham, Will Stabler, Robert James Carlson, Travis Shaw, Trevor Loflin and Trevor Law…

…When I saw trooper Sean Groubert shooting Levar Jones I thought about Joseph. Trooper Sean would still be shooting black men if he had not been caught on camera. In policing and in prisons we still have severe systemic and institutional racism. And we must address it with deliberate speed. But time and again we see where black cops (and prison guards) will treat or beat black inmates even worse than white ones will. So we have to make some complex and systemic changes in corrections and in policing. Unless we wish to continue "*creating monsters*"… I could lecture at Harvard, Morehouse, Stanford, Emory and at Yale regarding the segregation and racism in jail which retards prisoners. I repeat: To enter a California prison in 2015, 2016 – 2020 etc. where there is still systemic cell segregation destroys men. And it inhibits and retards their ability to adapt to societal norms upon discharge…

How can a person come into a "time machine" and live (if you call this living) for 10 – 15 years? Reside in an environment where blacks must cell with blacks and whites must cell with whites etc. And beyond the racial celling we have subsets or a kind of sectarianism. A black can't cell with just "any" black. He must cell with a black from his gang. The Mexican, Asian and white inmates are also housed accordingly. This housing is mandatory and prison authorities promote it; while simultaneously swearing to the courts that "there is no segregation in C.D.C." Prison administrators are pathological liars…

I want to conduct workshops, academies, clinics, conferences and seminars on these issues. I'd like to go to Emory University, Clark Atlanta, Georgia Tech, Harvard and U.C. Berkeley etc. and give presentations which explain how prisons retard inmate's ability to reintegrate into society. And we must examine what can be done to ameliorate this problem. These are issues which ought to be examined by the United States Congress. And I intend to talk about it on radio stations and in interviews etc. across this country. I hope Ryan Ferguson, Christopher Bird, Brian Banks and Daniel Kovarbasich will join me…call 916-321-3000 and ask C.D.C. to fire correctional guard Joseph Stratton. C.O. Reyes (guards call him Ghetto Reyes) watched Stratton slam an inmate's head into a cage. Reyes refused to snitch Stratton out. And they fired Reyes. Stratton's dad (George) helped I.A. decide to put the blame on Reyes. I wish I knew how to reach Reyes. Anybody know how?...

# **Attorney Robert D. Blasier**

    Barry Scheck, Peter Neufeld and Bob Blasier are the best 3 DNA experts in the world. Bob graduated from Harvard Law School. I've known Bob for many years and he's assisted me for years. Bob has also represented me in my lawsuit against C.D.C. Bob became so outraged by our stolen, destroyed, delayed, missing and interrupted mail etc. that he left the lawsuit… I've spent hundreds of hours with Bob on the telephone. He's a great lawyer. And his wife Charlotte Blasier is a brilliant private investigator.

    When Johnnie Cochran was alive I routinely corresponded with Mr. Cochran. I've also corresponded with Carl Douglas and F. Lee Bailey (not to mention my many correspondences with Gerry Spence…). But although I mention Bob in various places in this book, Bob is responsible for "none" of my O. J. Simpson data. And Bob (for the record) contributed "absolutely nothing to this book". Yet, I'd defer to Bob on interviews. Not because he "supports" (he might not?) this book. But because he has an encyclopedic knowledge of the O. J. Simpson case. So if this book makes you want to talk O. J. you should call Bob Blasier. Bob is the man…

Attorney Robert D. Blasier with Johnnie Cochran

Attorney Robert D. Blasier with Sherman D. Manning

# **Alec Loorz**

Alec is a terrific young man and he's the partner that should have been… (We'll talk about Alec in a moment. I need readers to locate the following folks: Alisa Block, Daniel Jensen, Daniel Jennings (Tiburon, CA), Ian Webb, Dan Abramson, *Alex Adame*, Jordan Adams, Jack Dale, Matt Clunie, Michael Dennis, (Grapevine, Texas), Steven Sowards, Roger Walthorn, Charles Lutz, John Foraker, Cody Baetge, Cameron Messindes, Weaton Clark, Tucker Hipps, Andrew Lohse, Jake Greene, David Hellyer, Cameron Polom, Steve and McKenzie Schultz (Iowa), Nick Fink, Justin Brewer, *Logan Paul*, Jesse Thompson (Stockton, CA), Bobby Mitchel, Jr., Devin Dwyer, Ryan Jeeter, Blake White, Thomas Burk (Ft. Worth, TX), Loic Hostetter, Austin Ho, Adam, Rachel, Michelle, Leslie and Matt Shepard, Nate Walejeski, Eugene Langford, David Joyner (in Georgia), Sam Fuick, Kenan Gebiz, Esteban Miranda, Charles Chad Pocher, Peter Nowalk, Michael Hernbroth, Jordan Bianco, Justin Frazier, David Reynolds (Chesterfield, VA), Nathan Hand, Tyler Batterson, Ralph Cannon, Eddie Cannon, Ronald Wright, Joey Grissett, Eric Sarnello, Josh Scannell and Mike Corsetto. Find Dillon Banionis, Tyler Grady, Tim Urban and Victor Smalley. And tell them to contact me…). If they contact me I would hope their experience is not like that of Alec Loorz.

I wrote Alec regarding my books several years ago. He went to my website and wrote back to me. He wrote, "Sherman I think what you're doing is amazing work and I'm going to read your book and…" When C. O. Couch read the missive from Alec (prison officials can read any of our mail. And since I write about their malfeasance they read everything which I write) to me he decided to block it. He telephoned the Loorz's family to turn them against me. He basically claimed, "He's a dangerous predator (i.e. molester) and Alec should not write to him ever." And…had I been the recipient of that call I, too, would have been alarmed. But if *Alec* is reading this Ryan lied to you. They hate me because I expose them. I want Alec to keep up the great work and I hope he'll drop me a line…

"You can never solve a problem at the level of thinking in which it was created." The problem(s) of judicial bias, correctional malfeasance and police brutality etc. will never be solved by mere internal investigations. It's hard to examine the picture when you are in the frame. I want the people (i.e. Alec Loorz, Alec Torres, Zack Torres, Josiah Lemming and Joshua Wotila etc.) outside to look inside these prisons. I want Cody Freisen, Alex Blench, Trevor Day, Timothy Goebbel, Gabe Herrington, John Garvin, Christopher Durbin (his family used to own a skating rink in GA), Marvin Stone, John Jodie Bear, Alexander Dugdale and Brian Devin Graham etc. to look in. And when you see what goes on inside these houses of horror you'll understand why they produce such broken, dysfunctional and evil misfits. The inmates are running the asylum? The inmates are the asylum. And I want to talk to political science and global studies classes about this. I want to talk to Max Wiseltier, Nathan Beckopec, Greg Pugh, Sean Zane, Joshua Orapello, Sam Cox and Timothy Hill etc.

…I will go on a crusade of sorts. It will be a nationwide campaign. And a campaign is like war. And…once I became aware that the courts (Allison Claire) were going to allow Ryan Wenker, Layton Johnson and others to get away with stealing my Valley Fever lawsuit.

When I found out that absolutely nobody would be held accountable for intentionally exposing me to Valley Fever due to retaliation; *this means war*... If prison officials are bold, arrogant and pompous enough to steal "my" mail and to try to kill me? What won't they do? There are guys who can't defend themselves. And they get dogged, beat, tortured and raped (figuratively as well as literally) by guards. And nobody helps them. I intend to be their mouthpiece. I'll be their flashlight. I won't let America forget about the 2.7 million people who are trapped in correctional quicksand...

Michael Gorman? I won't let you forget that he was raped by his celly (after begging to be moved), killed and had a T.V. guide shoved up his butt... I'll ask Ronald Cotton, Daniel Kovarbasich, Christopher Bird, Ryan Ferguson, Derek King and Marcus Dixon to help me tell this story. It's an incredible story... Mark Kashirets (I'm unsure of the spelling of his last name). He should be a nurse in Sacramento. We need to reach him. Jeremy Hudson, Joshua Stipp, Ian Webb and... We demand justice... They (C.D.C.) tried to kill me. But God said no. And because He spared my life I can remind you of Gary Webb. (Get the DVD "Killing The Messenger"). He was blacklisted because of what he wrote. I hope his son Ian Webb will read this book. I salute his father...

I'm living in a zoo and somebody benefits from my captivity. And everybody has some kind of cage. There are emotional, spiritual and psychological cages. And sometimes your experiences validate your cage. My writing can even be a cage. But I can't stay in this cage. I can't stay in this trauma and in this bondage. I will come out of this cage by any means necessary... Speaking for professors Bryan Stevenson, Michelle Alexander, Cornel West, Michael Eric Dyson and Charles Ogletree etc. will be my new opportunity and a chance for a new start. And I will go forward. If I have to call Steve Harvey, Floyd Mayweather, Tyler Perry, Jeff Deskovic or Byron Allen etc. I will call them and say, "Help me." I will not stay in this cage. To you who read I say get me out of this cage!...

One day I hope I can share a platform with *Alec Loorz*, Jimbo Spalding, Alex Hayes and Nathan Hand etc. I want Luke Johnson (Richmond, VA), David Moton (could be Morton but he's in Richmond also) and Curtis Sykes to join us. We must fight against the correctional terrorism inside American Gulags. ...A young white guy once told me that "since people and police treat all black men as potential and probable criminals, why don't they treat white men as potential and probable child molesters?" A white guy asked me this. He said he knew most white guys are child molesters. Yet, nobody criminally or racially profile white men...

And...I want to work with Sean Dunne, Jeff Gerber, Alexander Berki, Alex Weinberg, Alex Bernhart, Jaron Brandon and Barry Gibbs... I want to work with you... (As an aside: Donald Trump is a very good friend of Phillip Bradbury...Google Bradbury). ...I want Justin Birkhead, Ryan Jeeter, Cody Harlton, Allen Swift, Gabe Barajus, Gabe Teague and Dave Jessop to get this book...! The *Gangbangers* for *God* has awarded Attorney Robert Borrelle (in Berkeley, CA) with our "*Man of the Year*" award. We salute and applaud Robert. He is a brilliant, compassionate and powerful disability lawyer. The 2300 females in *G.B.G.* asked us to publish a picture of Attorney Borrelle in a *speedo* in this book. That's not gonna happen (LOL). Perhaps we will on our website so stay tuned...

On October 1, 2014 I was awakened by an I.S.U. prison guard. He was returning to me a confidential request which I'd mailed to the warden. Warden Macomber obviously sent the request to Lieutenant Faris with I.S.U. And rather than Faris responding in a confidential manner he handed his reply to a low level guard and told him to bring it to me. But this is how the Green Wall works… The photos in this tome (in underwear only) are of a prison guard who (as I wrote) was involved in some rapes. He is no longer at this prison. His name was in the request. Their plan was to leak his name. So when a person close to him (i.e. a relative or a friend) finds out inmates have accused this guy of "rape," they can *transfer* me and state that it's for my own safety. What's more? When the guy was committing the rapes the inmate filed a 602 and gave it to Lieutenant Nielson. Nielson shredded it…

On July 15, 2014 I mailed (for the victim) a confidential 602 to Warden Macomber regarding the rapes. And…two months later that appeal had disappeared also. Why? If the inmate tries to sue the guard for rape Kellie Hammond etc. will argue that the inmate did not "exhaust." Although reporting it to I.S.U. and writing the I.G. and writing Assemblyman Tom Ammiano and Congresswoman Jackie Speier and reporting it to Judge Claire etc. should be considered exhaustion… What really, really boils my blood is the fact that this guard blackmailed the inmate victim and sent an email to his friend asking for nude male photos. And any *forensic computer technician* could (indeed) tell I.S.U. exactly *where* that email originated. But C.D.C. protects their own. And they don't want to know… If Ron Jones (KOVR) or Mike Teselle (KCRA) want to know who that is on the photos. I will give them his name…

(Readers find Sean Farmer for me. I need to reach Scott McKinsey, Clarence Schoenberg, Bobby Mitchell Jr., Rob Godshaw, Nate Walejeski, Ryan Jeeter, Loic Hostelter, Austin Ho, Logan Paul, Matt Shepard, Daniel L. Swain, Casey Campbell, Alistar Arvin, Keith Jordan (culinary teacher at SACTO), Matt Easley, Brandon A. Hughes, Hugh Michael Hughes, Daven Torbett, Peter Kneght, Grant Arnette, Daniel Jennings (Tiburon), Ian Webb, *Alex Adame*, Remington Korper and Cassius Harti…). I need input from Paul Tassi and Nick Prugo etc. I face a powerful enemy in C.D.C. But my enemy is the people's enemy. I still believe that the power of the people is greater than the people in power…

If you read my book "*America's Richest Pedophiles*" you'll see where I say that real estate mogul Michael Lyon is a pervert. He had been given a slap on the wrist by a (Judge Gary Ransom) black judge in 2011. He's a pervert and if he'd been black, Mexican or poor white he'd been under the jail. But the judge gave him "probation." On October 1, 2014 my prediction came true. Google Michael Lyon…

I want to give workshops, seminars and conferences etc. Around the country on how to recognize (and predict) a pervert, a molester and/or a murderer. And…I intend to assemble a team of experts as we figure out ways to involve our youths on matters of criminal justice etc. I'll ask *Alec Loorz*, Jack Andraka, Joe Breen (Yale), Kory Corico and Timothy Hill etc. to join our team of experts. I'll seek out Allen Wright, Tim Griffin, *Alex Hayes*, Jimbo Spalding, Kyle Pratt, Kiel Pratt, Cody Hassler and Cody Baetge. And we will declare wars. War on illiteracy! War on police brutality and judicial inequality etc. etc. And I hope *you* join us… Remember – some readers receive a bonus copy of my *"Creating Monsters"* in this book…

Congressman Elijah Cummings stated, "I want to know what culture allows that to happen…" speaking of the Secret Service allowing the security breaches etc. which led to the Secret Service Director resigning. As I watched lawmakers grapple with a culture of top down complacency and try to figure out the culture. I thought of the California State Senate. In a story dated September 30, 2014 the article in the Sacramento Bee begins, "They didn't trust a colleague. Felt their boss wouldn't listen. Feared a powerful official would retaliate if they complained. That workplace culture described Monday by Sergeant-at-Arms of the California Senate when they took the witness stand in SACTO Superior Court." Gerrardo Lopez, a former Senate peace officer killed a man robbing his house. Lopez is close friends with Chief Sergeant-at-Arms and Lopez is the son of Dina Hidalgo who is the Senate's head of Human Resources…

The article goes on to say, "Lopez's Senate colleagues testified Monday that they felt helpless to air their concerns about Lopez because his mother was a powerful administrator and his boss trusted him like a son"… He tested positive for cocaine and he killed a man. But the culture of fear which permeates the Secret Service and the local Senate etc. this culture permeates prisons. I compare Lopez to Stratton. And I know guards who want to air concerns about his misconduct but they fear the culture of retaliation and reprisal. I would like to testify before Congress about this "culture" of fear which runs rampant in corrections, police departments and…the Secret Service. I believe that C.D.C. can be instructive and can elucidate a culture of corruption, retaliation, fear and reprisal…

I hope that readers will reach (for me) Jeff Gerber, Daniel Jinger, Dax Holt, John Foraker, Logan Paul and Daniel Jennings (in Tiburon, CA). I have a job for John Jodie Bear. We also have a job for Clarence Schoenberg… I need readers to reach Clayton Burnham, *Alex Adame*, Grant Arnett, Cody Hassler (in Vacaville) and *Bobby Mitchell, Jr.* (Bobby is in Lowell, MA). We have a job for Bobby Mitchell, Jr. right now. We have a job for Justin Frazier and Maxwell Hanger right now. Charles Jackson lives in Fairview Park, Ohio. We have a job for Charles. And we have jobs for Jordan Simon, Jacob Goodin, Scott Czeda and Nathaniel Mullinnex (Atlanta, GA). We want to hire Cody Baetge, Johnny Walker (in LA), Lane Garrison, Tim Quinn, Vincent Thomas, Ryan Ferguson and Christopher Bird…

We need Keenan Harris, John Spurlock, Will Stabler and Max Hodges… I need an army of gladiators to expose this book. When we have money (John Zwick, Mike Corsetto, *Alec Hamlin* etc.) we will pay you. When we don't we need volunteers. We must counter this culture of corruption, neglect and abuse… And to you young folks who have made mistakes. I remind you that you are bigger than your mistakes. You are better than the worst mistake you ever made. You can start all over again. God loves you… I want Christopher Eavey (Chesterfield, VA), Mike Cowder, Christopher Rousche, Gary Browning (Richmond, VA), Chad Sherman, John Garvin and Scott Johnson (Warner Robbins, GA) to join us. We need Trevor Law, Trevor Loflin and Austin Prentice (could be Austin Prentiss? He went to college in Texas). We want Angus McCloud, Angus T. Jones and Scott Cozza…

Justice too long delayed is justice denied. Justice is supposed to be indivisible. There is supposed to be equal protection under the law. At this juncture those are myths. And you and I can change this. We must work together… I keep writing all of those names because I'm cognizant that Matt Maloney, Aaron Maloney (in Green Bay, WI) and Cody Baetge etc. could all be the next Michael Gorman. And Michael Gorman has become one of the causes of my life. I shall never forget that he begged and he pleaded with guards at New Folsom State Prison to move him out of "that" cell. And they laughed at him. And the next morning Michael woke up dead, sexually assaulted with a T.V. guide shoved up his anus. And the Strattons, Wenkers and Bunnells etc. covered up correctional malfeasance. Because even if we (prisoners) have "open and shut" lawsuits etc. the CCPOA has trained guards in the trade-secrets to prevent us from successfully suing them. When I file appeals I've discovered that C.D.C. "lawyers" reply to my appeals. They make sure that I don't get due process…

Michael Gorman was somebody's son. He was a human being. He was paroling in 17 months. Michael Gorman could have been *Michael Dennis* or Daniel Jensen. And my goal is to tell his story to some young people who have no idea that Gorman existed. I'm crazy enough to believe that Cody Harlton, Cody Hassler, Cody Baetge and Kyle Pratt etc. would give a damn if they knew about 17, 18 and 19 year old guys being raped, beat and murdered in prisons. And these rapes and murders are swept under the rug. I want to get guys like Daniel Kovarbasich, Derek King and Justin Berry etc. to read this book. And I believe that they will care. I believe that *Anthony Baker* and Greg Baker will care. All I need to do is put this book in their hands. Having seen and read the truth they can't turn their backs. They shall not turn their backs on justice, the truth and what is right…

I get missives from young folks all across this country. And it seems like everybody that writes me seems to be "frustrated." They're frustrated because they feel they have potential to be what they are not. And to do what they've not done. Do you feel frustrated too? Do you feel like there is more in you than you've ever developed? I studied this frustration methodically. You can feel that longing in your soul to be more. And to do more. Most youngsters feel like they're built to do 100 mph but they're stuck in a 30 mph zone in life. You need life to take you into environments that will not tolerate that old lifestyle. And you need people who won't tolerate your old habits.

You have unborn seeds inside of you. You have all of that potential which is untapped. And you need help. The reason you've not developed that potential is because you need rain. You need rain for more seeds. And when you're in an environment that offers no rain for your seeds you get stuck, frustrated, lonely and even angry. Prison (for Joseph) was the great lesson. And prison has clearly taught me how lonely one can be when one's environment conspires to bury one's seeds. The same dirt that plants a seed can be used to bury a seed. And prison is the killing fields. It is the master burial site for vision, seeds and for dreams. And without a vision, "the people perish." I have to surround myself with books and with CD's because I need water. I reside in a place where…

"Lieutenant Kukrall is a racist, anti-Semite homophobe" a prison guard told me. "Kukrall refers to President Obama as a 'monkey'" the guard told me… And such is my environment. What is spooky and even scary at times is when I think about the dudes who run this Hard Rock "hotel hell" in which I live. Warden Jeff Macomber, Associate Warden Ross Meiers, Dave Baughman etc. Mike Todd, Konrad etc. etc! Not one of the aforementioned is a Democrat. And...these guys generally hate the President of the United States. And yet, I've authored books such as *"Why They Hate Obama"* and *"Why Republicans Go to Hell"* and they hate me. And my environment is built on violence, anger, hatred and racism. And when you add perversion into the mix it is toxic.

There are guards (here in C.D.C.) who torture us. We are fed like cattle. And the guards bank on the moral hazard that you need prisons. We have to have a place that we put vicious, violent and evil people in. Why do they do what they do? But this is not a place for rain. Prison does not fertilize dreams and visions. So I believe that God allowed me in this drought, this "valley of the shadow of death" to teach me. And it will be my job to teach others.

If you are frustrated I suggest you find rain. Do whatever it takes to get in an environment that will nurture your potential. And you might have to improvise. I've had to learn to master the art of improvisation. I live in a place where they hate black people. The guards who run the yard hate Mr. Obama. The guards for whom I work hate the President. People don't watch the news in prison. Gambling is more important than intellectual debate in a prison. "Two and a Half Men" is more important than "60 Minutes." It's pathetic...

But while housed in hell I've written 22 or 23 books. And I *write* my books. I have no ghostwriter. I have no editor. I write my own books. And 99% of the books written by celebrities are not written by celebrities – I'm like the actor who does his own stunts. When you read my books it's like seeing an actor with no make-up on. It's the real thing. And I *write* because writing creates rain for my seeds. And I write because I know even if the media ignores me right now, books are like diamonds – they are forever. My books are my *legacy*. They will live beyond me. And one day (2015, 2016, 2026 or 2036?) some students (at Morehouse, Clark-Atlanta, Emory University, Rutgers, Howard, or U.C. Berkeley etc.) will pick up my books and say, "How did he *write* that in jail?"

Writing has become my lifeblood. I've had to escape into my books. The books I read as well as the books I write. And...when I pick up this pen it is music. My pen is the handcuff key. It unlocks my creativity. My pen is the prison key. I transcend the place that holds me when I write. I think it (I'm not certain) was a South Korean President who spent years in prison. And when he got out he talked about imaging. He said he visualized his way out of prison. He said (while he was in prison) he used to visualize himself giving lectures and speeches etc. And I apply those same techniques.

I often visualize myself at U.C. Berkeley, Georgia Tech, Hampton, Stanford, Harvard and at Yale. I lecture, teach and speak. I see myself asking Spike Lee to help me do one-man shows as does Mike Tyson. I visualize myself asking Tyler Perry, George Soros, Floyd Mayweather, Steve Harvey, Byron Allen or Jeff Deskovic etc. to help me underwrite my vision. And my vision is to have an entire team of speakers. I see myself with Christopher Bird, Daniel Kovarbasich, Ryan Ferguson, Brian Banks, Marcus Dixon and Chris Ochoa etc. I want a team of speakers to make videos with me. And our videos will be shown to college and high school students. They'll also be shown to juveniles etc. And sometimes we'll do live clinics, seminars and conferences etc. I see us doing conferences in colleges, churches and at companies...

I see myself having Freddie Parrish to find the evidence to prove that I did not commit rape. I see us (Justin Brooks and/or Alissa Bjerkhoel) getting my record cleared just as Bryan Banks did. I see myself going to Rev. Michael Pfleger, Bishop James Morton, Bishop Paul Morton and other pastors and asking them to please let me tell my story. And I see my ministry and my message being more candid, powerful and impactful than ever before. I don't have to fake it. I can be frank and real with folks. I know what it is to be gifted but afflicted. I clearly understand what Paul meant when he talked about the flesh being at war with the spirit. The spirit is willing but the flesh can be weak. I know what it is like to be in dirt and to be dirty. But I am a seed. And a seed can't grow unless it has been in dirt and been in darkness.

I've come to realize that God allowed me to go through all of this darkness and dirt because I'm a seed. And when you stand above the ground you can't see what's going on underground. My seeds have been planted. It's like writing this book. If you could see (my typist can see it I'll betcha that) how sloppy and how pathetic this page I'm writing is you couldn't imagine the book you are reading. But by the time you see this it has been to Atlanta, Georgia. And a group of professional typists have done their magic. And they press a button and this (writing) shows up on a computer in Zürich, Switzerland. And they press a button and we have a book. And then...my words (seeds) are in bookstores, in libraries, in colleges and on Amazon.com etc...

If you feel like you are not living up to your potential, I want you to visualize yourself doing it. And then go look for rain. If I get out of here I'm running to find rain. I'll call Mikhail Khodorkovsky, Steven Fabian, Anderson Cooper and whoever I've got to call. And I will say, "Help me to prevent others from going through the hell that I've just come out of." I'll call *Jacob Gabriel, Joseph Latham*, Logan Paul, Curtis Sykes and Billy York. And I will ask them to help me to tell this story. I'm gonna look for "*Andy*" the volunteer (he used to work at Homeboy Industries. If you know how to reach Andy tell him to email me) and I'll ask Andy to join our crusade. I'm looking for John Mandern, Noah Zatz, Janice Bellucci, Matt McGorry, Peter Nowalk, Alex Back, *Scott Romano* (in Colorado), Nathan Beckopec, Aaron Katersky and Ari Shapiro. I need their input, ideas and suggestions.

I need *you* too. (Readers find Jeff Gerber, Michael Dennis, Jack Dale, Joshua Stipp, Jacob Faulkenber, Dillon Banionis, Daniel Coverston, Matt Maloney, Michel Castro, Tyler Grady, Gabe Herrington, Sean Farmer, Brian Devin Graham, Gary Browning, Eddie Cannon, Harvey Lashler, David Joyner, Jais Malcolm, Aaron Kelly, Collin Keys, Collin Orcutt, Collin Finnerty, Charles Askew, Taylor Matthews (Matthews lives in Alexandria, LA), Trevor Law, Trevor Loflin, David Hellyer, Maxwell Hanger, John Caudell, Sean Zane and Greg Pugh)...

We will give criminal justice, anti-crime, "*Hands-up! Don't Shoot*," "*Let Us Make Man*™," "*Creating Monsters*™" and "*Let It Rain*™" clinics, seminars, conferences and workshops all over this country. And...I am asking youngsters to share this book with your friends today. If you are in a frat, sorority, club, association etc. tell others to read this book. You can hold book parties in your dorm, student union building or library etc. And invite us to your group... Go online and start discussion groups about this book. Pick up topics which the media has forgotten and discuss them. What do you think about trooper Sean Groubert (in South Carolina) and what he did to Levar Jones? What about the black college football player (sadly – I don't even recall his name) who had been in an accident. He knocked on a white lady's door for help. She saw a black face and called the cops. And a cop murdered him. What do you think? Christopher Dorner? Let's not forget about issues merely because they're no longer in the media…

I'd like to see panel discussions regarding Dorner, Groubert, Michael Gorman, Stratton, Wenker and Mike Bunnell etc… Can I repeat what Eric Holder and Mr. Obama can't say? There are a lot of old racist, anti-Semitic drunks in the U.S. Congress. They are guilty of D.U.I. They *deliberate under* the *influence*. That's why they consistently block and fight this President. We have a bunch of Kukralls, Bunnells, Strattons and Tuckers in the U.S. Congress. They are racist bastards. Period… Every time I see these lawmakers on T.V. advertising about how great they are. I get upset.

I remember how sick I was with Valley Fever. I remember how I was told there were only 27 cases like mine in the world. And I spent 14 months of my life chained to a hospital bed. And I was not allowed to write, send mail or make telephone calls etc. And…I was heavily medicated even after I got out of the hospital. It was probably a year before I could even think clearly. And yet…with all of these great lawyers in California I can't find even one who will argue my Valley Fever case for me? It is absolutely sick… If Johnnie Cochran was alive he'd take my case… Geri Green could win this case…

I want you (the reader) to send this book to *Nick Jonas*, Ronan Farrow, Hunter Johannson, Kevar Gebiz and to Scott Romano. Send this book to a firefighter by the name of Brendon McDonough, Kevin Lynn, Scott Cozza, Scott Kauffman, Billy York and Raider Runner. Send this to Doug Pieper Jr., Patrick Crowe, Stuart Campbell and to Kyle Pratt. Let's put this book on front street. I need you… Again I apologize from my heart (Helping Educate At-Risk Teens) to *Alec Loorz* and to his wonderful family. I clearly understand how I would feel if I got a call from a guard alleging "Don't let your son write him he's a child molester" etc. That call was complete mendacity, improper, defamatory and wrong. And it clearly chilled my free speech. I pray that Alec and his family will read this book and let me know they read it…

(Before we move to Judge Claire I need the *Shermanators* to go online and find these people. If you want them to pay you for notifying these people they will. But contact Nick Thompson (San Francisco), Neil Davidson, Nate Kelly, Luke Kelly, Kyle Day, Justin Braun, Sam Pritchard, Charles Costello, Brian Devin Graham, Tim Combs, Michael Evers, Cody Lloyd, Jonathan Shaw (Dallas), Josh Lyle, *Jake O'Donoghue*, Creighton Baird, Dominic Burrows, Jonathan Dececchis, Jeremy Buendia, Jordan Spaschak, Tyler Straub, Christian Spaschak, Justin Hoop, Jake Tracy, Alex Sutaru, Colton Dixon, *Pelle Wall*, Austin Sisneros, Tommy Beard, Robert Leslie, Daniil Turitsyn, *Daniel Hamidi*, Hasib Habibi, A. J. Ali, *Tyler Yagley*, Daniel Chesmore, *Raymond Flores*, Sam Lomsky, Dan McShane, Tadd Carr, Jacob Darling, Anthony Villareal, Bobby Mitchell, Jr., Winston Tam, Matt Wendt, Christopher Cox, Brad Alexander, Tyler Kolb, *Alex Adame*, Michael Hernbroth, Elijah Wood, Ben Honeycutt, *Matt Fender*, Christopher Kluwe, *Joey* Arostegui, Trevor Sanford, Mark Japinga, Bryan James,

Brian Glasscock, John Schreiber, *Kaleb Leeper*, John Brandon, Derik Sweeney, Joy Sweeney, *Sean Aiken*, Christian Junsing, Austyn Whaley, Anthony Curcio, Phillip Urban, Kasey Schutz, Chris Hues, Robert Krybyla, Aaron Mize, *Grant Seidler*, Cody Sheldon, Vadim Trachuk, Shane Bruce and Jacob Gabriel. Find 'em and tell them to email me, they're in this book. We have checks for some of them…). Find Amy Nelson, Sterling Winter, Chris Owen, John Lucas, *Cody* (who wants to be Beyoncé. He was on YouTube) and Alex Lucas.

## **Honorable Judge Allison Claire**

I mention Madame Claire throughout this book. If you'd like her dossier just Google her. She is one of those judges Gerry Spence writes about in his books – judges who have no souls, no hearts and no spirits. They remind Gerry (and me) of concrete. They're hard, cold and cruel when it comes to their rulings against the *No J's*... If you assume this writing is designed to influence Judge Claire, wrong. She may or may not read this (I'll never know) book. But...by the time 'Madame Your Honor' reads this book (on the slim chance that she does) she will already have granted summary judgment to the defendants and dismissed my case. That's how they roll.

I state to you (under penalty of perjury) that Mr. Stratton told me, "My lawyer (Kelli Hammond) knows Claire good (sic) and Claire has already told her she will grant summary judgment. You will not get no (sic) trial..." Stratton old me that, "You see we got your Valley Fever case throwed (sic) out. And you had 3 or 4 lawyers and one by one we pulled the strings to get them off your case. And as soon as this is over you is (sic) on a bus again. Who are you gonna call Obama? You can't call Derrick (sic – real name is "Eric") Holder cause Republicans got rid of him." And I trembled.

Initially, I thought, *Lord I wish Allison Claire could hear this guy*. This man admits hands down that they (Wenker, Bunnell, Layton, Johnson etc.) stole my Valley Fever paperwork and delayed it (intentionally) to cause me to miss the statute of limitations. I wanted Judge Claire to hear this. But then it hit me; Claire does not care. She does not care. If she cared she could not look at my circumstances and not be inclined to move. How can they justify sending an asthmatic to P.V.S.P. so he can catch Valley Fever and write a book about that? And 6 months after I got there I was almost dead. And...I spent 14 months of my life chained to a hospital bed until 2008. And after I was released I was re-hospitalized 27 times. And I was clearly not allowed to write 602's while in a hospital.

I wrote and rewrote appeal after appeal regarding being transferred to the Valley Fever prison. I vividly recall (in 2009) coming out of hospital and writing another appeal because I wanted to protect the statute of limitations. I gave one appeal directly to Ryan Wenker. And it (too) disappeared. And during all of this time due to severe pain and aching I was on mind-altering drugs. Yet... After all of my missives (some of which actually reached their intended targets) to the court in 2008, 2009 and in 2010, the judge dismisses the most important Valley Fever case in the state. It's easy to see that Mrs. Claire does not care...

On October 3, 2014 a guard awakened me at 11:00 a.m. I'd written and prayed all night long... "Ain't you got a (sic) issue with Stratton and he told a judge that he don't (sic) do no cell moves?" I replied in the affirmative and then he told me the story. Let me give you a little bit of background for perspective. The prison building I'm in has 3 (A, B and C) sections. A-Section has the best digital T.V. reception. Most guys try to get moved to that section. But each section only has 20 cells (and 2 bunks per cell).

There were 2 inmates (I won't use their names without their permission. But call them inmate Battle and inmate Scott) in cell 206. They both have jobs. One works in visiting and the other works in the library. 206 is in Section-A. A guard went to the library and told inmate Battle that, "Stratton needs your cell so you and your celly need to pack and move your stuff to C-Section." One of the guys protested and asked, "Why?" Stratton came on the scene and put him (inmate Scott) in handcuffs. "I'll throw yo' (sic) ass in the hole if you don't move." Stratton calmed down and told him, "Oh it's a 'convenience' move." After getting out of cuffs they went to the building and packed their stuff and moved to C-Section cell 122. There were 2 inmates in that cell. Stratton gave them the cell. Inmates Battle and Scott are both African-Americans. The persons he gave their cell to are not black. Convenience move? There is a big memo in the building which clearly states that "convenience moves are done only on Tuesdays and Saturdays." The day Stratton did these moves was on a Friday. And… Convenient for who?

…Later that self-same day I talked to a Lieutenant and told him what Stratton did to these two black inmates. The Lieutenant replied, "If I had been working he would not have done that. That's just unfair on so many levels. Now if those guys went out and stabbed who he gave the cell to he'd be fired." I corrected him…"Stratton would not be fired. He'd dodge the bullet like he always does. And why don't you reverse the moves since you know they are unfair?" The Lieutenant replied, "Come on Manning. Let's keep it real. You know I stay out of other people's messes. And tell the guys to file a 602." And the guys are not going to file. And it is hard to blame them. Appeals get hidden, stolen, delayed and shredded every day.

And… As much as I used to like Warden Jeff Macomber, the truth of the matter is Jeff is not going to correct Stratton. Tim Virga would have. I guarantee it. That is too blatant for Tim to not have corrected. But Macomber? He keeps his head in the sands and he lets "Meiers run the yard and"… If Stratton thought there was any possibility that Konrad, Meiers or Jeff would discipline him for his *racist* move – he would not have done it. What boils my blood is the fact that just 8 weeks ago Stratton committed perjury. He submitted documentation to the Honorable Judge Allison Claire telling her that he did not have anything to do with cell moves! Period! And the Honorable Judge Claire quoted Stratton's statement (written under penalty of perjury) in her ruling as she ruled against me. Just 8 weeks ago I promise.

He blatantly lied to Judge Claire. Just as he lied to her claiming that when the mail arrives in his office everyday he's already gone home… I'd told Judge Claire (the truth) that Stratton plans to set me up (again) via a celly. I'd asked the judge to temporarily single cell me. And she conducted an "inquiry" (I shan't revisit the inquiry which I write about in other parts of this book). But he blatantly deceived the court. And… If the judge really (really) wanted to conduct an "inquiry" she'd call the prison and interview folks regarding the moves ordered (directly) by Stratton on 10/3/14.

…I also learned that in late September Stratton ordered the inmate in cell 131 to move to cell 132. That's unheard of. Stratton was just moving him to harass him. But the stunt he pulled on 10/3/14 I've never (ever) seen in prison. And guards lie for each other and cover for one another all the time. But I sort of believe that if a Federal Magistrate calls this prison (916-985-8610) and asks to speak with C. O. Reid and asked Reid (under oath) to "tell me why you moved the two inmates out of cell 206 – to – 122 on 10/3/14" Reid will reply, "My Sergeant told me to." "Who is your Sergeant?" He'd reply, "Joseph Stratton…" But by the time you are' reading this Judge Claire has already granted Stratton (and his cohorts) summary judgment. And it's a strong chance I'm in the cell with a celly who is planted by Stratton. And I'll end up transferred and/or in Ad-Seg. And who will stop Stratton? Obviously it won't be the courts…

And sadly, guys with no moral code, no sense of ethics or integrity etc. - guys like Stratton - end up becoming captains and wardens. And that is why we have a system in California that is run on a KKK model. And how dare you call these dudes racists? Even though I've seen many white guards (some who even have black wives and some who go to church every Sunday) running around here wishing that President Obama or his kids had been outside the East Room when that intruder got in. One guard told me, "You know the Secret Service let him in because Obama is black." One guard said, "If he could have gotten in while Obama's kids were in there and maybe mol----- (deleted) one of them. Then maybe blacks would stay in their place and stop running for President." After that I went to the cell and regurgitated (literally). What kind of human being even thinks about the possibility of an innocent child being violated?...

I thought a lot about Stratton's cell moves and realized he hoped the guys did attack one another. Stratton likes drama. He thrives on seeing inmates tear each other's heads off… Inmates are notoriously in disagreement with one another. You can't find 3 of us to agree on any one thing. And that is by design. There is power in agreement. In Genesis God saw that the people were all in agreement. They all spoke the same language and they worked in unity. They started building a tower and God said I've got to confuse their languages. Because if they stay together like this they can do "anything." God scattered them all over and He disrupted their unity…

Prisoners can't get out of prison and can't get better because we don't understand the power of corporate agreement. "How beautiful it is when brothers dwell" together in unity, "come let us reason together." The devil knows the power of people coming together in unity so he conspires to keep prisons disrupted with riots, fights, envy, jealousy and egotism etc. the devil (literally) possesses guys like Stratton, Spearman and Mike Jiminez. And he orders their steps. They "breathe out violence." Proverbs 10:23 says "To do evil is like sport to a fool." Read that again and think about the local jail or the prison. Doing evil (for a fool) is just like playing golf, basketball or football is to a normal person.

And I'm concerned that these people (Wenker, Bunnell, Stratton, May, Jiminez, Spearman etc.) are not normal. They inflict too much pain. They take pleasure in another person's sorrows etc. They can't be normal. "Violence covers the mouth of the wicked." If you come into a prison and listen to us talk all you will hear is violence. The Bible says that fools hate knowledge… I could take these three words (fools hate knowledge) and write a dissertation. But… A "fool" wouldn't read it!... If you could hear us talking you would beg us to please "shut up." My mom used to say that people can assume you're a fool but you open your mouth and confirm it… The "tongue of the wise uses knowledge rightly, but the mouth of fools pours forth foolishness." The tongue "is so set among our members that it defiles the whole body and sets on fire…it is set on fire by hell." The tongue? "No man can tame the tongue. It is unruly evil, full of deadly poison!" That's in the Book of James (in the Bible).

Prison is violent! And (Proverbs 16:29-30) "A violent man entices his neighbor, and leads him in a way that is not good. He winks his eye to devise perverse things; he 'purses' his lips and brings about evil." Did you read that? He just purses his lips and brings evil… Such is the subculture into which I've been embedded. And if we could get some of these judges (i.e. Allison Claire and Morrison England) to come off the lofty benches and come and visit these prisons which they preside over, they would not be so quick to dismiss us out of hand. They would not find it so incredible that a Wenker, a Johnson, a Bunnell and a Stratton etc. would intentionally delay, steal and sabotage my Valley fever lawsuit. And I'm not the only one. There are inmates all over California (and across the nation) who are being beaten, raped, set-up and tortured. And even if I can't help myself I want to help them…

I hope Houston Syvertson, Porter Robinson, Preston Hocker, *Connor Myers* and Jordan Bianco etc. will read this book. I pray that Ryan Ferguson, Brian Banks, Christopher Bird, Alex King and Daniel Kovarbasich etc. will connect with me and help me to tell this story. I hope we (Ferguson, Bird and I) can hold criminal justice seminars, conferences and crusades etc. Just like T. D. Jakes does with "Man Power" and "Woman Thou Art Loosed." We can even give presentations to judges, lawmakers and to the media… I pray that Tom Joyner, Roland Martin, Charles D. Ellison, Joshua Dubois and Otis Moss will get this book and share it. I want Elijah Cummings, Emanuel Cleaver, Barbara Lee and Steven Horsford, Alex Adame, Alec Torres and Josiah Lenming to get this book. And once you read about how horrible they treat prisoners, maybe that college education won't look so boring after all.

If you are a "fool we welcome you" to prison. "Come one and come all." But you must be a fool and *gay*. Yes you (and I have nothing against anybody gay. We're all God's children though He does not sanction all of our conduct) gang banger etc. You might carry a Tech-9 and sell cocaine but you are as queer as a three dollar bill. If you will risk freedom (women, p-ssy, food and a social life) to come sleep in a room with your homies (all male) you're gay, come…you will eat, sh-t and urinate in the same room. And the moment you get comfortable in a cell a Stratton will "move" you just because…

I hope that prison guards are arrogant, blatant and bold enough to disallow this book in the prisons. If they do that then I'll have some friends (Prison Legal News, Sanford Rosen, Donald Specter, Jeff Bezos and lawyers for Amazon.com) to help me in this fight. The book is free speech. I advocate (as I do in all my books) nonviolence. I tell inmates who may get a copy of my books to never threaten safety and security. "Follow the rules if you are in prison. And be nonviolent…"

I know some guards who would love to report Stratton (and Spearman, Tucker, Jiminez etc.) to the U.S. Attorney. But "I was fearful of retaliation from (Lopez's) mother, who was the head of Human Resources… You get on her bad side, she makes your life miserable if she doesn't try to flat out get you fired," said Jeremiah Wattenberger, a Senate Sergeant-At-Arms. I revisited Jeremiah's statement because his fears so remind me of the prison guards. The few who would like to come forth. I remember C.O. Deborah Paul. They ran her away for being a truthteller. I recall Sergeant Elsberry. She called Stratton a racist pig. And she testified against Sergeant R. N. Saunders and Lieutenant Scarsella for beating an inmate. They ran her out of Folsom also…

People can teach you everything you want to know about them if you just listen. I talked with a guard today who hates Sergeant Stratton. And Stratton hates him also. Yet, when I inquired about that "cell move" (from 206 – to – 122) he "defended" his "enemy." He rambled on and on about prison is not fair and if you wanted fair "don't come to prison" etc. I was amused. He then went into "race" and Obama etc. This man told me that "any guard here will tell you that 80 percent of the inmates who masturbate in front of female staff are black." I was caught off guard. A, I'd never heard that. B, I could name (off the top of my head) fifty white, Asian and Mexican inmates whom I know that masturbate in front of staff. C, where was this topic coming from? D, who thinks like that? F, what was that supposed to prove?

I disagree with anybody pulling their privates out in front of a nurse or guard and masturbating. In my opinion it's pretty perverted. But (and that's a big "but") I don't have a life sentence. And if a man has a life sentence his entire mental infrastructure changes…I replied by stating, "That's not true but let me ask you: Did you know that well over 86 percent of child molesters are white?" He said, "It's probably true and I can't dispute that." But the redness of his face said "gotcha!" What is sad is that this is the kind of stuff he and his white buddies sit back in the office and discuss. They sit in offices and… "Yeah – I'm not racist but facts are what they are. And… Blacks use crack way more than whites do. And… They masturbate more than white inmates. They were bred that way." I guess the black guards could (if they wanted to) sit back and talk about, "Who do you see abusing animals? Who has sex with cows and molests kids? White boys. I guess while the slave masters were raping black women and lynching the men. They bred their boys to molest." Touché. But why are "we" (he and I) still discussing black and white? (Tell Jamie Parsons, Ravin Wooten, Kabir Kapur, Norris Henderson, Ray Hill, Margaret West, Wyatt Hselm, Kyle Hill, Molly Rodgers, Leeav Sofer and Matt Swatzell to read this book.)

## How To Get Away With Murder

With all due respect to Shonda Rhimes; I'm talking real life murder. If you want to get away with murder there are two sure-fire ways. Number one is to be rich and number two is to own a badge. Police officers routinely get away with murder. And surprisingly, prison guards get away with it twice as much and three times easier than street police. Prisoners are considered as nobodies. Most of us will never write a book. And if we do write one it won't get published. Most of us don't know how to contact the media. And (as Dale Schornack can attest to) if they do reach persons in the media they will get dismissed.

This author called Dale (local SACTO News Ten anchor) 20 or 30 times asking him to mention "*Creating Monsters.*" And Dale insinuated that they ignore prisoners because they don't want us to be "celebrated." But that theory was proved a lie when they began to cover inmate/gang member Jeremy Meeks. Schornack (as I said before) even went so far as to offer modeling advice to inmate Meeks. It seemed as though Dale had a bromance going with Meeks. Google Jeremy Meeks. …Because he's a black dude with "green" (or blue?) eyes. But…if he was a black dude with a green thumb (or pen) for writing books etc. you would never hear his name; period…

C. O. Joseph Stratton, C. O. Ryan Wenker and Sergeant K. Porter all got away with murder. In 2009 (as I write about later) they murdered inmate Edwards. Had they not had badges – they'd be in prison as inmates right now. It was an open-and-shut murder. Here's "*How To Get Away With Murder*," kill a prisoner. Nobody will care. The beat will go on and on. It's only a prisoner. "He shouldn't have gotten locked up." The main problem with this type malfeasance is what it does to the psyche of the guys who will be (eventually) released from prison.

Every time I see a parolee shooting a cop. Each time I see a parolee holed up in a house refusing to come out I understand. Once you've been here and you see rogue guards literally get away with assaults, torture, theft and "murders" etc. If you ever get out you don't want to come back. You'd rather die. (But what needs to happen is more guys need to get out and speak-out-stay-out of trouble and go talk to churches, the media and professors etc. about what you saw in prison. I've witnessed nine murders in prison. And six of those were guards murdering inmates. Who cares?

## **Congressman Elijah Cummings**

Elijah is a great brother. I've watched two black men stand up to Darrell *ISIS* on T.V. One was A. G. Eric Holder. And the other was Elijah. Congressman Darrell *ISIL* is in love with himself. He is a bigot, racist and he's a criminal. He's worth over $300 million and a lot of this is drug money. Congressman Darrell Issa (we call him *ISIL* or *ISIS*) is a thug. He hates President Obama. He and guys like Joe King have disrespected this president in unspeakable ways. When have we ever seen a president asked to show his birth certificate? When have we seen a president called a "Muslim" (not that being Muslim is bad). The stuff they've done to this president is unheard of. We should arrest Darrell ISIL for treason. He disrespected Eric Holder and tried to talk over him. I know guys who worked for his car alarm company. And I could tell you stories worthy of Star Magazine…

(…Deputy Jordan Thomas told our team that he has arrested C. O. Ryan Wenker several times for possession of meth!... Deputy Bryan Payne claims to have arrested Mike Jiminez (the CCPOA president) for a number of unseemly crimes…). I hope to testify before Congress concerning correctional malfeasance upon my release. I'd like to elucidate why prisons *produce* killers and molesters etc. I want the nation to hear the truth. Over the past two decades America has fallen deeper and deeper into a statistical mystery.

Poverty has gone up while crime rates have gone down, but the prison population has doubled. Fraud by the rich wipes out 43 percent of the world's wealth – yet the rich get massively richer, and nobody goes to prison. Basic rights are now determined by poverty or wealth, which allows the super-wealthy to go unpunished. And *poverty itself* has been *turned* into a *crime*. I want to testify before Congress. I want Emanuel Cleaver, Barbara Lee and John Lewis etc. to hear these truths. We have a perverse new standard of justice: A system which devours the lives of the poor, turns a blind eye to the horrendous crimes of the rich, and implicates us all. There are a few folks talking about income inequality but who is talking about justice inequality?

…(I want readers to find the base player for Josh Shook, Nick Hogan, Nick Niccoli, Scott Dangerfield, Matt Susac, Billy Bell, Justin Johnes, Jody Searcy, Ryan Sill, Nick Fink, Taylor John Williams, Indio Downey, Daniel Malinovsky, J-Si Chavez, Steven Sabados, Zoard Janko, Cole Wilkinson, Guy Penrod (and his lead guitar player), Taylor Phelan, Kevin Shoop, Ryan Fitzgerald, Tyler Fehr, Austin Sisnores, Jimbo Spalding, Alex Hayes, Tom McFadden, Chris Kerny, Josh Band, John Brandon, Justin Tribble, Ricardo Angelino, Ricardo Angelina, Alexander Berki, Brett Westcott, James Merryman, Shaun Rushforth, Grant Seidler, Cody Sheldon, Matthew Fender, Kaleb Leeper, Stephen Tonti, Jacen Lankow, Joseph Breen, David Holycross, Michael Snowden, Jason Boyer, *JustinTankersaey*, Carlos Quintana, Scott Kauffman, Ryan Smallwood, *Anthony* Baker (Dad is Gregory), Trevor Hiltbrand, Daniel Wetter, Christian Stoinev, Charles Jackson and Ryan Satin etc… Please find them for us…).

I've felt a lot of emptiness while trapped in hades. But I know that the emptiness and the loneliness is actually a gift. It is a gift which draws me back to God. Only God can fill that void. When He created Adam He saw that Adam was lonely. And… "Adam what you need is not around you but within you. So go to sleep and I'm going to perform a C-section on you. I'm gonna pull something out of you and call it a wo-man." Sometimes we must look within ourselves to find the answers to that loneliness. …I can't over emphasize how lonely it has been for me in a California jail cell. And I would have never thought I'd meet so many backwoods, hillbilly rednecks in California. And I must remind Congressman Cummings and Congressman Cleaver etc. that Darrell *ISIL* (Issa) is also from California. You'd think there would be a lot of progressiveness out here. But don't confuse Hollywood with Bakersfield, Kern County and a lot of other places in California…

All the stuff I learned from *Rev. Hosea Williams* and from *Ambassador Andrew Young* etc. has been tried and tested by California racists. Just today a white guard was telling me how people are out there starving because they have to pay for "*The* Obama-Care." And when he said "Obama" I could see the horns… But… we (the progressives) must move forward. We have to erect barriers around the Constitution. And we must protect the least of these our brothers. I hear Mitt Romney told another lie. He said he'd "never" run again but now he's reconsidering. He told 900 (verifiable) lies when he ran against President Obama. And now…he may re-manufacture a pack of lies. I wonder if he'll tell us more secrets about the Mormon family. I want to know if Joseph Smith was really a homosexual.

I hope that we can pull together a team (Cody Hassler, Keenan Harris, Matt Fender, Cole Wilkinson, Ricky Manning, Houston Syvertson, Quyem Pham (San Jose), Timothy Hill and Christopher Eavey etc.) and that this team will develop a sophisticated PR machine. I want people working with *NAPS* (*National Association* for *Public Safety*) who know how to get Dax Holt and Max Hodges etc. on the telephone. I want Daymond John to be able to call anybody on my team and have them articulate the vision. This (*G.B.G.*) *Gang Bangers* for *God* must be bigger than me. Anything that stops because of one man was not worth starting in the first place.

My job is to recruit Jacob Gabriel, Daniel Job, Cory Laymen, Daniil Turitsyn and Gabriel Herrington etc. and to get them to catch this vision. If ISIL can recruit 15 year old Americans to go and behead people A, we are in trouble! B, we can do better… I want people who want excitement, meaning and purpose. Let's behead hate and ignorance. Let's perform psychological reattachments. We can make this great country better. Let's get busy…

…A lawyer told me the other day that they should put an ATM machine in the lobby of the Federal Courthouse because 90 percent of all Federal judges are on the take. And I can personally attest to the fact that if by chance you end up in prison with some money, there is an ATM in the lobby of every prison. And it is not for bail money. It too is for buying and bribing… Back to the child molesters? Stephen Collins of Seventh Heaven? Caucasian and rich and just admitted to molesting children. Sick… I should ask C.O. McCartney does he think Collins will "masturbate" when he comes to prison…

Officer Charles Turner (in Hamilton, Indiana) just broke out the window on Jamal Jones' car. And Turner tased him while his two kids were in the back seat. Why? For "riding" (not driving) while black. Turner has been sued numerous times for excessive force. The police department has settled all of the lawsuits. Prisons do the same thing. Stratton, Wenker, Couch, Layton Johnson and Bunnell etc. have all been sued before me. C.D.C. has paid $

hundreds of thousands of dollars to settle these cases. And even though they'll pay to settle the case(s) nobody goes up to Stratton and says, "Hey dude you're costing us too much money. You've got to stop this misconduct." Prisons just allow these Strattons (aka Trooper Sean Groubert), Wenkers (Charles Thomas) and other abusers to continue their wrongdoing. The beat just goes on and on and on.

And... I'm asking Zachary Dickinson, Cameron Brown, Brett Westcott, Patrick Ludlow, Daniel Hamidi, Justin Hempfling and Eric Lotke etc. to help us to tell the world about these happenings. If each of you will tell two people about this book we could do this. I need you to tell two people to read this book. If they cannot afford it tell them to email my team and we will send them a gratis E-copy. That's how much I want to get this message out there. I want professors and students (i.e. Kevin Droniak, Matt Fender and Quinn Halleck) everywhere to read this book...

The prison gangstas (i.e. guards) never cease to amaze me. Let me give you a brief overview of just one day (10/8/14) in the life of prison guard shenanigans. On 10/8/14 a prison guard (from New Folsom State Prison) was arrested for the cultivation of marijuana. That same guard admitted to this author that, "I know Stratton, Compton, Wenker and Layton are stealing your mail dude..." On 10/8/14 Lieutenant Faris (from I.S.U.) told me that, "The appeal you submitted regarding the guard...(name deleted, but the guard he was speaking of is the guard who is pictured in this book.) has been lost. And we are not going to find it and it's too late to rewrite it. Get the message Manning. Let it go... The guard may have transferred to another prison. But he has a relative still working at this prison. And we can use his presence to *get rid of you*. So chill..." That's a threat to blackmail me. I hope Geri Green and Stewart Katz are reading this. I hope Mark Merin and Donald Specter are reading. They stole the appeal to prevent exhaustion and... This kind of C.D.C. trick is not new. It happens every day of the week...

Also on 10/8/14 I received a missive from C.O. Ryan Patrick Wenker's lawyer. Keep in mind that you (the taxpayers) are paying for this lawyer. He has a private law firm at taxpayer's expense. I want you to read the missive for yourself.

October 2, 2014


Sherman D. Manning, #J-98796
Plaintiff In Pro Se
California State Prison, Sacramento
P.O. BOX 290066
Represa, CA 95671-0066

    Re:    Sherman D. Manning, Peter Andrist v. Bunnell, et al.
            USDC ED, Case No. 2:12-cv-02440-AC

Dear Mr. Manning:

I am writing to follow-up on the interrogatories, requests for admissions, and request for production of documents that Defendants Ralls, Wenker, Humphries, and Johnson each served on you on June 13, 2014. We have not yet received your response to any of the discovery requests. As you know, your responses were due on July 14, 2014. Please inform me of the status of these responses as soon as possible.

Sincerely,

KRISTINA DOAN GRUENBERG
KDG:tm

    She wrote that to me on 10/2/14 and I received it on 10/8/14. And…it is another play, a trick and a game being played to persuade their judge, Allison Claire, to dismiss the case. Attorney *Bob Blasier* was kind enough to do the interrogatories etc. for me and he returned them to me on July 2, 2014. I mailed all of the documents etc. to Kristina Gruenberg and Kelli Hammond on 7/10/14. When I mailed them I made two statements to my celly: A, I said (half-jokingly), "I wonder if those clowns are going to pretend not to receive these." And B, "I hope none of Stratton's boys gets a hold of these and steals them." And lo and behold I get this missive.
    Yet, I'm not certain who I believe less. Do I believe they were stolen en-route? Or do I believe she received them and pretended not to get them. Why would she wait almost 100 days to mention, "Oh by the way, your stuff was due 3 months ago? Where is it?" And since I mailed Attorney Hammond (as I've explained the State gave 4 of the defendants one lawyer and the other set of defendants another lawyer) her interrogatories simultaneously (with Gruenberg's) obviously Hammond received hers.
    And… Moreover I am suing these people for stealing my mail. My regular (non-legal) mail as well as my legal mail. And their defense is basically, "Okay we did find 800 pieces of your mail hidden in the mailroom. Some of it was *five years* (incoming and outgoing) old. But…yours was not the only mail we found. We are innocent because you are not the only one we did like that!" That is a helluva defense. Although all of my mail goes to special investigations. Although 3 months prior to the discovery of this large cache of mail Peter Andrist (in Switzerland) notified Warden Tim Virga that we believed Couch and Layton Johnson were stealing my mail. And Virga assigned Sergeant L. A. Quinn to conduct an investigation. And in January Quinn emailed Mr. Andrist to state that he'd investigated and there was a "slight delay in mail due to the holidays" but that neither "Couch, Layton Johnson, nor anyone is stealing" my mail.
    And… I've filed 200 appeals regarding missing mail. But "Oops you were right we even withheld a missive from Congresswoman *Karen Bass* for three years." And they found the Karen Bass letter hidden in the desk drawer of mailroom supervisor Layton Johnson. Next to it was a request from me asking, "Where is the letter?" from Karen Bass… Virga was so

appalled by the way my mail was stolen and hidden etc. that he had them to tape every locker, closet and desk drawer shut in the mailroom. But I'm up against a machine. And they've perfected the art of getting lawsuits dismissed... And that was just October 8, 2014... This is malfeasance on steroids... And it's painful.

But I've learned to journalize my pain. And I must use my pain to work through my pen. And pain won't stop me. Tyler Perry was abused and beat by his father. And even though he's now a star his dad said to him, "If I had beat yo' (sic) ass one mo' time you probably would have been Barack Obama." Tyler was also molested by a man. Tyler says, "Predators know when a child is vulnerable. It's blood in the water and they're sharks. He 'used' God to molest me," Tyler says... Tyler went to church because he said that it was only in church that he would ever see his mother smile. And he said, "I wanted to know this God that made my momma smile." Tyler says, "What you feed will grow in your life; what you starve will die." We're in *Tyler Perry* School for a moment y'all! Tyler Perry says, "Take the pain of your past and let it destroy you or you use it. I use it in my life and in my work." He says, "Hollywood closed the door on me so I had to tear a hole in the window. 'He who owns the gold makes the rules.'" Tyler says, "I know I've been changed." Flopped. But he used his own money. He says, "They control the content, rewrites and they say what goes. I couldn't handle that. I had to do my own thing." And he went on the chitlin' circuit...

I may have to put the *Gang Bangers* for *God* (*G.B.G.*) tour on the chitlin' circuit. We'll do workshops and seminars etc. I want to be a part of the positive. And I want to help people become politically literate. And there are far too many youths (white, black, Asian and Mexican) who know zero about American politics. I started studying politics when I was six years old. And I'm a political junkie. I know crackpots like Ted Cruz when I see them. But rather than proselytize I'd just like to educate. Rev. Hosea Williams used to say, "Vote as you please but please vote"... Perhaps I'll go on YouTube and post political reviews. I can review books and politicians like Marques Brownlee reviews tech gadgets...

Like the recent interview of Leon Panetta. I was taken aback. President Obama appointed this dude to two of the highest offices in the land. And as soon as he's gone he (a Democrat) writes a book which is more critical of President Obama than a book by Bob Gates (a Republican). Some of Panetta's criticisms are just Klannish. He's a Clintonite. And he wants to bolster a platform for Mrs. Clinton to run on. If he really had these criticisms he should have waited two years until Mr. Obama was out of office... We have no Kings or Queens in America. But do we really need dynasties? Jeb Bush might run. Bill Clinton happens to be very close to the Bush family. And Hillary happens to be running. So yet another Clinton or Bush? Is the joke (pun intended) on us?...

I couldn't sleep yesterday. I kept thinking about Valley Fever, stolen mail and what Bunnell and the CCPOA did to me. I can't forget how they tortured me. Not only because they did it to me. But because I know they do it to others. I know that I am not the only one. These people (Stratton, Wenker, Bunnell and Layton Johnson etc.) are *correctional terrorists*. George and Joseph Stratton etc. They're not smart enough to build or create anything; therefore they peddle only vindictiveness and hate. No God condones this corruption. No regulation justifies their actions. There can be no reasoning – no negotiation – with these agents of evil. The only language understood by rogues like this is the language of litigation. So we need a broad coalition (of lawyers, students, professors and others) to dismantle this network of corruption (aka the Green Wall)…

I'm so appalled by the court's (Judge Allison Claire) strong bias in favor of these crooks etc. that I'll do anything to get the word out. So…this is unheard of and my publisher's will kill me. But (here goes) *any college* or high school *student, professor*, *dean* or *teacher* etc. can get a gratis E-copy of this book. I will *give you* (every student) this book (E-book) for free. So…I'll ask every person reading this book to tell each and every college student and professor that you know to *read this book gratis*. I can't get justice from the courts. The deck is stacked against me. And lil' shade-tree lawyers like Jeff Kravitz in Carmichael, CA are too weak, timid and "flexible" to take on C.D.C. So the only way that I can truly pay them (George Stratton, Joseph Stratton, Ryan Wenker etc.) back is to *write* it down. If it's not written it didn't happen.

So I want readers to notify David Roddy, Oliver Mikkelsen (UC Davis), Alex Bernhart (US Berkeley), Quinn Halleck (UCLA), Trevor Jones, Kevin Droniak, Charles J. Couch, Caleb Lamb and Christopher Clubb etc. that this book is out and they should read it. They simply need to email Hallopeter@Sunrise.ch for a free E-copy of this book. I want students to analyze the contents of this book, and send me suggestions on what you think should and can be done to correct corrections. Send me a letter today.

Now… I need readers to review this list of names. And I want each of you to email them and tell them to email me. I want to work with each of the people: Curtis Sykes, James Nesmith, Scott Hoover, Adorian Deck, Keith Jordan (Sacto), M. Hiscel, Zoard Janko, Ju Hong, Serge Verobyov, Ryan Fitzgerald, Andrew Maillet, Kevin Shoop, Ryan Fehr, Justin Johnes, Luke Niccoli, Scott Dangerfield, Hernan Parra, Dante Mazza, Jacob Williams, Stuart Campbell, Ricardo Angelina, Robert James Carlson, Caleb Lamb, Caleb Butler, Dr. Seth Myers, *Matt Fender*, Zack Clark (Sacto), Zachary Sampson, Corey Janecek, Jared Gaber, Steven Retchless, Alex Back, Walter Michael (Willow, CA), Robert Roldan, *Matt Kwiatkowski*, Alex Adame, Bobby Mitchell Jr., Cody Lloyd, Ryan Neller, Randy Gyllenhall, Matt Jones (UC Davis), Jared Michael, J-Si Chavez, Grayson Pangilinan, Ryan McAndrew, Daniel Levine, Greg Smialkowski, Josh Bennett, Andrew Baggaley, Luke Clark Tyler, Adam Newkirk, Alex Attardo, Brett Loewenstern, Dylan Brant, *Austin Sisneros*, Nick Fink, Scott Dangerfield, Krystof Lopaur, Andy Dimitrov, Yancer Strickler, Jimmy Rock, Greg Bonetti, Jordan Simon, Hairo Torres, Zack Torres, Ryan Coolley, Dillon Waniecki, Derek Friedhoff, Matt Stuart, Devin Dwyer, Ryan Baker (Sacto), Nick Doss, Steve Sowards, Bryton Meyer, Ben Murphy, Brad Hinkle, Tim Franzen, Jon Tyler Straub, Jacob Faulkender, William Zander, Tadd Carr, John Brandon, John Dececchis, Robert Krybyla, Daniil Turitsyn, Robert Leslie, Daniel Hamidi, Hasib Habibi, A. J. Ali, Tyler Yagley, Patrick Hughes, Cameron Hughes, Jake Tracy, Brandon Hughes, Joseph Latham, Chris Wilczewski, Justin Brunner, Peter Knegt, Marko Beslach, Yarn Shcherbanyuk, Matt Wendt, *Brad Standiferd*, Brent Sebati, Joel DeFranchesca, Professor Noah Zatz, *Trenton Dorsey* (we have a job for Trenton), Scott Romano, John Mandern, Noah (in Mission Six or Cay Lights), Lane Garrison and Ari Shapiro…

...Tell them they have a free E-copy of this book waiting right now. Also Joshua Thornton, Joe Kirk, Brennin Hunt, Jacob Tenbrink, Robbie Burmeister, Jack Horgan, Daniel Asare, Kyle Evans, *Dakota Sotto*, Nathan Kavenik, Anthony Fedorov Bogdan Pishtoy, Robert Bowling, Matt McAndrew, Alex Blench, Trevor Day, Alex Hayes, Zach Freisen, Gary Jiang, Justin Hofstetter, Keith Semple, Bradley McClain, Tal Safron, Matt Clunie, Sam Burchfield, *Derek Pacque*, Paul Jolley, Levi Weikel, Moi Navarro, Adam Ben-David, Garrett McCain (Davis, CA), Josh Ogle, Sean Zane, Sean Farmer, Mason Porter, Patrick Ludlow, Brett Westcott, Cameron Brown, *Justin Hempfling*, Steve Kaufmann and Billy York… I want Blair Casey, Kory Carico and Tyler Grady to join my team today…

I'm dealing with officers Darren Wilsons right here in the California penal system. Guys who will murder a black inmate without batting an eye. Because they (Stratton and Bunnell etc.) know that their union (CCPOA aka the Green Wall) is like the white citizen's council. And their victims (i.e. Michael Gornan etc.) are usually an illiterate group of have-nots who can't get the New York Times to care about their well-being because they're not "Jeremy Meeks"… "Hands Up: Don't Shoot"… We need to put more hands down and start writing. We need to engage and get engaged in the transformative power of reading and education… I hope barbershops on Del Paso Boulevard and all over Sacramento, California etc. will put a copy of this book up in the window. I hope barbershops and beauty salons in Los Angeles, Atlanta, Chicago, Detroit, Ferguson and St. Louis, Missouri will put a copy of my book in your shop. And people will pick it up and read it. Google this book and talk about it. Chat about it and tell your politicians, your pastors and your educators etc. that they must read this book…

Pray for me please. I'm not playing around when I say pray. Ask Almighty God (through Jesus Christ) to bless me, to protect me, to empower me and to expedite my release. And…if I ever get out I will teach, speak, lecture, preach, write and I will never stop telling this story. I want President Barack Obama and the "new" Attorney General to read this book. And if I ever get out I'd like to talk to President Obama. When I meet Mr. Obama I believe that Rev. Hosea Williams (my mentor), *Dollie Mae Manning*, and…Dr. Martin Luther King will smile. I am "the least of these my brethren" in St. Matthew Chapter 25… Read this book…

# **Robert Shapiro**

Shapiro is the founder of Legal Zoom. And he was initially O. J. Simpson's lead attorney. And (as I share later) Robert is credited with assembling the Dream Team for O. J. And had he not assembled that "Dream Team" O. J. would be sitting in a California prison doing "life" without parole right now. But when the trial got started jealousy and envy began to set in. And Shapiro became very jealous because the media began to follow this flamboyant black lawyer Johnnie Cochran around. And they began to ignore Shapiro. And for the American media (which is controlled and owned by the Jews) to choose to follow a black lawyer over a Jewish lawyer in 1994 was unthinkable.

So one day Shapiro barged into Johnnie's office to announce that he wanted to cross-examine some key witnesses as well as do the closing argument. Johnnie, Carl Douglas and Lee Bailey told Shapiro that he'd lost his mind. Shapiro was a "fixer" and a notorious "deal maker." He usually pled all of his high-powered cases out. And lo and behold, Johnnie pointed out that, "Bob you have never tried a murder case in your lifetime." Shapiro insisted. And finally they got the "Juice" (aka O. J.) on the telephone from the jail. And O. J. made it clear that Johnnie was now calling all the shots. He said that Johnnie was the quarterback. So he ultimately could call his own plays. But Shapiro could still be the head coach. Keeping Johnnie Cochran in charge of the trial and in front of that jury was perhaps the best decision Mr. Simpson ever made in his lifetime.

In late 2013 – at age 75, Shapiro decided to actually do a murder trial. He inudated the court with paperwork (a sharp lawyerly move). But when the DA insisted on a trial Shapiro argued the case himself. And… When the jury was returned to announce their verdict Shapiro did not even bother to show up for the reading. He should have sent another lawyer to try the case also. He *lost*… Brilliant trial lawyers such as Clarence Darrow, Bobby Lee Cook, *Willie Gary*, Gerry Spence, *Johnnie Cochran* and Roy Black etc. come far-and-few between. There were some brilliant (Barry Scheck, Peter Neufeld, Alan Dershowitz, F. Lee Bailey and Blasier etc.) lawyers on O. J. Simpson's team. But there was only one man (here's – Johnnie) who could connect with that jury and tell them that, "Truth may be out there on a scaffold. And wrong may be in here on the throne. But that scaffold sways the future. And God standeth above the dim unknown. And He watches above His own… And He will be watching you as you render your decision. Do the right thing…" Johnnie's performance was so spectacular that the DA dropped the charges against Calvin Broadus (Snoop Dogg) and said, "We need to keep Cochran out of the courtroom for a while." If I could get a Johnnie (a Geri Green, Stewart Katz, Mark Merin or Mr. Francke etc.) on my case against Bunnell etc. C.D.C. would be shell-shocked!... I hope Logan Paul, Daniel Jennings (Tiburon, CA), Joshua Thornton, Cole Wilkinson, Dakota Sotto and Tommy Beard will get this book. *Advertise this* book on your Facebook page or on Twitter etc. And *we will pay you!*... We hope *Justin Boatman* is reading this…

And Cody Baetge, Daniel Jennings, Jeff Gerber, Jacob Faulkender, Cole Wilkinson, Keenan Harris, Matt Fender, Quinn Halleck, Bobby Mitchell Jr. and Scott Dangerfield. This chapter has their names in it because I'm asking each of them to become *G.B.G./HEART* (Helping Educate At Risk Youth) ambassadors right now. If you (whoever you are) received this book gratis, if you bought it at a legal store or if you bought it online, please do me a special favor and please (right now please) email the ten people above and ask them if they have this book. If they say no tell them to send me an email. Tell them "dude you are in the book!"

And…if you can find them online please do. *Cody* lives in Sacramento and he's a very affable youngster. *Daniel* lives in Tiburon, CA and he's a very intelligent dude. We are not certain where *Jeff* lives but he's very upbeat. *Jacob* lives in Carmichael, CA – and *Jacob* is very, very intuitive. *Cole* lives in South Lake, TX and he's brilliant. *Keenan* attends Wake Forest and we have high hopes for Keenan. This guy is eloquent. *Matt* attends the College of the Ozarks. He is super motivated. *Quinn* attends UCLA and he's a future mover and shaker. *Bobby* lives in Massachusetts and he wooed Judge Judy. Scott used to live in Milwaukee. We have high hopes for Scott. We want each one of them on our core team. Whether they believe I'm wrongly convicted or not is irrelevant. Do they believe in justice? Do they believe in equal protection under the law? Do they believe that we've got to stop beating, raping and killing each other? If so, I want each of them to be our Ambassadors. And we need you to preach literacy, the power of reading and education. Reading wakes people up.

I need you guys on my core team. I want all ten of you to send us a photo today so we can put your face in the next book and on our website. And I need *Ambassador Baetge* to call, email and contact local barbershops (i.e. black barbershops and white ones, etc.) and churches etc. in Sacramento. And all Ambassador Baetge needs to do is ask, "Have you all read *Sherman Manning's* new book yet? If not can we send you a copy for barbershop talk?"… I need *Ambassador Jennings* (*Gerber*, Faulkender, Wilkinson, Harris, Fender, Halleck, Mitchell and Dangerfield etc.) to simply use your computers to tell people about this book. And if you (the ambassadors) can give us 2 – 3 hours every Saturday or Sunday etc. we will "pay" you. I.E. if Cody emails us and says, "I contacted 100 people about the book and I spent 3 hours. I volunteered my time but I could use $30 bucks," we will send you (Cody, Daniel, Jacob, *Keenan* etc.) $30 bucks or so. The help we need is y-o-u. Just tell everybody you know to read (love – or – hate) this book.

I want Professors Brittney Cooper, Dylan Rodriguez, James B. Rule, Creed Archibald, Alan Dershowitz and Cornel West etc. to tell their students to read and critique this book. If *Ryan Regan*, Max Wiseltier, Jonathan Kassan (at UCSB), Cody Cook, Michael Hernbroth, (URNV), Zack Everhart, Teddy Coffey, Casey Askew, Jordan Bianco and Charles Askew will join us. If we get *Trenton Dorsey*, Aidan Sheehy, Tory Russell, Jeff Vinokur, Khulay BiBi (in Pakistan), Chris Wiczewski and Bradley Rayford on our team we can begin the work we need to promote schools over prisons. Education over incarceration. Picking up books and putting down guns. The more educated a people are the less crime they have. It doesn't take a rocket scientist.

I promise you that Bill Gates would tell you that if you take any trailer park, barrio or 'hood in this country, and get a Mitt Romney (who has a half $billion) to adopt the trailer park and send tutors and mentors in etc. Inundate those communities with books etc. Twenty years from now more kids will all be successful. We can't do it? They told Barack Obama, "You can't defeat Clinton." Even the great Vernon Jordan told President Obama that, "It's not your turn; it's not your *time*." You can never win me with an argument about what can't be done. *Floyd Mayweather* can be persuaded to buy twenty thousand copies of this book and donate them to churches. Floyd, Tyler Perry, Daymond John, Byron Allen etc. can be persuaded to *underwrite* our campaign and tours. Spike Lee can be persuaded to "sign *Manning* up to do a one-man" show. I believe all things are possible to him that believeth. But they (Spike, Floyd and others) have to see the book. So I need you to use the internet to leave no stone unturned.

I'm locked up in a cage and I can't reach them. It took a 16-year old boy to read Rubin "Hurricane" Carter's book and… Lesra Martin was moved by a book written by a man convicted of a terrible homicide. I am convicted… And it is wrongful. And I've poured my heart onto these pages. But words mean nothing if you don't read and hear them. I need Christopher Bird, *Justin Tankersaey*, Professor David Schwebel, Zachary Dickinson, *Daniel Sample*, Daniel Asare, *Kenan* Gebiz and *Austin Sisneros* etc. to read this book. If they (Shane Bruce, Ryan Fehr, Moi Navarro, Freddie Fox, Ben Schnetzer, George Mackay and Charlie Tschudin) read this book it will change them…

Police officers must stop racial profiling. Because we are not going to stand around and watch them stop, suspect and check the computers of crazy middleclass and rich *white* men looking for child porn… Stop profiling!... Dr. King was a prophet: He said stop judging people by the color of their skin. Because he knew how many McConnells, Issas and other older white men were child molesters and pedophiles. He desegregated the country because he knew that a white woman from Kansas and a black man from Kenya would produce America's first black President. Martin Luther King, Jr. (I'm serious) was absolutely a prophet!...

In prisons forgetfulness or oblivion settles like quicklime on the spirit, intelligence and bodies of exiled, demoralized and illegalized young people. A sense of responsibility to the community is replaced with rage. And beneath all posturing is despair, self-degradation and suicide. Help me to find Narcisco Morales, Daniel Kovarbasich, Daniel Job and Clayton Burnham etc. and get them to read… And we will read our way out of despair. We will read our way above racism and partisanship … "It's a one in a million chance that Obama will read your book" someone told me. But…if it's a one in a million chance that it happens, that means it happened to 311 people in 2012; a thousand if you include China… Hernan Parra, Stuart Watkins etc. read this book… Jessica Pierce and Molly Greider? Read this book…

## A Nation of Cowards

    Darrell Issa is the most divisive U.S. Representative in modern history. Mitch McConnell is the most divisive U.S. Senator in modern history. And with people like Issa, McConnell, Ted Cruz and Joe King in D.C. we will never become the nation that we can become. The media downplays the amount of animus which has been directed at President Obama by members of Congress. Out of all of the elected officials (including former Presidents) in this country only President Jimmy Carter has had the integrity and the audacity to state (emphatically) that, "A lot of the problems he (Obama) faces from the House is because of 'racism.'" Since Leon Panetta alleges to have a strong desire to see this president succeed. It would have been loyal and righteous if he had made that case. Panetta could have stated (factually) that, "A lot of the problems Obama faces is because the House (of Representatives) is too old, too male too pale and stale. And they need to stop being so racist." If Bob Gates had been the warrior he claims to be he certainly could have made that case…

    Argue politics with me all day long. Some of my views are conservative and would be considered "Republican." Some of my views are liberal and progressive. And I'm willing to debate political views all day long. We can be civil, intellectual and studious. But we can disagree all day long. And I'm okay with that. I love the art of a good debate. I love the Socratic methodologies. But if you put me in a room with a group of old white men who don't think I belong there. Who want me to leave. And who would celebrate if I was assassinated. No matter how articulate or eloquent I may be, I will not win those people over. The reason that neither Panetta nor Gates would include a chapter in their tomes on Issa, Mitch or Ted Cruz etc. is because Attorney General Eric Holder was right-on in 2009. He gave a speech in which he stated that we remain "*a nation of cowards*" when it comes to race. We are afraid to talk about it. And as long as we have former *KKK* members in the U.S. Senate (i.e. Mitch McConnell! Mitch was a Grand Wizard) we will continue to retrogress. Even reporters are "cowards" when it comes to race. No reporter has ever asked Mitch if he was in the Klan. Nor have they asked Issa if he is a racist. Yet, they (the media) had no problem asking Mr. Obama if he was a "Muslim" even after he became president. Nor did they have any problem asking to see his "birth certificate" after he was already a sitting president…

    But thanks be to God that our young people are not cowards. I have full confidence in *Adam Newkirk*. Adam lives in Sacramento and he's a great young man. I've every confidence that when it comes Adam, Scott Dangerfield, Nick Fink, *Hayden Voss* and Daniel Swain etc. This country's future is absolutely bright. And my goal is to find *Joe Kirk* (in Nashville), find Aaron Jackson (In Delaware, Ohio), Collin Stark (in California), Josh Stipp (Temecula), Zachary Pritchard and Brandon Urbas. I want to bring them together online and have think tanks, discussions and forums etc. I want a street team (i.e. Steven Evenhouse, Creed Archibald, Dakota Sotta, Frankie Edwards, Sebastian Demers and Jacob Williams etc.) to come together and to begin to plot strategy on how we overcome racists like McConnell.

    I want to bring together Daniel Job (i.e. Nick Topete, Trevor Leja, Stephen Karr, Tim Ballard, Laurie Holden, Scott Romano, Keith Semple, Derek Pacque, Mason Porter, Cole

Wilkinson, C. J. Sheron, Taylor John Williams, Jody Searcy, Keith Jordan, Matt Easley, Justin Johnes, Luke Niccoli and Caleb Butler etc.) with others and let's devise a set of plans to kick off a literacy campaign. I want to do voter registration drives etc. We are in the process of building a new *NAPSUSA.org* website on Facebook (so go to Facebook and look up *NAPSUSA.org*) so we can reach more people…

    Lieutenant Jimmy Guyton told me that "a lot of the reasons Couch and I.S.U. have called people like Loorz and told them not to write to you are because you're black. And black inmates ought to be gangbanging, playing cards or doing drugs. You are not supposed to be writing international books." Lieutenant Guyton told me to, "Please understand that these corn-fed, hillbilly cowboys like *Lieutenant Kukrall* are still living with the mentality of the 1950's era." And thus it is… I never thought of myself as facing the same kinds of problems (in a prison) as the President faces in the Congress. But the more I analyze it the more striking are the parallels.

    The average California prison "manager" represents the average U.S. "Representative." In fact, I found it strange the other day when I saw a big white guy with grey hair on T.V. and he was doing a commercial which is speaking out against "healthcare." I looked closely at this dude and finally realized who this was. This "expert" on healthcare is actually the former C.D.C. Director. And I don't mean Center for Disease Control in Atlanta. This C.D.C. is in California. This is the California Department of Corrections: Matt Cate. The guy who was "running" California's prisons as recently as 2 years ago is now on local T.V. as an "expert" on "*Why They Hate Obama.*"™

    Politics are "local." Any California warden can be an Associate Director of prisons tomorrow. And these guys are "all" Republicans. Half of them can't tell you why they are Republicans. But if Mr. Obama switched parties they'd all become Democrats. I look at the guards who work in this prison. They are clearly in the "47 percent" of the "takers" that Mitt Romney said would never vote for him. But they are "proud Republicans." I asked a guard to "spell Republican." And he said, "R-e-p-l-ub-l-i-c-a-n" and I was about to… But I just said, "Yep: You got it"…some of these fools? You can't change 'em. The only way they are gonna change is with death. I won't waste my time…

    If *Adam Newkirk* (Kory Carico, Tyler Kolb, Clayton Burnham or Max O'Rourke etc.) is reading this right now I need you. Adam please find Josiah Lemming, Daniil Turitsyn, Jacob Faulkender, (in Carmichael), Maxwell Hanger, Scott Czeda and Jacob Goodin. Tell them they are in this book. Tell them my team has small checks for each of them. And they have checks for Joe Kirk, Cole Wilkinson and Kent Boyd. *Adam*: Please tell them to get this book and to email (or snail mail at Sherman D. Manning J98796, C-15-239-480, Alta Rd., San Diego, CA 92179) me…

    The news media has done a terrible job of showing how well the first year of healthcare went in this country. The Affordable Healthcare Act is a really startling policy success and a defining achievement for Mr. Obama… Reagan is touted as a "great" President. But other than good speeches Reagan did not really deliver much. President Obama is even more eloquent than Reagan was. Plus Mr. Obama has delivered more. Thanks to President Obama healthcare is now a "right" as a permanent resident of the United States. And Mr. Obama did what no president from Truman on down has done. He is a transformative president. And Obama owes a lot of thanks to his opponents for his historical legacy. Medicare and Medicaid are historical but ask any person 40 years old or younger which president passed Medicare and they don't know. But because Republicans insisted upon referring to the AHC as "*Obamacare*" there will be no doubt (100 years from now) that *Obama* is responsible for *Obamacare*! It is awesome how good God is. He will use your enemies to bless you. Obama is more important as president than Reagan was. Mr. Obama is one of the most consequential and successful presidents in history…

The problem with the Senate and the Congress is that we have a lot of Donald Sterlings in D. C. If you could record McConnell, Cruz, Boehner and Pete King etc. they share those same views about black people as Sterling does. So does Mitt Romney. I personally know Newt Gingrich and he is just like Sterling. William Morley is a racist and he claims that Darrell Issa once stated, "I'd pay to have a N - - - er killed." He did not know who Issa was speaking about… (Ty Herndon, Billy Gillman, Jessica Pierce, Chris Nachtrab, Tory Russell, Phillip Joubert, John Emery, Matthew McRae, Ryan Tallman, Matt Swatzell, Jason Fagerlie and Drew Clover are you reading this?)

(I want a team of *Shermanators* to help us. We'll pay as many of you as we can. I want Benjamin Prado, Garret Smith, *Jacob Hageman*, Chris Thormann, Michael Braunstein, Will Niespodzinski, *Chad Elledge*, Jack Forsyth, Chase Friedman, Ben Beard, Alex Hayes, Jimbo Spalding, Alex Hayes, Justin Strada, John Garvin, Daniel Swain, Mitchell Thorp, Oswaldo Hernandez, Zack Clark, Ryan Fehr, M. Hiscel, Justin Jankersky, Ricardo Angelina and Tommy Beard etc. Help me reach them!)…

President Obama once said about racists that, "Ignorant folks want to advertise their ignorance. You don't have to do anything, you just let them talk." And I utilize that Obama tactic 8 days per week and 25 hours per day. And oh the stuff I hear coming out of these people's mouths. These people who have fallen in love with their own 'rectitude.' Those white prison guards who secretly hate blacks but their daughters are dating blacks. These people who have one foot in the trailer park and one in the prison but they're Republican and they're being looted every day. I shall repeat: If you are not a millionaire you're foolish (speaking fiscally) to be a Republican…

Ages ago I met an older white dude who hated black people. This was in Chicago. And…three weeks later when his 22 year old (I was 25) daughter was performing fellatio on me I said to myself, "If your daddy could see you now"… Racists are "cowards" by nature; period… Somebody Tweet that "we've gotten a lot more from Obama than from anybody else since LBJ." Period…we've surely (without question) gotten way more out of Mr. Obama than we got out of Clinton. And I know that the James Carvilles of Life will argue about how much Bill loves politics and how he was so affable. Clinton is the "darling" of the Democratic party. He's the comeback kid and all that. But the fact remains that Mr. Clinton tried (*and failed*) to pass "healthcare." Mr. Clinton does not have a single piece of signature legislation (and I know that he does not want to talk about PLRA and AEDPA etc. He's certainly locked up millions of black men for non-violent crimes and he gutted the right of appeal) that will outlive his name. Mr. Clinton is a flawed man (like all of us), he was a 'good' president and he's a good politician. He was not great; period. If you look (meticulously) at PLRA and AEDPA you could think he's a bit "racist"…

I'd like to debate and lecture around the country about these issues… If you know how to set up a podcast I'll need you in 2 months. I'll just get on the internet and pontificate. And… If Scott Dangerfield, *Hayden Voss*, Cody, Josh Brown, Chad Elledge, *August Clary*, Joe Redmond, John Garvin, Scott Johnson (Warner Robins, GA), Lane Garrison, Nick Prugo, Van Harris, Jordan Bianco, Shane Bruce, Cole Wilkinson, Joe Kirk and Brandon Urbas are reading this. Let me hear from you. Email all of your friends and tell them to read this book. We want to work with lord Charlie Cotton, "Rob" (a TMZ bus driver in New York), Rev. Osagyefo Sekou, Adam Newman (in New York), Cody Tow and Joel Northrup. We need college students like Keenan Harris, Will Stabler, John Spurlock and Izzy Gardon. We need high school students like Jacob Hageman. Jacob is a star varsity football player at Oakmont High School out in California. Garret Smith is a soccer player at Oakmont. Joe Kirk is an 18 year old in Nashville. If we get a team like Tyler Grady, Taylor Mathews (in Alexandria, LA), Andy Hines (GA), *Benjamin Prado* (Modesto) and Adam Newkirk etc. we can transform the nation.

When I met Joe Stratton, George, T. Negrette, Marion E. Spearman and Mike Bunnell etc. they had no idea that I'd make exposing their corruption (on steroids) the cause of my life. I will write, lecture, podcast, teach and testify about Ryan Patrick Wenker and Aron Ralls etc. until the day I die. I will talk about the so-called "suicide" of Captain Doug Pieper, his wife Yvette and son Doug Jr. until I'm dead… And remember: The guard who is photo'd in this book (in underwear) is a rapist. And I have email and computer evidence which *any FBI tech could use* to prove (conclusively) his corruption. He raped an inmate in 2011 and in 2012. Prison officials *shredded* the inmate "*appeal*." Why? To prevent "*exhaustion*" because (thanks to Mr. Clinton) the inmate *can't sue* as long as the prison "*claims*" he didn't *exhaust*. I've personally told Allison Claire about this inmate being raped. And I was threatened (by J. Stratton) that if I published these photos I'd be *transferred* and/or given a "*horrible*" *celly*. I hope Gerri Green, Sergio Garcia and Stewart Katz etc. are reading this. I also want Attorney General Loretta Sanchez and the FBI Director to read this book. And I hope "change" will come… Every California prison guard (due to all of their "hate-Obama" rhetoric) needs mandatory diversity and sensitivity training. Well over 90 percent of California prison guards are hillbilly racists…

I hope we can find Trenton Dorsey, Alex Back, Daniel Jennings (in Tiburon, CA), *Justin Tankersaey* (he witnessed the Stockton County Bank robbery), Jay Davies, Cody Baetge and Max Wiseltier. I *need* their help. I need Indio Downey, Vincent Thomas, Dominic Burrows, Justin Hoop and *Bianca Graulau*. If we work together, pray together, think together and write etc. we can transmogrify the world. When people are corrupt we must disrupt their messaging campaign. I can't do it alone. Remember how they lied to Alec Loorz. I need Brooks Randolph, Chris Jamison, Tyler Smith, Kyle Rieman, David Hellyer, Trevor Law and Nolan Wong etc…

Dr. Parsa Zadeh (DDS) is a Beverly Hills dentist. He is a complete crook. Dr. Zadeh should have his dentistry license pulled. But guys like him usually end up being sent to work in prisons…

If you are a student (i.e. Josh Ogle, Paul Jolley, Max O'Rourke, Jacob Williams, Derek Pacque, Chris Kluwe, Moi Navarro, Mason Porter, Benjamin Prado, Garrett Smith, Jacob Hageman, Keenan Harris or Cody Hassler etc.) and you are willing to be a *Shermanator*: We will *pay* you!... We need all the volunteers we can get. But if you do special projects like holding up signs or directing people to our books etc. we will pay you. It won't be tons of money! But it will be money! So please let *Trenton Dorsey*, Daniel Jensen, Daniel (in Tiburon), Logan Paul and Austin Whaley know we need them. If you make a video (on YouTube) that tells people about this book etc…we'll pay… Now read this book…

I spoke with Donny Thompson on 10/14/14. The call was a blessing and it was absolutely unbelievable. I could not believe that I was actually speaking to the Donny Joe Thompson of "The Bold and the Beautiful" and of "Big Brother" fame. After our active chat I asked Donny to pray for me. Donny is a good man. I hope Donny will tell Amber, Cody, Hayden and Zach to read this book… Guys like Donny can help heal the racial wounds of our country. And you (Dan Childs, Zachary Pritchard, Willie Steed, Peter Grasso, *Josh Klein*, Spencer Adams, Spencer Perry, Ramses Pringle, *Shakia Pennix*, Jack Falahee, Conrad Ricamora, Ann Kindberg, August Clary, Eliot Sudal, Kevin Lockhart, Mike Mowry, M. Hiscel and Dan Wetter etc.) can help to heal this nation. Don't ignore the issues. Let's deal with the issues.

# **Behind the Scenes with F. Lee Bailey**

I'm not going to reveal my confidential sources so forget it. But if you know anything about O. J.'s murder trial you'll know that I've done my homework. When Bob Blasier and I began our friendship (years ago) I'm certain he thought I'd be writing an O. J. book sooner. Why not? I'm a writer. Yet, it has taken me ten years of studying this case to decide to write it. And it turns out to be a much different type book than anyone would anticipate. It's got a lot of No ' J issues in it. I wanted to bring a fresh, analytical and candid voice. You know the media reported "facts" of the case. But this book is different. First of all I actually (yes I repeat) *write* my own books. I'm one of the few authors who really writes his own work. And I do not allow a publishing house, editor or a book doctor to do any rewrites. I "write live." That's either extremely "*impressive*" or pitiful (depending upon your perspective)…

Here's what didn't make the news. Behind the scenes the Goldman family worked frantically to suppress the fact that their son (*Ron*) had not just worked at the restaurant. He was also an escort. Ron had been a meth addict and did gay escorting. He'd recently started doing "straight" escorts. So many were wondering was he really returning Nicole's glasses or was he "servicing" Nicole. And perhaps (I'm told) O. J. knew Ron was a gigolo and this lead to him exploding. But O. J. had a ton of skeletons in his closet also. Not only was he coking it up with his male (live-in) house guest, O. J. was also freaking with that house guest. Ipso Facto, O. J. and Attorney *Robert Kardashian* had also did a threesome (with Mrs. Kardashian). And Robert's wife became livid because she saw "Robert *fondling* O. J.'s penis"… What's more is the fact that one day Lee Bailey came into a defense meeting drunk. And Lee Bailey blurted out, "Rob was O. J. f--king you in your Jewish ass or what?"

Lee Bailey continuously showed up for key meetings intoxicated. Alan Dershowitz states, "They called us the "dream team" but we were actually the *nightmare* team. We hated each other." But Lee Bailey was the most famous lawyer (prior to the trial) on the team. He'd written tomes on criminal procedure and on cross-examination etc… As recently as 2012 he called *Bob Blasier* to get the trial transcripts from O. J.'s trial. He was going to write a book about the case. Bob sent Lee Bailey everything. Lee Bailey got drunk and forgot all about it. I say this not to make fun of Lee Bailey. I grew up with strong respect for F. Lee Bailey. He's a brilliant lawyer. But I'm a literary evangelist. And I have to use Lee Bailey as an example of what alcohol or drugs can do to a great man. I have to try to inspire youngsters to never surrender to alcoholism and to drugs…

To get something you never had you've got to do something you've never done. Life is not all – fun. The battle (if you serve God) is already won. You just have to keep aiming (and shooting) your spiritual gun… I hope that Danny Frishmuth (in Philly), Ernest Griffin (in Georgia), David Hartline, Daniel Rogers (Canyon Lakes, CA), Nick Topete, Michael Strange, Dan Childs, Dakota Sotto, Hugh Murphy, Trevor Leja and Brandon Urbas will hear about this book and read it…

Even if they are not interested in O. J.'s trial, it is still a story of a life gone wrong. O. J.'s life is a Shakespearian tragedy. He had it "all." And he risked it by "killing two people."

*Johnnie Cochran*, Bob Blasier, Barry Scheck and Peter Neufeld etc. got him "off." And he still did not stop faking. What else do you need to wake you up when you get lucky, blessed and… You get a big enough break that you are acquitted of two counts of murder. I don't know any black man (in the 20$^{th}$ or 21$^{st}$ centuries) who has been tried for the murders of two white people and *lived* to *talk* about it. Much less walked out of the courtroom as a free man. And that was still not enough to *humble* this "sick" brother. Bob Blasier tells me how affable and gregarious O. J. is. And Bob genuinely "liked" O. J. But… At one point I liked Eric Menendez. But I also *know* (beyond any doubt) that he viciously murdered his own mom and dad.

My research assistant spoke with several inmates who say that "O. J. is taking it up the" posterior right now. I can't verify that. We know (for a fact) that Suge Knight was sexually involved with fellow prisoners. Suge received a write-up (written by Lieutenant Cherry at MCSP) for performing fellatio on a man… With O.J. I'm told "it was absolute chaos behind the scenes. I don't know how Johnnie Cochran was able to keep that team together. And I don't know how we were able to win that case. But even as a "team," well over 90 percent of that case was won by Johnnie. What a f--king lawyer that man was." And Attorney Ben Brafman echoes those sentiments regarding his friend Johnnie. The only other lawyer on the team who had actually had arguments with Johnnie was actually Robert Shapiro (the man who brought Johnnie into the case). Envy and jealousy are absolutely deadly…

…I suggest that readers ought to call C.D.C. (916-323-6001) and demand that they identify the guard pictured in this book in underwear. Demand that I be treated fairly. Ask them not to transfer me as *retaliation* for publishing this. And I affirm under penalty of perjury that he *raped* an inmate. And there is an intentional conspiracy (unfortunately aided by a judge) to cover it up. *Why* won't *I.A.* analyze the handwriting on missives "he" wrote to an inmate? I know where the missives are. No one has asked to read them. Why? They cover up crime… Ask Narcisco Morales…

(I need to reach Alexander Mosanto, Hayden Voss, Brandon A. Hughes, Aaron Kelly, Alex Lambert, Alex Hayes and Raymond Flores…) O. J.'s life reads like an "oh what a tangled web we've weaved" novel. I suggest that law students (Justin Cash and Kevin Johnson in New York) study O. J. Simpson. I wanna reach Alec Blench, Zach Freisen, Creighton Baird, Clint Scott, Kory Carico and Cassius Harti. I want Remington Korper and Hugh Michael Hughes to read this book. I am a writer. And writers wanna be read. And the more you read the more you'll know. And I want America to know how Judge Allison Claire treated me. I want the world to know what Mike Bunnell and what C.D.C. did to me. "Who do you think you are?" a guard asked me…

And that is another major problem for President Obama. "Who is he and how did he get there?" says McConnell. Mr. Obama did not come from the right family. His grandfather was a Muslim. And President Obama was just a "community organizer." How in the hell did he get to the White House?... "Figure it out for yourself my lad." What is frightening is that by the time you are reading this Mitch McConnell might actually be the leader of the Senate. God forbid… I hope not…

When I talked to (Big Brother star) Donny Joe Thompson I asked him what were different people's last names. And when we got to Cody he said, "It's an Italian name; I don't know how to spell it but it's something like C-a-l-a-f-e-u-r-i-e," so I'm not sure how to spell it but we want Cody to get this book. I need an A-team. If you'll be so kind (as a reader) I want you to locate Kyle Pratt in Sacramento. We want Kyle, Daniel Jennings (in Tiburon), Logan Paul, Benjamin Prado, Casey Campbell (he used to live in Oklahoma), Joey Grissett, Eric Lotke, Avery Hughes (Sacto), Will Niespodzinski, Bianca Graulau and Brooks Randolph. I figure that Max O'Rourke (and his dad Mike) can read this book. And Max can share it with teachers and with students who agree and disagree with me. My aim is not to pontificate. I'm very interested in people who disagree with me. I can learn from them. I'm not looking for friends and buddies etc. I want a posse and a team includes skeptics. I don't discriminate against folks who watch me with a skeptical eye. If you're not skeptical of a prisoner I'm skeptical of you.

Be careful who you trust. Just a few weeks ago Sergeant Eric Lund was arrested. He is the spokesperson for the California Highway Patrol. He was about to retire. This man has a gun, a badge, a uniform and stripes. He is trusted by many. Yet, they found kiddie porn on Sergeant Eric Lund's computer. He's been downloading child pornography on his police computer as well as his home computer for years. A sick bastard who is a cop! Be very skeptical and careful! Parents should closely scrutinize every adult!... I want Jacob Williams to share this book with his parents, teachers and fellow students at Bear River. I want Sabrina Foster, Ramses Pringle (US Berkeley), *Danny Frishmuth*, Scott Czeda, Janus Getty, Michael Dennis and Willie Steed to get this book. I want Mike Oleginski, Sam Burchfield (Athens, GA), Trevor Leja, Andrew O'Brien (Keller, TX), *Brandon Urbas* (Michigan), Jared Goetz, William Haskell, Josh Klein, Gene Wallis and Daniel Jensen to read this book… Some of these people can help us. We want to change the world. I want to get students back to reading. I want to get inmates and ex-cons etc. reading. Readings open up the mind…

Anytime you are anointed you are a dreamer. And Joseph (in Genesis) can tell you that dreamers are dangerous. People who walk in the favor (of God) often have sleep disorders. The enemy doesn't want you to see (in a REM stage) the dream. I want to tell students like Jacob Williams, William Haskell, Keenan Harris and Dave Jessop etc. to be encouraged. Your own family may not believe in your dream. Sometimes family members don't celebrate young dreamers. Jesus' own brothers didn't believe in Him. Success stirs up jealousy. And…dreamers are often overlooked when you're young. David's father (King David in the Bible) didn't even consider David when they were looking for the next King. His father didn't even bring him in because he was just a shepherd boy. Even after David became the King he never convinced his brothers that he was "qualified." Jesus couldn't do any miracles at home. They boxed him in as a "carpenter." Jesus knew his critics didn't understand Him. Don't get involved with battles that don't matter.

I'm writing this right to *you* youngsters (Jacob Williams, Trevor Law, Trevor Loflin, Kyle Pratt and William Rains etc.) right now. God will give you the grace for where you are. Sometimes Jesus didn't even answer his critics. The best answer to critics is success. Go where you're celebrated – not where you're hated. Go where you're celebrated – not even where you're tolerated and deep down they are jealous of your *gift*. This has nothing to do with O. J. Simpson or justice etc. I know… But I'm leaving the book (I digress) and I'm led to (go off script) write this right now. Go where you are celebrated. (And if God blesses me to get out of prison in 2016) I must remember that myself. There will be pastors and leaders etc. who hold the *scams* of my *past* against me. David could not sing "praises" for you if all you thought about was his adultery. And David was an adulterer and a murderer. And if Jasper Williams only remembers that I disrespected him and I insulted him. If he doesn't forgive me and embrace me etc. I can live with that. I still apologize…

There will be people who actually believe that I'm "guilty" of this crime. I can live with that. Everything you go through now is preparing you for where you're going to. I'm surrounded by people who believe I did "it." They know nothing about the case or me. They've never seen me "rape" anyone. They don't think I act, look or "think" like a "rapist." But that's all irrelevant to them. This is prison and since they did "it." They murdered people etc. then I "must" have did what they "say" I "did." So God teaches me in the now for what I will face in the future!)… You should read St. Matthew 10:14 and it will make sense to you. That (St. Matthew 10:14) will be my mantra when I get out of here.

As I hit the "chitlin circuit" I'm gonna preach for those who let me preach. And I'll speak at the places that want me to speak. But if you don't wanna be bothered with me, I certainly can live without you. I'm living without you right now; right? I've survived for more than a decade having never met you. And still I've survived. God is an awesome God. (If you are an Atheist, Jew, Muslim, or Agnostic etc. I respect your beliefs. And you don't have to have my beliefs to be on our team). I want to tell Charles Jackson (Fairview Park, OH), Trevor Day, Alec Loorz, Brian Devin Graham and Jacob Williams etc. to be who you are. *You* (Baetge, Hassler and Pratt etc.) are the *leaders* we've been waiting for. If not now when? If not *you* (Danny Frishmuth, Tyler Kolb and Adam Newkirk etc.) who? *You* have the power to change yourself. You can change your school and your *community*.

No matter *who* is in charge of the United States Senate right now (even if it is that Klansman Mitch); Frankly? *Especially* if it's Mitch McConnell. One thing Barack Obama's life and legacy can tell every person (black, white, lesbian, gay, woman etc.) is that even if you are a small-time "community" organizer; with a middle name like "Hussein." With every odd against you; with $billionaires (i.e. Trump, Adelson, Romney and the Koch brothers) working against you; with McConnell, Cruz, Issa and McCain calling you a "Muslim," a "terrorist" and with Cruz comparing your political ambitions to "the rise of *Hitlerism*": In spite of all of that you can rise up (with a Kansas mother and a Kenyan father) and become the *President* of the *United States*. If Mr. Obama can become *POTUS*! What can't you (Jacob Williams, Brandon Urbas, Benjamin Prado, Kenan Gebiz, Bobby Mitchell Jr. and Shane Bruce etc.) become? I intend to spend my life teaching a master class (if Barack can become POTUS – I can teach) on *Obama*, on *Joseph*, on *Mandela*, on *Banks*, Ryan Ferguson and on Christopher Bird! *You* (the reader) can do anything!...

# **Andy Wu and UC Berkeley**

    Andy Wu has applied to UC Berkeley, Stanford and a few other universities to study business and computer science. I personally hope he goes to UC Berkeley. I have a strong affinity for Berkeley because of their strong stance on "free speech" and artistic expression. And great students like Nolan Wong, Alex Bernhart and Shawn Lewis etc. have gone to UC Berkeley… Andy Wu is a senior at Bella Vista High School in Fair Oaks, California. I don't want people to define Andy by an accident or by a temporary limitation etc. so I'm not going to write anything (zero) about his accident! He is co-president of the student body and he's nominated as the homecoming king. Andy has great parents and he's a brilliant student. His girlfriend is Natalie Caraway. Natalie is a senior at Granite Bay High. *Steven Bush* is one of his best buddies.

    I salute and applaud Andy, Steven, Natalie and their friend Hanna Johnson. Jinee Sargent is an adviser to the student government team and Jinee teaches Andy calculus. I hope Andy (Steven Bush, Hanna, Natalie and others at Bella Vista) will show this book to his parents (since Andy is not yet 18) and get their permission to become an "Ambassador." And… I hope Andy, Steven and others will go online and contact 20 or 30 of the people we name in this book (any person who can prove that they contacted 80 or more people whom we name etc. we will send that person a small *check* to say thank you.) and tell those persons to read this book. I want government studies, social science, criminal justice and political science students to read this book. I want them to also read "*Just Mercy*" by Professor Bryan Stevenson. Read "*The New Jim Crow*," "*Creating Monsters*" (www.cafepress.com/Manning) and read "*The Miraculous Journey of Rubin "Hurricane" Carter*." I want *Ambassador* Andy Wu (*Ambassador* Bush and *Ambassador* Caraway etc.) to help us to develop creative and innovative strategies to motivate and stimulate a reading revolution. I want people to read. Readers become leaders. The more you read the more you learn. The more you learn the more you earn. Even the Bible says, "Brethren I would not have you be *ignorant*." Doctors become doctors and lawyers become lawyers because of what they read… Help us to start people back to reading…

    If Andy (Steven and Hanna etc.) is reading this book I want you to know I'm not looking for you to agree with everything I say. The more you don't agree with me the more I can learn from you. And the more I learn the more I can earn. I just want you (Wu, Bush etc.) to contact others (i.e. *Alex Smith* at UC Davis, Nate Zavaleta, Barrett Foa, Logan Lorman, Cody Linley, Lane Garrison, James Lewis in Valdosta, GA, Josh Orapello, Greg Pugh and Tyler Stanley etc.) and tell 'em that "you are in this book dude." Andy if you go to UC Berkeley you'll meet a student named *Eric Wilcox*. He's cool… Email Eric and tell him to get this book. We want Tyler Gattis, Daniil Turitsyn, Roger Walthorn, Steven Sowards, Charles Lutz, Nathan Peterson, Josh Klein, Greg Deekins, Maxwell Amadeus, *Will* (Nederland, TX), Nick Doss, Alexander Monsanto, Nick Doss, Moi Navarro, Christian Jordan, Jais Malcolm, Cory Laymen, Zac Sunderland, Andy Hines and Scott Johnson. Scott is from Warner Robins, GA etc. to read this book.

I did Navy boot camp with a guy from Floyd, Illinois. His name was Steve or Scott Coffman and/or Steve or Scott Kauffman. I'd like students to help me find him. We were in company 048. Our company commanders were Senior Chief Petty Officer Franklin and CPO Beauchamp. If Steven Bush, Andy, Natalie and others (at Bella Vista Rocking High etc.) will help us we will be grateful…

# John Grisham

Throughout this book I've mentioned the fact that parents can *not* trust their children to anybody. Not even the police (remember Sergeant Eric Lund). I've also ruffled a few feathers by pointing out that most child molesters look a lot like *Mitch McConnell* (i.e. Mark Foley, Larry Craig and Jeffrey Dahmer etc.) and Darrell Issa. And that less than 12 percent of child molesters are black. And any statistical data will inform the reader of this fact. I'm sorry that this is true but it is absolutely true. And nobody has the gall or the audacity to state it. Yet, in a roundabout, foolish, convoluted and controversial way *John Grisham* concurs with this statistic. He made some "telling" comments which he ended up trying to walk-back. After I read his "cleaned up" comments I asked myself, "*Who* says this?" Grisham apologized for saying in an interview that many men imprisoned for child pornography offenses in the U.S. probably just had too much to drink and pushed the wrong button.

John told British newspaper The Daily Telegraph that U.S. prisons were "filled with guys my age; sixty-year old *white* men in prison who have never harmed anybody, would never touch a child!" John made a distinction between "real pedophiles" and those he said were being punished too harshly. That lost me because his statements are convoluted and contradictory. He starts out insinuating that he's defending drunk, "white" men who hit the "wrong" button. The he seems to insinuate a defense for 60-year old white men who "have never harmed a child." That leads any rational person to assume that he means that these guys crave children or fantasize but would never actualize. I have a problem with the premise. If a 60-year old "white" man is craving children he needs a psychologist or a jail or both… Then he contradicts his "wrong button" and "too much to drink" claim by stating that pedophiles are being punished too harshly. He said offenders did deserve to be punished but "we've gone nuts with this incarceration." I say Grisham may be a pedophile himself. We know he's a racist already. And I love his legal thrillers. I am a fan of his legal novels. But he is definitely a racist…

Child welfare advocates criticized his comments. He later issued a statement through his publisher, Random House which says his comments "were in no way intended to show sympathy (that is exactly what he intended to show!) for those convicted of sex crimes, especially the sexual molestation of children." This publisher said he regrets making those comments. But I guarantee you he meant exactly what he said. A bestselling author is a master with "words." He knew what he was saying. Random House knew he might cost them money (and the CEO of *Random* House is probably a "60-year old" white *pedophile* just like Grisham!) so they cleaned his words up.

It bothers me that we are naïve enough to "buy" that bull. I am uniquely qualified to detest his comments. I am *wrongly convicted* of raping an adult. And I believe sexual "violence" is a sin, a shame and a crime. And sexual deviants deserve *punishment* and *correction*. And that "correction" can involve therapy and treatment. Not sympathy! And Grisham was very specifically and clearly defending "*child* molesters." And… I've written books about the light sentences being given to pedophiles. But lo-and-behold John and I are on different planets.  He said (clearly) that "pedophiles" deserve (some) punishment, but "we've *gone nuts* with this *incarceration.*"  Random House can't delete that statement.  I keep seeing pedophiles like Dr. Melcher (a psychiatrist in Sacramento) get convicted of molesting little boys.  And…Dr. Melcher received "probation."  And during my research (in 2012) I reviewed 463 child molestation cases.  93.7 percent of those cases were white men over 40 – molesting kids.  64 percent of the molesters received probation.  15 percent received five years or less in jail…only 8 percent of the pedophiles received sentences of ten years or more…

Someone should email America's favorite legal thriller author and tell him that America's non-fiction author calls him a 60-year old pedophile.  John Grisham is a sick man.  And Random House is sick also.  And parents should beware…  To be fair I always warn parents.  I'm transparent.  I'm wrongfully convicted so I expect people to be hesitant around me.  And…I will get *Freddie Parrish* and Justin Brooks (or Deidre O'Connor etc.) to prove I did not do this.  But…  If I were released tomorrow (although my conviction does *not* involve *children*) and if a principal wanted me to speak to high school students, I would *not* go without *police* escorts.  The police (and parole officers) would have to go with me.  A grown ass man over 40; who just got out of prison for "anything" does *not* have any business "kicking it" with kids who are not his kids…

I want to find Pastor Corey Watson and ask him to help me build our team.  I want to find Rev. Willis Johnson and Pastor Pfleger.  I'll ask Rev. Larry Rice to help us.  We will find David Pate, Brad Standiferd, Jordan Bianco, *Eric Wilcox* (UC Berkeley), Alex Smith, Brent Sehati, Dhoruba Shakur and Attorney Jaime Dorenbaum.  I'm looking (right now) for Christian Gamboa, Cameron Polom, Josh Stipp and *Hayden Voss*.  I wanna locate Devin Dwyer, Tony Varatip, Charlie Cotton, Moi Navarro, Alexander Monsanto, Josh Klein, Nick Topete, Jake O'Donghue (Tampa, FL), Matt Kwiatkowski, Matt Harmon, Tyler Caldwell, Kevin Droniak, Will Haskell and Mike Wiseltier etc…  I need readers to reach them and tell them to read this book.  I want to spark a movement.  We need college students to get back in the fight.  Start back reading, writing and voting.  This is a joint effort.  I want students to help heal the world.  If we are`the world and we are the children…there are people dying…  We must make the world a better place; just you and me.

I have some secret tactical strategy which I shall not discuss in this book.  But once you (Cody Baetge, Michelle, Kris Beall, Clayton Burnham, Daniil Turitsyn and Doug Pleper Jr. etc.) become a *"Shermanator"* we can disseminate our confidential strategy.  Remember Alec Loorz (and his dear mother Victoria)?  C.D.C. lied to them.  They (the CCPOA) play dirty.  They've mastered dirty tricks…  Look at the photos of the *guard* (in this book).  He is still a guard!  He raped an inmate in 201 and 2012.  And (I repeat) to keep him from suing – Lieutenant Nielsen shredded the victim's appeal.  He rewrote it in July 2014 and sent it directly to Warden Macomber.  It disappeared.  And he's threatened that if he pushes the "rape" they will *transfer* him…

The *CCPOA* is like the Mafia!  Ask *Narcisco Morales*…  The rapist guard sent emails to (actually a semi-*black* mail) a friend of the inmate's seeking "photos."  A forensic examination of the guard's computer and/or the email would prove (conclusively) that the guard sent those emails…  Why won't *CCPOA* follow-up?  The inmate "victim" is not "popular" and guards don't want to be sued. (If they knew Allison Claire like I do they'd fear not)... But I hope Geri Green, Mark Merin, David Ring, Stewart Katz or Jeff Wozniak will read this and help this inmate. He can *prove* he was repeatedly *raped* by this guard... I want justice for this inmate. Perhaps John Grisham may be soft on sex crimes. I am not. I want the guard to be prosecuted to the full extent of the law. The fact that a guard has any kind of sex with a prisoner is a crime. An inmate cannot consent!

...I want to thank Fred and Helen Powell for their missive(s). It is not every day that I get mail from "Simi Valley," California... I also want to reiterate our campaign to get a new team. I want Cristina Mitchell (in Sacto), Montana Hull, Tyler Bogdanos, Ryan Sill, Kory Carico (Sterling, VA), Charlie Cotton, Adam Glyn, Mark Friedman, Rev. William Barber, Clayton Burnham, Nathaniel Mullennix (Atlanta, GA) and Joshua Avery etc. to join us. We need you all to go online and start "discussions" about this book etc. My team will *pay you* (Josh Avery, *Cody Baetge*, *Cody* Lloyd, Joe Kirk and Steven Bush etc.) to start discussion groups about this book. We want to see students (i.e. Alex Smith at UC Davis, Eric Wilcox at UC Berkeley, Keenan Harris, Jonathan Spurlock and Keenan Gebiz etc.) to start discussions (online) at your university. We will pay you a small fee just to start the discussion. (It will be a private confidential fee. Just send us an email with proof of the "discussion group")... We want young folks to stand tall. *You* (our youth) can do anything you put your mind to. You (Hayden Voss, Austin Sisneros, *Cody* and Dylan Heath etc.) are the leaders we've been waiting for. If not now, when? If not you who?... Follow me on Twitter at *@ShermanManning*. And email us at Hallopeter@sunrise.ch. Look at www.NAPSUSA.org and www.cafepress.com/Manning... Tell everyone you know (Like Tim Quinn, Vincent Thomas, Nick Prugo and Lane Garrison etc.) to read this book. ...Special thanks to my Chief Administrative Assistant (and P.A.) Mr. Jacob Paske. And I could do none of this without God and (my brother-in-law and his wife – in Zürich, Switzerland) Peter Andrist... Sherman D. Manning – December, 2014... I hope to work with Steve Madden, Zack Everhart and Joe Kirk etc. We can make short films,
movies and do workshops etc. I'll work with Anthony Fedorov, Scott Dangerfield, Nick Fink and *you*...

# **Jacob Paske**

Jacob Paske is a bright young man who appeared on a lady justice case aka "Judge Judy." Jacob is an avid reader of my books and he's been very instrumental in our work at "*Gang Bangers* for *God*" (G.B.G.). Jacob is my Chief Assistant and he was recently promoted to "Chief Executive Assistant – to the President of *Gang Bangers* for *God*." We've included a few photos of Jacob wearing our t-shirts (you may purchase these t-shirts at www.cafepress.com/*Manning*.) Jacob met us through our books. And… A guy on Judge Judy connects with a wrongly convicted author. And now we have a 23-year old youngster working for a 41-year old author. And my team in Switzerland coordinates it all. I applaud, salute and I commend Jacob. If I had ten more people who worked as hard as Jacob we would revolutionize the world… I need a few more people who can see through B.S. and understand how often our justice system gets it wrong.

I plan to find Tammie Counts and *Christopher Bird*. And I want them to join *Gang Bangers for God*, *HEART* (Helping Educate At Risk Teens), Jacob and I as we tour across the nation. I plan to get Christopher Bird, David Quindt, Ryan Ferguson, Josh Avery, Matt Fender and Ricky Manning etc. together. And we will do justice "revivals," crusades, workshops and seminars. We will conduct clinics and trainings unlike anything which has been seen or done in this nation before. I will ask *Spike Lee* to help me. Perhaps Spike can do with my wrongful conviction (via one-man shows etc.) what he's done for Iron Mike. Maybe Spike (or Daymond John, Jonathan Jackson, Byron Allen or even Tyler Perry etc.) will help me to promote our justice clinics, seminars and workshops etc…

I am ordained minister of the Gospel. I've preached all over the country (prior to my incarceration). And I've owned a successful business. I've authored 23 books. But when I get home a lot of preachers will not accept me. Because (in their opinion) I'm not Joseph. Joseph had a "right" to get wrongly convicted of *rape*. And "Rev. *Manning* ain't Joseph." Plus Joseph was convicted of attempted rape on a woman. And "they claim Manning raped a man." That's a tough pill to swallow. And I was worried "Lord where am I gonna preach? And why did you allow this to happen to me?" God told me to shut up. I'm gonna have this wrongful conviction in my background forever. Just as Paul had that thorn in his flesh. And God will order my steps. I may not ever be invited to preach (again) for so-and-so. But there are 320 million people in America. And if God only softens the heart of 10 percent of Americans (which means that 90 percent of them are against me) and causes them to want to hear me preach that will be 32 million people. If I have 32 million people to preach to that's a pretty good audience…

But I want to do more than preach. I'm an entrepreneur, an artist, an activist and a survivor. And after all the hell and high water which I've had to come through I have a message. I've watched what can happen when justice goes astray. I lean Democratic and I support President Obama. But I also know what can happen when government gets it wrong. The California Department of Corrections is state government. And it is government gone wrong. This department is run by a *code-of-silence*. I have photos (in this book as you see) of a guard who *raped* an inmate in 2011 and 2012. And he got away with rapes. And when the inmate built up the nerve to tell Lieutenant Nielsen and write an appeal they shredded the appeal. He told Dr. Wiggins and Dr. Stabbé. And Dr. Wiggins, Lieutenant Nielsen and Dr. Stabbé covered it up…

As recently as July 15, 2014 the inmate reported the rapes to Lieutenant John Mayhew and to Lieutenant Farris. He resubmitted his appeal on the rapes to Warden Jeff Macomber on July 18, 2014. He sent the appeal via legal mail to the warden (confidential due to the sensitive nature of the appeal). And that 602 has gone missing. He wrote and rewrote Warden Macomber (over 14 missives) in August, September, October and November asking, "Where is my appeal?" Lieutenant Farris made it clear to him that the appeal is gone and if he does not want to transfer he must forget it. My problem is I happen to know that *Judge Allison Claire* is aware of the *rapes* by the guard. She is aware of this felonious assault and rather than intervene she has joined the "cover-up." It sickens me to my stomach to know that a sitting judge will sit her ass in Sacramento and cover for a rapist prison guard. It is happening right now. And I submit to any Federal agent that if you review the "Cloud," cellphone and/or the email evidence etc. It can clearly be proven that the guard raped this inmate and then blackmailed him. And he cannot explain away the emails. And please remember that the only reason C.D.C. has shredded and lost appeals etc. is they don't want a Stewart Katz or a Mark Merin to file suit against the guard for rape. A, C.D.C would have to fire him. B, they'd have to compensate the inmate…

I want to get teams that we can pay to start book reading clubs. I want to visit some of these barbershops (on Del Paso Blvd, on Auburn Avenue and on Martin Luther King Jr. Drives across the country) and beauty salons etc. and talk about this book. I want to (do the unthinkable) start some think tanks in odd places. I'll start a think tank in a barbershop, a church, a sports bar etc. And I'll ask *Faris* Tayeb, Christopher Staggs, Travis Nagler, Henry Chang, Cristina Welcome, Max Wiseltier, Hairo Torres, Christopher Nachtrab, Matt Fender, Jacob Faulkender, Francisco Corona, Pastor Justin Boatman, Daniel Darr, Alex Hatch, John Mandern, Seth Weidner, Blair Casey, Steven Hune, Ramses Pringle, *Josh Klein*, Danny Frishmuth, M. Hiscel, August Clary, Joe Redmond, Eliot Sudal, *Robert James Carlson*, Michael Mowry, Bryan James, John Brandon, Kaleb Leeper, Logan Nordgren, Grant Arnette, Aaron Mize, Robert Krybyla, Scott Dangerfield, Nick Fink, A. J. Ali, Austin Whaley, Josh Sundquist, Tanner Linford, Ryan Sill, *Ricky Manning*, Jody Searcy, *Joe Kirk*, Triston Syron, Lucas Thorington, Bryan Santiago, Nick Topete, Taylor Fannell, Barrett Foa and Josh Stipp to help us.

If you can find Chris Jamison, Brian Zimmerman, Taylor John Williams, Dakota Sotto, Tyler Smith, Zachary Tierce, Kyle Rieman, Jake O'Donghue, Logan Paul, Aidan Sheehy, Justin Hoop, Dominic Burrows, Tyler Caldwell, Kelton Pisano, Will Haskell, Jerome Jarre, Paul Jolley, Brenin Hunt, Devon Franklin, Alexander Monsanto, Moi Navarro, Devin Dwyer, Lucas Murray (UC Davis), Eric Wilcox (UC Berkeley), Nate Zavaleta, Alex Smith (UC Davis), *Kenan Gebiz*, Will Niespodzinski, *Hayden Voss*, Jacob Gabriel, Jacob Karr, Hernan Parra, Ty Hemmerling, Johnny Keyser, Tyler Grady Alex Lambert, Tim Urban, Nick Boddington, Kyle Pratt, Stephen Pond, Josh Wingrove, *Jake Dodridge*, Gabe Teague, Cody

Harlton, Steven Sowards, Daniel Wetter, Aaron Burke, Shane Miller, Garret Smith Jr., Benjamin Prado, John Foraker, John Toraker, Matt Clunie, Nick Dean, Jamieson Knopf, Phillip Lomax, Jacob Mullins, C. J. Sheron, Michael Castro, Anthony Fedorov, *Tyler Bogdanos*, Montana Hull, Casey Campbell, Rev. William Barber, Stephen Tonti and…*Jay*…

    I met Jay (as I said) in October 2014. He works for NWN Corporation (he plans to go to work for the State soon). *Jay* is an affable, gregarious and unbiased person. *Jay* is the kind of guy that I wish would run for mayor or for governor. If Jay (or Niel Davidson, Eugene Langford, Nick Prugo or Vincent Thomas etc.) ran for office the world would be better. Youngsters (like "*Mario*" who's only 19 and he works in maintenance, Daniel Bugriyev or "*Glen*" in food services etc.) need to become politically active. I want to see Chef Flynn, Mike Weinberg, Maria Herrera and Daniel Jennings etc. learn "politics" so they can retire hate-mongers like Mitch McConnell and Darrell Issa… No profits from this book will go to O. J. Simpson or his ex-legal team. Although my writing has been fully endorsed by Bob Blasier he did *not* participate in this tome. I (alone) am responsible for the contents. Although I strongly recommend *Bob Blasier* for interviews etc…

    *Sherman D. Manning…*

# The Truth About O.J. Simpson

Prisons are the new slave ships on dry land. They are the plantations of the 21$^{st}$ century. The American prison, juvenile and jail system houses almost 2.7 million people. Because they are outnumbered, 300,000 white boys are raped in prisons yearly. Every 19 seconds a Caucasian inmate is raped in a U.S. prison. America houses over 10,000 kids in adult prisons. These kids are sexually abused and molested by inmates, guards and counselors etc. These kids are 8 times more likely to commit suicide than adult inmates. America incarcerates more people than any other nation on the face of this earth. Violent crime is lower than it has been since 1968. Yet we continue to pass new laws to lock down more citizens.

There are more black men in U.S. prisons than there were black men in *slavery*. And our prison systems are run, managed and operated by drunk cowboys. Most prison administrators are *pale*, *stale* (old) and male. And by and large they are racist. We have taskmasters and Klansmen running some of the largest prisons in this country. There are dumb, bumbling and drunken prison guards in California who earn more money than college professors. Many guards earn well over $125 grand per year. And these are often guards who did not even graduate high school. And they treat prison inmates like scum, *cattle* and like rabid dogs…

I used to say that I was glad I didn't grow up during the time of slavery because I'd be dead. I could not kiss up, suck up or do what it took to survive slavery. Then I thought that I was glad I didn't grow up in the 1940's, '50's, or in the '60's etc. If whistling at a white woman would get you lynched I'd be 'a' dead and gone. I likes (sic) 'em white, black, brown and bronze. But I'm growing now and I've come to realize that many great men survived slavery. And had they not survived I would not be alive. Moreover, I had a powerful 'aha' moment which shook me to my very core. It dawned on me that as a prisoner in the California prison system I too, am considered "a *slave*." Something turned in my stomach and I had to grab my ink pen and begin to write. I figured the *written* words (of a judge) sent me to prison. Some would say I allowed myself to get *written* into slavery. So perhaps I might be able to *write* my way out of here. Maybe writing can be the road home for me. But more important than *me*; maybe this writing can educate or elucidate this new slave system. And it can turn somebody around.

There are boys (and girls) in Watts, Compton, Oak Park, Del Paso Heights, the Bronx, in trailers, suburbs and in ghettos right now; who are growing up and preparing themselves to become *slaves*. When gangs recruit boys they are preparing them to come to prison. In many neighborhoods the gangs are operating under the *mandatory draft* initiative. It is mandatory that kids in certain neighborhoods join a gang. It is literally join or die. When you serve as a gang member that (per se) is a kind of slavery. Then the actions which gangs engage in will usually result in a prison sentence. And prisons are plantations…

Perhaps you are wondering when am I going to elucidate the O. J. Simpson matter? Well I'll get to Mr. Simpson in chapter two. Since O. J. Simpson is now in a prison himself that is all the more reason to write about prisons. O. J. presents a fascinating example of a *celebrity slave* (oxymoron?). And I use the term "celebrity" in regards to prisoners quite sparingly. Because I get upset when folks confuse celebrity with infamy. I had that debate with both Eric Menendez and his brother Lyle Menendez.

I knew Eric for years at New Folsom State Prison. Then I got to (unfortunately) know his brother Lyle at Mule Creek State Prison. They both believe (erroneously) that they are celebrities. Neither of them has been celebrated for having achieved anything in civilian life. Whereas, O. J. was a star football player and actor. The Menendez killers' claim to fame is simply the fact that they viciously murdered their parents who were wealthy. Had they not murdered their parents we would have never known them (Lyle or Eric). Had O. J. never been accused of killing Nicole Brown Simpson and her friend we still knew who he was. There are very few celebrity slaves. I'll get back to Mr. Simpson later…

I struggled with this book. As an author you can only write one letter, one word, one sentence, one paragraph, page, chapter etc. and one book at a time. I wanted to write "*The New Slave System*" as well as the real *O. J. Simpson* book at the same time so I decided to merge the two books… Professor Bryan Stevenson has authored a powerful new book titled "*Just Mercy.*" I highly recommend it. Attorney Michelle Alexander (a beautiful sister) has authored the tome "*The New Jim Crow*" which I also strongly recommend. And I also recommend a book called "*The Divide*" by Matt Taibbi…

America now spends $80 billion per year on prisons. We have incentivized keeping people in prisons. There are 245 lobbyists working in 30 states to keep people in prisons. The lobbyists are funded by private prisons. Prisons are big business and they've become deeply entrenched into America's political and economic systems. Rich and very powerful folks, including former Vice President Dick Cheney, have invested $millions in private prisons. They are focused on expanding the market — increasing the supply of prisoners. Corporate and political interests have a vested interest in crime. Politicians use fear and anger about crime to argue "tough on crime" initiatives. One in three black kids born in the 21$^{st}$ century expect to go to jail or prison. Because private prisons are in cahoots with politicians. There are people serving life sentences in prison for writing a bad check…

And teacher unions ought to be reading this book and talking about it. School budgets have been disrupted and compromised by prison budgets. I am sitting in a prison right now which has a $100 million budget. And drunk cowboys are responsible for managing (with very little oversight) that budget. This prison is run by a bunch of stomp jumping, tobacco chewing, and hillbilly racists. The guys who run this prison would shoot President Obama on sight. This prison has had only two black captains (out of over 500 captains); one captain, Beecher Welch, back in the '90's. Then it took 14 years before New Folsom promoted another (Rhonda Carter) black captain.

As I write these words Warden Jeff Macomber has just replaced Captain Carter with Dave Roth. And he's promoting Lieutenant Konrad to captain. Never mind the fact that just last year Lieutenant Konrad was placed in the mailroom (aka employee ad-seg) for calling a guard "a rat." Never mind the fact that a female staff member accuses Mr. Konard of sexual harassment. Skip over black Lieutenant Riley because Lieutenant Riley has never been assigned to the mailroom. If he wants to become a captain he needs to transfer out to promote.

Because Folsom is Dick Cheney land. So we have hundreds of prisons across the country being run by white people. This is a human rights crisis and America seems to not even be embarrassed by this. We need to join the Divestment Movement...

And black people? I wish that Elizabeth Warren were to decide to run for president. Because otherwise sometimes we have to fight with our friends. But we keep hollering about how much we love Bill Clinton. And Mr. Clinton is the "explainer in chief." Well if Bill Clinton loves black people so much why did he sign draconian laws which only affected blacks, browns and poor whites? Bill signed the 100-to-1 Crack (to powder) Law. That law was a "racist" law. There are entire black, Mexican (and working-class whites) neighborhoods that are empty of young black men thanks to Bill Clinton. There are perhaps more black lesbians (and more black ladies marrying white men) thanks to the Clintons because some laws codified by the Clintons sent millions of black boys to juvenile, jails and to prisons. And nobody in the media ever asks him about it. But if Hillary runs for President, Rand Paul is going to ask her about this.

Bill signed AEDPA into law. Consisely? If an inmate can prove (even scientifically) that he's sitting in prison (serving life) for a crime he did not commit, thanks to AEDPA if he's beyond *two years* of his conviction the court *can't* (ever) release him. If inmates are being abused in prison, thanks to the PLRA (signed by Clinton), a juvenile being raped may not be able to sue. Bill Clinton's tenure was the worst (mass incarceration) presidential tenure (in history) for poor people. Perhaps Kanye West could have directed his comments "We all know that George Bush (or rather Bill Clinton?) doesn't care about black people" toward the Clintons. Black people have been bamboozled by Bill Clinton. He has no problem with a crack addict serving a life sentence in prison while white child molesters get probation. Bill Clinton was worse to black people than Cheney and Bush were...

We are all better than the worst thing we've ever done. We are *better* than the *worst* thing we've ever done. And just because we did it doesn't mean we have to be it. Some of these draconian laws condemn people (for life) for mistakes they made 20 years ago. But there is money in prisons. Crime pays. Crime pays politicians, magnates, medical service providers and private prison owners etc. They are prison profiteers...

I shall repeat: there are more black men in prison than there were in slavery; the fact that you read that without weeping is evidence of the sad state of affairs in this country. There are more black men in prison in the U.S. than there are black men in college! Did you read that without jerking? Something is wrong! Every 19 seconds a white male is raped in the American prison system. And in more than 80 percent of those rapes the perpetrator is black or Mexican. You won't see this on the local news. Because when I call News Ten (i.e., reporters like Dale Schornack etc.) they are not interested. Journalists used to have a mistrust of power. They were often iconoclastic. Becoming a journalist was similar to becoming a plumber etc. Now journalists are Ivy League students with ambition. People enter journalism now for the proximity to power. There are too few real journalists willing to ask tough questions and to seek out real answers... So politicians (i.e. John Boehner, Ted Cruz, Darrell Issa etc.) are able to stir up fear and anger and pretend that "violent predators are getting a free ride" and pass new laws and build new prisons. All while they are accepting millions of dollars from the private prison lobbyists. And no major news outlet is covering it…

I shall repeat: there are people who are serving *life sentences* without the possibility of parole for *writing bad checks* in America. If that happened in North Korea or in Russia you could not shut John McCain, Issa, Cruz or Boehner up. Our red-faced politicians would be calling Kim or Putin despots, madmen and vicious. If Putin had somebody incarcerated for "life" for "writing bad checks" you would hear John McCain: "Putin is an evil man. No real human being would allow a life sentence in prison for a non-violent crime. We reserve that type of sentence for serial killers and serial rapists etc." But when the recipient of that type sentence is a poor white, black or brown man in America, we find that all of them (Cruz, McCain, Issa and Co.) are silent. Why are they silent? Because 90 percent of American politicians are money grubbing crooks. John McCain has a fortune worth well over $100 million. Darrell Issa is worth over $200 million.

John's wealth comes from his wife. John divorced his last wife (while she was in the hospital in critical condition) so that he could marry into money. McCain has 8 mansions. Small wonder Mr. McCain can't relate to those poor white citizens in your city who want to see the minimum wage raised. A man with 8 mansions, $100 million and body guards etc. cannot even fathom living off of a budget. And nobody in the media is talking or writing about it. They'll write about do-gooder liberals who want to give away the shop.

But I read six newspapers per day. And I read 200 books a year. And I've not read a single book within the past five or six years which mentioned the fact that 75 percent of these Republican politicians who want to cut all funding to the poor (who are mostly white) in this country are rich. Those who shut down the federal government etc. are all multi-millionaires. That's like a 125 pound man using his own personal appetite and his food intake as a guideline for how much food a 400 pound man should be allowed per week. Now a Republican would argue that this man needs to lose weight. And I would concur. But we keep arguing over how he should lose the weight.

I simply find it cruel and unusual to utilize the diet of a 125 pound man as an example for how much we should feed a 400 pound man. We might not need to feed him cookies and donuts with every meal. Yet, we do need to consider his appetite. It is advisable to put him on a diet and to motivate him to exercise. But it is unconscionable to torture people. And when you bring together a group of pale, stale, all male multi-millionaires and ask them what we should do about poor people in this country; They are looking at the habits and needs of the poor through the lens (and from the paradigm) of a 125 pound man. And they are making decisions for people who weigh (if you will) 400 pounds.

Aside from all of that they are hypocrites. I'll just be candid. We still have a group of racist people in this country. And usually they are older like Mitch McConnell. And several of McConnell's aides admit that he routinely refers to President Obama as a "N" (he actually says the word). And what happens is McConnell influences and he molds others (on Capitol Hill) into his thinking. And most human beings are followers. And we have a United States Senate which is damn near all white. Ipso facto, they don't need to segregate. They're all white (but two).

And our House of Representatives is divided. It is as segregated as Alabama in the 1940's. Many members of our House of Representatives to this very day are affiliated with the *KKK*. And many of them also refer to President Obama, John Lewis, Maxine Waters, Barbara Lee and Gwen Moore etc. as "N-ggers." I spoke with Darrell Issa (personally) and (he thought I was Caucasian) he stated, "The country will be better off when we get rid of this 'N-gger' president. We have enough problems with these N's in the Congress. I'm sick of Bass, Cummings and Waters. I have to sit next to that greasy N-gger, Cummings every day. And I wish I could spit on him and lynch him." This came out of the mouth of *Darrell Issa* (in 2014)…

Do you still want to talk about a post-racial America? It'll be a racial country until the McConnells, Boehners and the Cantors etc. *die*. I'm being politically incorrect I know. I'm supposed to be diplomatic and sugarcoat it. But I don't have time to play games. If you want gamesmanship or a "proper" (poll tested) book go read "*Hard Choices*." The hardest choice Hillary had to make about that book was *choosing* who would *ghostwrite* it. I'm sorry; I know she was Secretary of State. I know she's done a lot of good. She will probably become President. And I do respect Mrs. Clinton. But speech writers write these books. Yet, I am *Sherman* (J. D. Salinger) *D. Manning* and I (without a ghostwriter) am writing this book holed up inside my bunker. *I* am the *writer*.

I write from my head as well as from my heart. I am one of the so-called originals because I write like authors used to write. Nowadays when you read books by celebrities and by politicians etc. it is almost like listening to Britney Spears sing. The singer's autotune is the writer's ghostwriter. If you sit Britney on a stage with nothing except a microphone and tell her to sing she'd freak out. Sit any of those celebrity or politician book authors in a room (alone) with a computer and say write they could not. So when you read a book by Ted Cruz I have some very bad news. The news is the book was not written by Cruz.

One of my chief goals now is to motivate and inspire people to read. Reading good books can unlock creativity and innovation. I encourage every person to read. Read for information, pleasure, guidance, education and also for liberation. I have never seen a door which a book can't unlock. I've found no mountain high enough which a book can't climb. Read, read, read.

For those who grow up in poverty, it is criminal not to read. If one is in the trailer parks or ghettos of life it is suicide not to read. Many poor kids who are 15 and 16 years old have never left their side of town. Some of them are 18 years old before they even venture outside of their own zip code. But books are passports that can take you all over the world. Books build things inside the mind and the psyche which help people to lead better lives…

We are witnessing the dumbing down of America. And a dumb, uninformed, unenlightened or uneducated person is a victim. They are victimized by bad politicians, bad preachers and bad teachers etc. If you don't understand how to read you can be persuaded to sign anything. I would tell any poor person or any minority person to read everything you get your hands on…

Prisons are predominantly built to house the poor, the dumb and the damned. And prisons are predominantly run by the poor, the dumb and the damned. Revisiting Folsom State

Prison I can tell you that Jeff Macomber is the warden. He probably reads on a 12th grade level. I'd estimate his I.Q. at 112. He's Caucasian and has no black associate wardens and no black captains. He has only one black lieutenant (Lt. Riley) and it was Tim Virga who promoted Riley. And if that seems redundant (it is) it's just that it boils my blood. I've watched Joseph Stratton commit federal crimes at New Folsom State Prison. He has *blood* on his *hands*. (See my book "*American Dream/A Search for Justice*").

Stratton is responsible for inmate Rocky Salazar being murdered by Frank Christian. Stratton participated in the murder of inmate Edwards (along with Ryan Wenker and Sgt. K. Porter). They pepper-sprayed him to death while holding him in a dog cage. And Stratton continues on unabated as pompous and arrogant as ever. Stratton is very close to Konrad. Stratton is also very close to Associate Warden Ross Meiers. And Meiers and Konrad etc. would all be totally happy if Folsom never had a black captain or a black associate warden. And yet many inmates under their care are black. And what do you do when you are black and you have to be subjected to the subtle, hidden and the camouflaged racism of an all-white prison administration? And…

By and large, the black guards at Folsom are 'suspect,' i.e. C.O. Edington. Mr. Edington purports to be a Christian. And he may, in fact, love God. But you cannot love God and hate your brothers. Edington is as close as you can come to full Uncle Tom. He is a bootlicker. He has 28 years in the department. He plans to retire in 2 weeks. Stratton has 12 years in the department. Yet Edington (to this day) still runs around calling Stratton "boss." President Mandela told me (in his book "*Long Walk to Freedom*") to never call a man "boss." Edington will talk Jesus Christ (whom I worship and praise) yet he bows down to The Code of Silence. And he supports "The Green Wall" (aka 723, aka The CCPOA). And you can have no other god before God. Yet Edington would violate every page in the Bible to support, back and to corroborate "The Green Wall!" I can remember one day I looked in the office window right at the window where Edington sits every day. And there was a racist, disrespectful and discourteous joke in the window. The joke was about President Obama. And Edington sat right there and allowed it which means that one of his co-workers (probably C.O. Hayes) had no respect for the President or Edington either.

Yet, Edington and Mr. Hayes get along well. Mr. Hayes has been known to run around the prison singing "Tote that Bell" which is a slave song. No white man (in the 21st century) has any right to run around singing a demeaning slave song. And why would you sing it if you were not a racist? And yet, day after day I see Edington kissing up to Mr. Hayes. But Edington is a Christian? He gossips, is vindictive and has an anger problem etc. But he's a Christian?

I'd like to see him be a man. A man will tell Stratton, "I'm not doing that. That's not my job." But these *nephew* Toms (like C.O. Friday, Edington, Tim Woods, Sgt. Holloway, Walker and Quinn etc.) will join racist white cops In beating and killing black inmates. I make a big deal about the fact that Folsom is known as a bastion of racist management which refuses to promote blacks etc. I am appalled by that…

Yet, I must reluctantly admit that there are tons of examples of prisons and jails which are run by blacks. And in many instances the blacks treat the blacks just as bad as white folks do. In Fulton County jail (in Atlanta, GA) there is a black sheriff. The jail commanders, majors, captains and the lieutenants etc. are all black. And the jail population is 85 percent black. And the guards treat the inmates like dirt. And if I took you to meet Sergeant Black Man in Atlanta, you would be led to believe that he was trained by Sergeant Joseph Stratton at Folsom. They're vicious, rogue and they're corrupted. And Stratton has taught me that they will never change as long as wardens (such as Jeff Macomber) tolerate these guys. As long as the Macombers of C.D.C. legitimize and refuse to punish and correct guards gone wild, they will continue to be thugs…

Joseph Stratton reminds me of Hitler. He is a cruel, sick and a wicked human being. It takes a certain kind of person to wanna grow up and become a prison guard; in an all-male prison. What 12, 13 or 14 year-old boy (who is heterosexual and who is not a psychopath) do you know who aspires to grow up and work in a prison? Not all prison guards are gay. But many of them (who are married with kids) are undercover. Many of them are rapists, sadistic and have other ulterior reasons for working in prisons. Hint, hint?...

(I need readers to Google and email Vlad Sonnik, Joseph Cox, Matt Fender, Paul Weubbe, Jacob Tenbrink, Julian Loy, Kevin Sullivan, Ryan Coolley, Frankie Grandie, Timothy Goebbels, Justin Chirigotis, Zach Barsuglia, Nick Dannenberger, Michael Evers, Zack "Danger" Brown, Dante Mazza, Russell Brandom, Kyle Day, Colin Guinn, Colton Dixon, Jaycob Curlee, Logan Paul, Daniel Jensen, Stephen Zinn, Grant Silow, Trevor Law, Joe Shetz, Evan Ross John Stapleton, Blake Gopnik, Tyler Yagley, Trevor Loflin and Justin Cash etc. and tell them this book is out. And tell them to get it)…

I've studied America's prison guards like a science. I know them better than their own mother's know them. I've not studied them in a vacuum. But I've consulted (at length) with psychologists and psychiatrists etc. while studying the mental apparatus of prison guards. I've learned that about 10 percent of them fall into the "necessity" column. Folks like C.O. Drake. He's 22 or 23 years old. He is basically a decent dude. He became a guard for one reason: It was the best gig he could get for which he was qualified. The problem with a guy like C.O. Drake is that he is a decent dude. But five years from now he will be fully indoctrinated into the "Green Wall." A combination of peer pressure, environment and the survival instinct etc. will lead Drake to know that the only way he can survive in this line of work; the way to keep his job and not become an outcast etc. is to follow the rules: "Green before blue." Green meaning the color of a guard's uniform vs. the color (blue) of inmate's uniforms.

Next: The code of silence, which means you never snitch on a fellow guard. Whether the guard beats, maims or even rapes an inmate. If you see it you don't say it. And slowly but certainly prison guards begin to compromise their own integrity. And after a few years the prison guard realizes that he belongs to an armed militia. Ipso facto, there are 33,000 California prison guards. And there might be 300 – 500 who would report misconduct by another prison guard…

Guards own the gates and I've often stated that nothing light, bright or authentic can grow inside of a person. Prisons destroy everything and anybody who comes into contact with them. The very nature of a prison is to destroy. I would not wish prison on my worst enemy. They break, disrupt, distract and destroy the human spirit…

But God can do anything. And he has the power to build, to teach and to inspire even in the midst of destruction. Sometimes the system will lock you out. And *if* I actually get out of prison (Because God can do anything! He can get me out in 2016 and even *before* 2016. And He can bring you out of anything that you are trapped in.). But great things are often born outside of the system. Who but God would birth a King in a barn? God births great things in strange (prisons? jails?) obscure places. God will birth something great in a prison. And when I get home there will be pastors wondering why they should let an ex-con preach. And…

God will birth somebody great in a prison. Don't allow circumstances to intimidate you. God has taught me not to allow my circumstances to intimidate me. So I've sat in the bowels of this dark and deadly prison. And I've written 22 books while locked up – outside of the system. Some of you reading need to get outside of the system. You may need to get outside of the system and redefine history… Jesus was born outside the system. And nobody hated Jesus Christ like church folks hated Him. Church folks tried to kill Jesus. Jesus died outside of the gates of Jerusalem. He was put in a barn so I could reach Him. I can't reach Him in a palace. But I can find Him in a hog pen…

So when I exit the confines of this dank and dastardly prison I will (by necessity) have to work outside the system. But I'll make the system catch up with me later. Nobody (as an ex-con and a parolee) wants to *give* you anything in the barn. But when you get in the palace anybody will give you anything. When Joseph was in the prison he was a convicted sex (*Sherman D. Manning*), Brian Banks, Ronald Cotton etc.) offender. And nobody would give him a damn thing. But when he got to the palace and became the Prince of Egypt, every pastor (even at the mega churches etc.) would invite him to preach…

It's hard for me to believe this but one day I'm gonna thank God for the folks who rejected me. Because if they were helping me right now they could say they made me *who* I am becoming. I used to cry about being rejected. I'd hear preachers on T.V. and on the radio. And I knew I was as gifted as some of them were. But they were on T.V. and I was in the prison. They were wearing suits and I'm in a prison jumpsuit. I've been locked up (in 2015) so long that I've been forgotten. I'm not even a part of the conversation anymore. But God reminded me that He allowed Joseph to sit in prison for a similar wrongful conviction as mine. And God let him sit there for almost 14 years. But when God got ready He got Joseph.

And I wrote to Tavis Smiley, Cornel West, Steve Harvey and even Charlie Rose etc. and sometimes they won't write back. But when I get there I want Tavis and Steve etc. to know that God is not through with me yet. I was a rising star in the ministry. I preached all over the country. But God had a plan for my life. He chose to send me another way. And the rejection and neglect has taught me. I have learned…

I've experienced nothing but racism, abuse and opposition in prison. But God can hide your opportunity in your opposition. He hid Moses in Pharaoh's house. Although Pharaoh wanted to kill him. God can put you on the very stage of your haters… Moses was educated as an Egyptian even though he's a Hebrew… I've learned that the only way you can keep people from hating you is to lay down and play dead. But if you play dead you'll never accomplish anything… I've learned to use the rocks in my life. And the rocks will get you to the sword. And the sword will cut off the head of your enemies. The more influence you get the more people will like you. The more people who like you the more haters you'll get. As long as you do something you'll have haters…

I've studied the life of Jacob. And God basically says Jacob you will limp your way into your blessing. And God designed the limp to keep him humble. The fact that I'll be an ex-con will be my limp. It will be my thorn in the flesh. God will build a limp in you so that you never become high-minded. But don't let people bury you just because God planted you. People who are buried go into the same dirt. But only that which is planted will rise up out of that which it has been planted in. I am in the dirt right now. But God planted me. You may be in dirt right now but don't let them bury you. The enemy will send you haters to try to convince you to bury (curse) your ownself…

Jacob (prisoners and perhaps readers) "your captivity is a learned behavior." But I wanna serve notice on everybody reading this. If you learned to make do in the cave, you can learn to hunt in the wild. But you are a teacher on the first floor. But get on the elevator and go to the second floor. And you become a student on the second floor. Because you're on the next level. Your ceiling has become your floor. You are now sitting and walking on what you used to look up to. The ground moves under our feet whether we feel it or not. You can't waste your energy on your history. You need all your gas to get to your destiny.

When you get into a new place shut your mouth. Learn the terrain of the new territory. Faith is for the place where sight fails us. Being in a new environment does not feel good. Because I grope in the dark. Even though I signed the lease. With a new place comes a new language. And I struggle with that which is new to me. I'd rather gather with the gifted than hang around the dysfunctional. Am I packaged right? I need to synchronize with other gifted people. And I want to package myself right. And…I need to get in an environment so I can nurture my gifts. But God allowed me to land in this slave ship because He wanted me to shine a light on it. He knew it would change me. It would humble, teach and reach me. But He also knew He would use me to *change* prisons. Sometimes God will allow you to get in the unemployment line just because He wants *you* to *bless* somebody else…

I hope Timothy Nosal, Matthew Besler, John Alviso (Sacto), Kyle Pratt, Kiel Pratt, Anthony Curcio, Cody Baetge, Kevin Sullivan and Timothy Hill etc. will read this book… And I also want prisoners, guards, the families and friends of prisoners etc. to read this book. And there are persons in civilian society. You have no handcuffs on your wrists; you don't have any shackles upon your feet; and you're not in any physical prison. But your mind is incarcerated; your marriage is a prison; and you're a slave to drugs or to alcohol etc. I would like to write to you about the secrets which you are hiding.

I wanna write to that woman who is Nicole Brown Simpson in 2015, 2016, 2018 or 2020. From the outside your marriage looks good. You have a nice house and a nice car. Perhaps your husband has money and social status. But behind closed doors he is abusive. Maybe he beats you with his fists and sometimes he beats you with his words. And his words are so evil that sometimes you'd prefer he just hit you. There are women reading who have hooked up with boyfriends and even husbands etc. and you catch them looking at your child (who may be underage) in an inappropriate fashion. There are even women who have caught your man or husband etc. doing something to your child and you are afraid to report it.

You are afraid of the disruptive nature of a police report; scared that people are gonna look at you funny and say, "She chose him." You are afraid of losing your child and even afraid of losing him. Your whole life will be turned upside down if you call the cops. Now your family and the neighbors will find out what happened to your child. You are stuck in the middle of the quicksand of indecision. My suggestion to you is to call two people. Call the police and call your pastor. It won't be easy and it will be stressful. You will have to pray and seek the face of God. But in the end you will be glad that you reported the sexual misconduct etc…

Don't allow any man to beat you. And if he hit you one time he will do it again. And if you are hooked up with a man who feels it is appropriate to hit a woman, you are hooked up with the wrong man. In fact, he is not a man. I don't care how good he is in bed. I don't care how well you may think he is endowed etc. If you continue in a long-term relationship with a woman-beater you are incarcerating yourself, and you will become a slave to your "relationship." If you don't believe anything else I write I want you to believe me when I say get out of that relationship right now. Don't wait and don't hesitate. I don't care how far he can throw a baseball. I don't care how far he can run a football. If he beats you he is not a man. If he is controlling and dominating etc. run away from him.

I'm so very tired of these women who settle for abusive men. There needs to be workshops, seminars and clinics to help ladies to begin to know who they are. And to know that a real woman deserves a real man and real men don't hit, assault or abuse women. If you are a lady (or if you know a lady) you are special and not just the good looking ladies. Even if you are overweight or unattractive etc. a woman is special. You are the queen of the earth and mother of the universe. You are somebody in the eyes of divinity. And I love you very much. And any real man can't look at you and see a punching bag. So if he hits you leave him. And don't look back. Get over him. Bad won't taste good anymore when you've gotten better. Leave him and forget him. And your destiny is not tied to the one that left nor is it tied to anybody you left. The sun will rise again; you will take another breath; you will survive.

I know it will be difficult and it will be perplexing. But you must believe in the power of love and dignity. I don't care what his excuse may be: he was abused or beat; his mom was beat by his dad etc. All of that is very sad and it may be very real. But just because you were a victim does not give you the right to victimize me. I refuse to be your victim. And ladies must refuse to be anyone's victim. You are God's child. And you deserve to be respected and protected.

If you have been involved with abusive men, and if you are being abused right now, you must get out of that relationship right now. I command you to call the police right now. Put him out of your house. Get a restraining order. This may disrupt your life baby girl. But being disrupted is a whole lot better than being dead. I'd rather you see a judge than have a coroner seeing you. You have to get help for yourself. What has happened to you that made you feel that you deserve to be abused? Why are you so broken, hurt and traumatized that you feel that you deserve this? Why do you look down on yourself? You don't ever have to settle for the normal routines. You were built for greater and bigger things.

I want you to begin to seek out people who will help build you up and not pull you down. I want you to X everybody out of your life who seeks to denigrate you. I want you to seek guidance, counseling, prayer and books etc. which help to build you up. Know yourself because you can't have esteem for a self that you don't know. You are made from some good stuff. There is greatness all down in the marrow of your bones. You are not an afterthought or a has-been. You are worthy to be loved, respected and protected.

If your lover is beating you get away. He's angry at himself. And when he hits you it is because he's really fighting himself. He can't hit you without feeling the pain. But his real problem is with the man in his mirror. So when a man is angry with himself he does not need a woman. He needs a God and he needs a doctor. And you're not God and you are not a doctor. And the only thing an angry man can do is abuse and hurt you. And a broken and frustrated man will end up breaking you. And he will frustrate and stifle your growth. He'll frustrate and incarcerate your innovation and your creativity.

Angry men create broken and angry women. And then you begin to procreate. And when an abused woman has a baby by an abusive man they create abuse-prone children; or abusive-prone children. And this creates a chain of generational curses on your lives and families. So if you are not willing to get away to save yourself, do it to save your children or your future children. Do you really want to bring a child into the home of a man who beats you? If he will beat you what won't he do? If you are not willing to save yourself you must be willing to save the children *in* you. Get away from that man… Who thinks it's a good idea for a child to watch mommy being beat by a man? If you don't want your child to grow up witnessing abuse you know what to do. Get out of that relationship right now.

I have come to drive a stake through the heart of that dependency. I've come with a warrant in my hand. And I arrest that spirit. There is a spirit in you which makes you feel like you need him. Well you don't need anybody who abuses you. Not now and not ever. I want my words to shake you and to awake you. You are better than that. Look at your daughter (or son) and ask yourself would you want her hooked up with a man who beat her? Well she came from you and she is a reflection of you. You lead her by example. Now show her how to walk away from abuse. You might have to get a job or a second job. You might have to get temporary assistance. But whatever the inconvenience, it is well worth it to save your life. Get away from that abuser today. Leave him…

If an actor doesn't get new scripts they will perform old lines. You must update your scripts. Transform your life by transforming your thinking… Two broken people produce broken kids. And we must break the cycle by getting out and by getting help… Sometimes people will throw you away for being guilty of the same stuff which they did… I don't want you to let your sensitivity to assault, disrupt or deny your opportunity. Don't build walls to protect who you used to be. The Bible says to "*write* the *vision*" not the victimhood. Write the vision not the fear. How are you going to finish? You've got to *write* it out. You can't run it out until you write it out.

If the script (the journal or diary etc.) is good enough you can take a bad actor and make a good movie. Write out the script of what you want to achieve in your life. And then X out the habits, the people and the things which are hindering you from getting there. You have been writing a memoir of your pain and what you went through. Don't write out the script of your life looking in the rearview mirror. You deserve to move forward in your life. You deserve to be happy. And I am always shocked to discover how many unhappy people we have on earth; even people in America who have enough food and water. No matter how many movies we see or how many DVD's we own, we seem to be inwardly unhappy. We smoke up a lot of weed, drink booze and take pills. We try to medicate our way out of the prison of unhappiness. We try to anesthetize our sorrow, hurt and our pain. Well what does happiness look like to you? What does happiness feel like to you? When was the last time you were truly happy? What can you do now to be happy? Paul said, "I've learned to be content" no matter where "I" am.

Why don't you invest some time, effort, reading and energy into learning happiness? We've all seemed to master how to be angry. We learn early how to be mad and even sad. We know how to push each other's buttons and create friction. But maybe we need to take the time to learn the opposite. How can I be happy and how can I help others to be happy?...

I tell ladies to hang out with ladies who are happy. And hang around other ladies who refuse to be abused. Who you associate with can play a large part in who you are and who you become. I'm willing to admit that perhaps I'm not that smart. Maybe I'm not the sharpest tool in the shed. But I'll be damned if I'm gonna hang out with other ignorant folks. I don't have time to hang with folks who are just as limited as I am. What are we going to do? Sit around together saying, "I don't know what that word means." I choose to hang out with folks who are stronger than I am. If I'm lazy I don't need a lazy companion. I don't need anybody to keep me company in bed. I need somebody who will inspire me to get up out the bed and do something.

Be careful who you hang with. Brothers if you hang out with other men who call women "bitches." If you hang around with losers, gangbangers and perverts etc. it will rub off on you. If I'm paralyzed I don't wanna hang with other paralyzed people, because not walking starts looking normal when you hang with others who are paralyzed. I don't want paralysis to become my norm. I want at least to know I could walk. And a lot of poor people spend all their time around others who are broke. If you are indigent you need to find you a few friends who are not broke. Not so you can borrow from them or sponge off of them. But just ask them to mentor you. If people discover that you're not looking for a handout they'll often be willing to help you.

If you live in the ghetto get out sometimes. Get you a cute dress (or a conservative suit and tie) and go to the suburbs and hang out. Act like you belong there. Talk like you belong there. And walk like you belong there. And find you just one or two friends who live there. And at some point you can be transparent. You can (after you get to know them) say, "Listen: I don't live out here. I live in the ghetto. And I'm attempting to develop some strategies which will get me out of the ghetto. I'm not looking for a handout, a crutch or charity. I'm looking for strategy, advice and leadership. If you were where I am how would you get out?"...

Warden Tim Virga asked me, "Are you going to become a visiting professor or a scholar in residence at UC Berkeley when you get out?" Warden Jimbo Walker asked me, "Are you going to lecture as a scholar in criminal justice at colleges and universities when you get out?" I explained to Jimbo that, "Until I get my wrongful conviction overturned I'll have to register. And I'm not sure prestigious universities will let a so-called convicted 'sex offender' lecture." Warden Walker replied, "Bullshit, if you were convicted of child molestation it would be different. But you're convicted of supposedly raping a man and you've written 14 (actually 21) books now. Dude I have colleges right now who want me to allow you come and speak to their students. It would be a crime for you not to share your experiential knowledge. As Dr. Yablonsky told you, you are an experience therapist."...

Well, I'll certainly be available for Georgia Tech, Emory University, Morehouse, Clark Atlanta, Howard, Stanford, Harvard and Yale etc. I'm willing to divulge the secret torture, the malfeasance, the violence and the evils etc. which are bred and fed behind the iron curtains of prisons. I've conducted years of study into prison violence, guard brutality, in-custody rapes, in-custody murders and the prison subculture. I've studied the institutionalization of inmates, as well as the institutionalization of prison staff. I have a clear grasp and understanding of why prisons do what they do. I know who works in prisons. I know who goes to prisons. And... I would be honored to speak, teach and lecture at institutions of higher learning, at churches and assemblies etc...

I hope and I pray that God will intervene. And Steve Harvey, Tavis Smiley, Dr. Cornel West, George Soros or Tyler Perry etc. will intervene and help me underwrite a campaign against this slavery. Michelle Alexander has already elucidated the issues in the powerful tome "The New Jim Crow." Now I'd like to initiate a nationwide campaign which will wake brothers up. Michelle did her part by writing the book. I wanna do my part by sharing (teaching, preaching, promoting and exposing) her book. I know authors don't promote books written by other folks. But while Michelle teaches in Ohio, I want to be out in the field using her book to turn on the lights in some of those dark cities, schools, homes and minds.

I also want to promote the book "Just Mercy" by Bryan Stevenson. It is a book that should be required reading for every at-risk youth... I will carry copies of "Just Mercy" and "The New Jim Crow" with me to churches, to UC Berkeley, Emory University, Hampton, Grinnell, Wake Forest, UC Davis and to New York University etc. And I will give (gratis) as many copies to students as I can. I don't wanna just *write* (and preach) to the choir. And all too often we write books which only get read by scholars and pastors etc. But if we can get water to the most remote areas in South Africa; if we can invent ways to get cocaine and speed into every ghetto and barrio; if we can find ways to get porn into North Korea. We can finds ways to get "Just Mercy," "The New Jim Crow" and "Creating Monsters" etc. into the hands of at-risk youths. I want gangbangers to read these books. I want wanna-be gangbangers to read these books. I want kids who know somebody in a gang to read these books. And readers become leaders.

I'll go on a *crusade* to promote *reading*. If we can get young folks and old to read enough Harry Potter to make J.K. Rowling a billionaire etc...hell I know kids who read Harry Potter. And I've also seen men in their fifties (in prison) reading Harry Potter. So many folks read Harry Potter that they read J.K. from the welfare rolls to the $Billionaire Girls Club. If we can get guys on death row to read Harry Potter, we can get youths in high schools, colleges, churches and group homes etc. to read "The New Jim Crow," *Blue Eyed Blonde*," "Failing Up," "Long Walk To Freedom," "Just Mercy" and *Creating Monsters*." And I want to…

I will launch a national campaign to get youths back to reading. I will use my past to teach the future. God will set before me a large opportunity. The enemy wants me distracted and stressed out. The large place will start from my small prison cell. My opposition is my opportunity. I can't control other people. I can't control gossip, rumors or innuendo. I can't control the fact that there will be some people who think I actually did what the opposition said I did. I can't control the variables. I can only control my perspective…

As I get more influence and better known, the more people love you the more people will hate you. Lovers and haters both grow up together. Our success (remember this because this almost killed me before I ever saw the inside of a jail cell) creates an opportunity for people to envy you. The only way to keep people from envying you is to lay down and play dead. If you play dead (as I've said before) even animals won't bite you. The risk of getting bit is the cost of getting up. But bite me or not I'm getting up baby boy. You tell Tavis Smiley (tell George Soros, Cornel West, Michael Eric Dyson, Gerald Chertavian, Ken Chenault and Pastor Michael Pfleger etc.), Tyler Perry and Steve Harvey etc. that I'm getting up. And I'm getting up out of this small place. Tell them I've got a lot of baggage. I've got smut on my name. I've been broken and battered. But still I rise. If David E. Kelley or a television producer needs a consultant on prisoners or guards etc. here am I. If the president needs my input here am I. If a high school principal or the chairman of a social science department etc. needs a speaker here am I. I will use what I've learned to warn others…

The challenge of my life is to coexist between two things that are totally true yet opposing each other. And the only thing that makes the difference is my perspective… Are you so concerned about being bitten that you are willing to spend the rest of your life playing dead? I could get out of prison and play dead. I could hide out and hope nobody notices that I'm out. But instead I'm gonna manufacture a movement. I'll write the vision and then live the vision. I can't play dead…

I used to wonder why God would allow certain things to happen to me. I thought will I spend the rest of my life explaining that I was *wrongly* convicted of rape? How do you convince people that you are not a rapist? How do you prove "I did not rape that *man*?" And "I don't even like *men*" sexually? Do I need to spend the rest of my life bedding woman after woman to convince *men* that I don't want them? Then do I have to shun gay people for the rest of my life trying to prove I don't want a man? How do I also prove that I don't hate gay people and that I'm not insecure in their presence? Do I really have to spend the *rest* of my *life* proving that I *don't rape* people?

This is a stressful, difficult and fascinating position to be in. But I've chosen to look at it and say thank you. And I will use this pain to fuel the rest of my life. I have a sneaky suspicion that one day God can still sit me in a large place. And I believe that I will have power. The power to hire and fire. The power to make a difference. To inspire, uplift, educate and to elevate others. And all the while that God is raising me up I'll never forget. I won't forget the pain, the loneliness and the sorrow which I feel.

I have sat here and written letter after letter (from my prison cell) to pastor after pastor. A number of these are pastors whom I used to preach for. I've written to pastors with whom I used to break bread and fellowship with. And they don't write me back. They won't even dictate a missive via their secretary to say "Tell *Manning* I'm praying for him." And I'm not writing these pastors letters asking for money. Nor do I ask them to give me anything. I just ask if they still remember me and will they pray for me. And these guys don't write back. The only time I do get a reply is if a church ministry sends me an advertisement begging me (a prisoner) for money.

Initially this made me mad. But now I'm sad about it. To know that Jesus built His entire ministry around helping the locked out, locked in and the forgotten about. He said in Matthew 25 that He was hungry and we fed Him not. "I was in prison and you visited me not." And yet with millions of churches and… Hundreds of thousands of black churches etc. I could not find one (not one) to write me back. Only Rev. Michael Pfleger (in Chicago) took the time to have an assistant to write me back. And I thank God for Pastor Pfleger and Saint Sabina Church in Chicago.

I've never met Pastor Pfleger (although I've preached at several churches in Chicago. I preached for Rev. Leroy Elliott, Pastor Joseph Wells and Pharis Evans etc.). But when I was on my deathbed I heard the voice of Pastor Pfleger. I was in so much pain that I can't even explain it. The most pain that I have ever felt in my life. And Pastor Pfleger was on T.V. imitating Hillary Clinton. Explaining how Barack Obama had come along and stolen her show. But there was something in his voice that fed me. And it made me feel better. So years later I found his address and I wrote to him. And I don't want to live in Chicago when I get home. But maybe God has a plan for Pastor Pfleger to play some role in my life in the future. I don't really know.

But I do know that I'm gonna need the favor of God upon my life when I get home. I will be (in 2016) a 44 year-old ex-con. I'll have to register for a crime I did not commit. And I'm going to need somebody to help me. It used to be the church that would take you in and say we don't care what they said you did. We will embrace you and pray for you. I kind of believe that if my pastor (Rev. Moses Lee Raglin) were alive he would help me. Rev. Raglin would let me preach the gospel. He would give me a chance. Doc (Rev. Hosea Williams) would say, "Rev. Manning here is a $thousand dollars to help you get started. You going to need some suits and ties." Pastor Jean Barber would say, "Rev. Manning I'm giving you this $5 grand but you owe me a revival. In December I want a 3-day revival from you." These people would help me get started.

But Rev. Raglin, Rev. Williams and Pastor Barber are all in heaven now. And I've got to go out into a world where some church folk will hassle me more than prison guards do. But Jesus was rejected by His own. So I must expect to be rejected by many. But my message will be undeniable. No one can negate the power of my testimony. And I will embark upon a one-man crusade to educate the world regarding the criminal justice system. I will educate, entertain, inspire and elucidate criminal justice unlike any politician, preacher, teacher or lawyer in history. I will have to build my own platform. I must elucidate the so-called justice system in an awesome way. The message that I teach, preach and advocate must be gripping, candid and stunning. My delivery must be King- (Dr. Martin Luther King) like. I've gotta be so good at teaching, preaching and speaking that "the living, the dead and even the unborn will say there lived" a great speaker (and preacher) who spoke his job well.

America needs a speaker. We need someone with the passion of Rubin "Hurricane" Carter. The platform of a celebrity etc… And that is the hard work. I will have every odd against me. I will be an ex-con who is wrongly convicted. I will have to literally build myself a *bully pulpit*. They say if you build it they will come. I must build myself a bully pulpit from which to launch this crusade. I will have to try anything and everything to build this bully pulpit. I will have to call (or write) Byron Allen and tell him I know you've never invested in anything like this. But will you please underwrite this campaign…

I'll call Steve Harvey, Tavis Smiley, Dr. Cornel West, Tyler Perry, Professor Charles Ogletree and Dr. Alvin Poussaint etc. and I will have to just tell them the truth. Corporate America is not going to invest in an ex-con. And the Shark Tank ain't gonna fund this. And I'll be starting from scratch. I will need the Smiley Group (or George Soros, Levan Hawkins, Kerry Washington or Harry Lennix etc.) to get behind me. I'll call Mayor Michael Nutter and Senator Cory Booker (I think Cory will be our second black president) and I'll ask them to help me get started. All I need is to make and promote the first CD. It will be like a book on CD. It will be my words for gangbangers, suburb nerds and other at-risk youths. But I don't intend to preach to the choir. We've gotta market the CD on radio stations across the country. And we must market and promote it via the internet. And once young people hear this CD many of them will never, ever be the same again. I need Byron Allen, Tyler Perry, Steve Harvey, John Burton, Rand Paul, Bryan Stevenson, Professor Paul Butler and others to help me market it. And…

I'll ask Steve, Byron, Tyler, Tavis and Russell Simmons etc. to underwrite a *crusade* against the *celling* of America… It was absolutely chilling to me when I heard Rand Paul and Cory Booker talking about the celling of Americans. And the celling of minorities. Senator Booker explained that we now have more black men (in 2015) in jails, prisons (or on parole or probation) or juveniles than we had in slavery in 1850. What the hell is going on? We have a black president and a black attorney General. The state of California has a black attorney General (Kamala Harris). But with a black president we still have more black men in prisons than we have in college. I'll be damned…

If Dr. Martin Luther King, Jr. were alive today criminal justice would be his number one priority. He would eat, sleep, talk, sing, live and breathe this issue. We have got to get black men out of prisons. We have got to keep black men from going to prison in the first place. This is the new *slavery*. Slaves are now prison inmates. I'm not unmindful of the fact that violent rapists, molesters and murderers need to be in prison. But since I am *in prison* I have developed an expertise on *who is here*. I don't need to merely do a statistical examination of surface numbers. I am the statistic. I know who comes to prison, why and for how long. I know who should be here, who needs to come and who should have never come. I know who works in prison and why they work in prisons. I have read, studied, analyzed, scrutinized and examined the system from the inside out. And I am declaring *war*. This book is my war cry…

I used to think that when I got home I'd launch a campaign against gangs (I know the Bloods, Crips, AB, NLR, Nuestra Familia etc. inside out)! Then I thought I'd launch a campaign against corrupted police and prison guards. Then I thought I should launch a campaign against wrongful convictions. But the Lord let me know that my campaign and crusade must be against *politicians*...shocking? I agree but that's where the real issues get their roots. Politicians launched the "war on drugs." It was Nixon who decided that "we must do something about 'the' blacks." It was a politician who signed the PLRA, AEDPA and the crack laws etc. And it was a group of politicians who wrote the bills. And it was a group of lobbyists who wrote what the politicians claimed to have written. Cops could not do what they do. Judges and juries couldn't do what they do. Prison guards could not rape, beat and abuse inmates etc. Wardens could not do what they do if politicians did not write, pass and approve of these draconian laws. And Americans have been asleep. And my job is to serve a wakeup call.

Ted Cruz is one of the most dangerous men in America. And he has a lot of friends. And they all want to lockup the poor and to throw away the key. And I will attack any platform which calls for the mass incarceration of an entire generation. I will record a wakeup call (call to action) for North America. And I'll plead with Byron (Anderson, Smiley, Perry and Harvey etc.) to help me put it out there. I'll tell Byron Allen that even if he does not believe in me. Even if he's uncertain about me etc. just listen to my message and help me get the CD to pastors, teachers, leaders, students, professors and at-risk youths etc... And if, by chance, I can't get them to help me, it still will not stop me. I will survive. And I will thrive...

My war on politicians will also be a war upon the media. You can't fight politicians without fighting the media. If politicians are the automobiles then the media are the gasoline. Ipso facto, the politician would exist without the media (fuel). But how far can a politician (car) travel without the media (gasoline)? Without the coverage of the media no matter how great a politician is, he could be the most articulate, studious and professional leader in the nation. But neither you nor I would know who he is. And we would not know what he's doing. If I had a brand new Bentley and one gallon of gas, how far would I get? I'd have this big ole beautiful Bentley sitting by the side of the highway immobile. And at some point the cops would tow it away. And you'd have this beautiful automobile sitting in the impound lot. So we have a $200 thousand car rendered useless for lack of fuel.

There are many good men with dreams, visions and talents. But they had no exposure. They could not get the media to cover them. And so they ended up getting towed away to jail or a prison. And you have guys in prisons for doing the same things which Senators and Congressmen do (and get away with) every day. They lock men up and tow them away every day of every week. Men with no power, no exposure, no influence and no connections etc. They lock us up and put us in prison, for doing the same things which members of the City Council do (and get away with) every day of the week. If you don't have gas it doesn't matter if it's a Ferrari. You can't go very far. It can look good and be expensive. It can be made of the best parts. It can be flashy and ostentatious. But it will not progress without fuel. And these are some brilliant and skilled men and women who could not get any fuel to kick-start their dream. And they got towed away to prisons.

So I am gonna work with every ounce of my energy to expose the media. This war will be a dual war on politicians and on the media. And it won't be easy. How do you expose the media when they are the exposure? If I attack the New York Times do you think the New York Times will cover my attack? And if they actually cover my attack on them how well do you think they'd cover it? But I must build a platform. And I must invent, discover and create ways to expose that platform. I may not have gasoline (the corporate owned media) but I can tap into alternative sources of fuel. But I must find a way...

The media (and politicians) run the world. And their power is unchecked. And their biases, racism and prejudices are not exposed. I realize there are folks who believe that *hidden hands* run the world. And I can't prove that they don't play a part. But I'll have my hands full fighting the hands that I can see. And I can see Dale Schornack, Rush Limbaugh and Sean Hannity. I can see the hands of Ted Cruz, Mitch McConnell and Allen West etc. *You* deal with the hidden hands. My war is with Cruz, McConnell, Limbaugh and Hannity etc. I will deploy the weapons in my literary arsenal and utilize them to attack the enemy. This one-man crusade against the media shall transform into a mass campaign against politicians. It is a war in which our enemy is powerful. The media can put any spin on me that they want. But I'm launching a frontal assault herein.

I'm telling you the worst thing they can say about me right now: I am wrongly convicted of raping a man. His name is Ricardo Calvario. He lied. An all-white jury convicted me of crimes I did not commit. That's the worst they have. And they can't really use this from my past to try to destroy me. How can you knock a man down who is already down? I am a state prisoner. You can't go any lower than a prison unless you're in the cemetery. It's not like I'm asking you all to vote for me. I'm not running for political office. I'm not the pastor of any church. I don't (quite frankly) need you to believe in me. As a man wrongly convicted of raping a man I'll take major precautions to protect the integrity of the crusade.

I'm not even certain exactly what all my parole will entail. I'm certain I will have to register until I get this conviction overturned. But... Regardless of my parole I will also police myself (literally). I will not go to a high school to speak unless I have a police escort. It's easier that way. And I'll be very candid with students... "Now see this cop standing here with me? He's here because I'm on parole for 'rape.' And I brought him here with me to protect you and me"... I will not go to a high school without a police officer; period...

I will ask Brian Banks, David Quindt, Ryan Ferguson, Jeffrey Allen Walker, Ronald Cotton, Rolando Cruz, Marcus Dixon and Christopher Bird etc. to join me in doing workshops, seminars and clinics. We can speak to trial lawyers, The American Bar Association, to churches and law schools etc. I want to hold "Truth and Reconciliation"(^TM Sherman D. Manning), "Let Us Make Man" (^R Sherman D. Manning), "Creating Monsters" (^TM) and "The Joseph Project" ® crusades. I will (again) ask Byron Allen, Judge Joe Brown, Tyler Perry, Steve Harvey, Ken Chenault and The Robinhood Foundation etc. to underwrite these conferences (initially). Eventually they will pay for themselves.

I will ask Mayor Kasim Reed, Mayor Kevin Johnson, David Axelrod, Gerry Spence, Paul Morton and The National Urban League to help us. I want to put books and CDs in the hands of people all over this country. I won't light a lamp and put it under a bush. We will promote our "war" by any means necessary... If you're still waiting on O.J. Simpson I'll get there. But O.J. Simpson is now a slave. He's in prison. And my chief aim with this book is to expose the slave system. I must repeat (tautology?) that we have more black men under the judicial (aka "slave system") system than we had black men in slavery in 1850. We have more black men in prison than there are in college. And 92.6 percent of American judges are white. 74.9 percent of police officers are white. 84.3 percent of deputy sheriffs are white. 93.9 percent of sheriffs are white. Well over 82.1 percent of prison guards are white. In prison systems that do have black guards they are mostly low level guards...

At Folsom State Prison I've watched 24 and 25 year-old white guards promote to Sergeant over and over. Yet, C.O.K. Pinkard (i.e. he's black) was passed over time and again. He is a retired military man in the United States Navy. He was a high-ranking NCO (non-commissioned officer). He was a Chief Petty Officer. Yet, Folsom Associate Warden R. Meier elected to promote C.O. Sweeney over Pinkard. Sweeney urinated on a mentally ill inmate's mattress in Building Seven and forced him to lay in it. They promoted Sharma over Pinkard. Sharma is a dark complexioned Indian (I'm not sure). But his brain is white and he's as corrupted as Stratton. He's a follower. And if he saw me being beat down by 8 white guards he would join in and then swear I was beating them. But deceptive, duplicitous, corrupted, colluding, conspiring and conniving prison guards come a dime a dozen. And they get away with abusing, beating and mistreating inmates because they consider us slaves. And most inmates are too dumb to write a missive. We'd rather play cards, gamble, make prison wine and stab each other than to write a letter to the U.S. Attorney or media regarding correctional malfeasance. And...

What if we do write the media? They won't cover us. I watched Dale Schornack and even the national media cover inmate Jeremy Meeks like he was a rock star. He's a gang member facing ten years in prison. Most persons would refer to him as a "thug." But I watched local news anchor Schornack cover this guy like he was a saint. Why? Because a lot of women thought he had a "cute" mug shot. He's half-black and he has blue eyes. Dale said things like, "And maybe when he gets out he can pursue a career in modeling."

And my problem is not Meeks. Prisoners get denigrated all the time. I'm never offended when one is lucky enough to get positive press. My problem is with the media. They preach democracy but practice hypocrisy. Time and again I tried to get Dale to cover "*Gang Bangers* for *God*," correctional malfeasance or some of the books I'd written. Yet, he refused absolutely. They have a general rule whereby they don't want to celebrate inmates or give us any type of platform. Yet, the moment they figure out a way to make some money (ratings) exploiting us (as they did Meeks) all the rules are absolutely forgotten. They are hypocrites... Remember 286 girls were kidnapped in May of 2014. Remember "Bring Back Our Girls?" The media forgot about the girls. Forgot about the 300 missing people on the Malaysian plane etc... Where is Congressman Tom Delay? He should be in prison. He was convicted of bribing lobbyists etc. He's probably out on the beach because judges pamper the rich as soon as the media forgets them. Remember Ethan Couch? Why have most of you forgotten Ethan Couch (Google him)? Because the media decided Ethan did not need to be a slave...

I invite you (readers) to help me build a platform from which to fight this new slave system. They (the media) will hate us. They will try to neutralize, contain (ignore?) or destroy us. But if we are warriors we won't back down. We may only have rocks right now. But we will use the rocks. As I said before the rocks will get us to the sword and the sword will cut off the head of our enemies…

All the while I've been trapped in prison I've been studying, reading and praying. I've been waiting on something big. I'm working on something. It can't come quick. I've got to withstand some heartache… But I'm digging. And God is digging. I asked God to dig out my sensitivity and my insecurity. And often the shovel God uses is people. He uses people to dig you down to something solid. The reason people keep hurting you and letting you down is God is using them to get to the rock. Everybody wants to do the above ground work. But there is some underground work which must be done. Don't play dead and don't lay dead.

Dirt is a common denominator. Things that are buried go in dirt. And things that are planted go in dirt. But only that which is planted in the dirt will come out of that which it was planted in. The darkness you are in right now can be a blessing because a seed can't grow unless it has been in dirt and in darkness. And the reason I'm growing is because I've been in a lot of dirt and I'm in darkness right now. You have to be willing to work in places people don't see. The work goes down (into the dirt) before the building goes up (out of the dirt)…

If we are gonna wage war against injustice we will have to fight with our friends occasionally; and we may attract strange bedfellows. But we must be tactical and strategic. Politicians go where the power is. So let's get power or at least be where it is…

We are all better than the worst thing we've ever done. David did some bad and sick stuff. I'm worried about whether or not pastors are gonna let me preach and speak upon release. But if David was alive he'd have problems. Jack Van Impe would be on TV hollering "Oh Rexella this man is not of God. A man of God does not fornicate. A man of God does not lust and commit adultery. Rexella, a man of God does not get a married woman pregnant and then kill her husband. David is a devil."… But (as usual) Jack doesn't know "jack"…

David once found himself at a crossroads in his life. David was praying and asking God to reverse a curse. David would fall out on the floor and cry, repenting. He had moral failures and character flaws. But maybe the reason God blessed him is because he was a serial repenter. This mighty man of valor and power; this mighty man of God who brought giants to their knees; he was lying on the ground… How the mighty have fallen. David lay on the ground for seven days, face in the dirt, asking God to somehow save this nameless baby. David fasted and prayed for seven days. David is the first man we saw in scripture on his face crying for his baby. The mighty man of God is on his face weeping. It's real hard when you are trying to save something God is trying to kill. Seven days he prayed trying to save what God was trying to kill. Every great man goes through something (sooner or later) that will make you wonder—Lord, will I ever come back from this. Is this the big one? Am I going to "join Elizabeth?"

Even Paul prayed, asking God to remove the thorn from his flesh. But God said "no, I'm going to give you the grace to carry it." Who knows how many times Joseph prayed and fasted in that prison? Joseph probably asked God over and over to get him out of that prison.

"Lord, I'm wrongly convicted of a sex crime. And the only thing I did was have a coat of many colors and a dream; and my daddy gave me the coat and you gave me the dream. I am not a rapist, but I'm in this prison with all of these men. I'm surrounded by darkness, haters and by opposition. And the guards think I'm a rapist. And the warden thinks I'm a rapist. And the people who normally come to rescue me when I'm in trouble are not coming this time. When my brothers plotted to kill me you sent Reuben to save my life. But this time I'm all by myself in a dangerous prison. I'm hurting. How can I preach to guys about the awesomeness of your power? Because the first thing they'll say is 'why won't you get me out since I say I didn't do it?' Lord, get me out!" But God told Joseph 'not yet.' He waited 13 ½ years before he got Joseph out.

God is a healer but we don't want to get sick. We all want to have a powerful testimony but we don't want to have any tests. We just want God to endow us with greatness without suffering. We don't want to pay the price to be great. And if the test is difficult enough you'll find yourself asking, "Is there any way I can come back from this?" (Perhaps that's why I'm worried about whether or not I'll be invited to speak and to preach after I get out.) But you have to put it behind you. You have to keep the faith. I'll fight you all day long but what do you do when your greatest enemy is within you? The real battleground is in your mind. It is never in your circumstances. It's always in your mind. Stop wasting your weapons on what people say. You will never be defeated by what people say about you. You will only be defeated by what you say about you. You must win the war that you have inside of you…

David is the only man in scripture seen crying over his baby… Perhaps the questionable shadow over David's life made him love this baby more. Remember, David said, "I was born in sin and my mother conceived me in iniquity." Don't we work twice as hard to fight for people who are troubled like us? Have you ever been so low that nobody could raise you? Sometimes your history determines the fierceness with which you fight what's in front of you… You've gotta change your mind. Don't let the stain of the rumors of what people said about you destroy your opportunity. You've got to kill that negativity right now. The people that normally come to rescue you may not come this time. What do you do when what normally lifts you won't lift you? When bad has gotten worse what do you do? …

While the mighty man of God, David, lay on the ground weeping he looked up and saw they were whispering. And he perceived that the child was dead. To perceive it meant he knew in his mind… If you can kill it (or build it) in your head you can kill it in your life… Put it behind you… You have too much in front of you to let this trial destroy you. Put it behind you. No trial no triumph. No tests no testimony. Suffering breeds character; character breeds faith; and faith will not disappoint… I just wanted to get that off my chest because the people who are gonna join me in this crusade are gonna be attacked. The folks who join me in this campaign against the celling of America's youth, poor and minorities etc. are going to be talked about. Why are you helping an "ex-rapist?" Why do you wanna help prisoners? …

I'm fascinated by people. I'm even more fascinated by God. And I'm fascinated by how we overlook the flaws of great men in the Bible when and while we are finding fault with today's human leaders. David was an adulterer and a murderer while he was saved. What if your pastor got a married woman pregnant and then killed her husband? I can hear you now:

"I can't sit and listen to a murderer preach." I think God let mighty men have conflicts, issues and demons to show you that there is hope for you and me. And He also does it to keep us from becoming conceited and narcissistic. Paul said, "Lest I become conceited." Is that why he gave Jacob a limp? David, a whore-mongering spirit? Paul, a thorn in the flesh? ... A limp will keep you humble... But (I repeat) don't allow people to bury you just because you are in dirt. God has planted (Joseph, Brian Banks, Christopher Bird, Ryan Ferguson and *Sherman D. Manning* etc.) you in that dirt (or prison)...

But to my fellow slaves I remind you that captivity is a learned behavior. Laziness is a learned behavior. If you learned to make-do in the prison you can learn to swim with the sharks. But you must humble yourself and learn. Don't allow your history to hinder you from your destiny. Change your mind. New environments are very uncomfortable. You will grope like a blind man in a new apartment. The new apartment may be a blessing but it feels like a curse. But keep the faith... I signed the lease and I wanted a change but I grope as I struggle with this newness.

The actor needs a new script so I don't perform old lines. I've got to heal because I've been broken. Many of you are broken. Poverty has broken your spirit. Loneliness has broken you. Sometimes affluence can break you. But we have millions of broken children in juveniles, jails and prisons. And broken boys hook up with broken girls and two broken people produce broken kids... Write a new script. Write the vision and not the victimhood. Write it out. You can't run it out until you write it out. Don't write the memoir of your pain or where you used to be. Don't write from the rearview mirror. But forward march. It's time to start forgetting those things which are behind you. And if you no longer want to be a slave you must press forward to those things which are ahead of you. You must know thyself. And you can have esteem for a self that you know. And don't allow the cracks in you to destroy that which is great in you. Don't allow your weakness to destroy your greatness.

David knew that he had issues. Jesse didn't even choose him. He was not Jesse's first choice... So perhaps this shadow over David's life was rooted in his conception? And since David knew what it was like to be overlooked as a child; since David knew what it felt like to be rejected by his own father, maybe he grew up and said, "I'll never give up on or reject my child." There had to be a reason David wept so horrendously over this child. He is the first man ever recorded in scripture who wept over a child. And the Holy Spirit is so discerning that He wouldn't have included this seven days of weeping unless there was a reason. A novice would say that God wanted to show us that men do cry. But I'm not a novice. I believe God was showing us that there was something in David's childhood or past that gave him a special attachment to this child. And David did not want to let him go. He said, "Fearfulness and trembling have come upon me. And horror has overwhelmed me... Oh that I had wings like a dove I'd fly away and be at rest." David almost sounded suicidal. That means that God understands your sorrows. He understands your pain and my hurt. As hurt and as depressed as you and I may be—God understands...

David was a mighty man of God. David was an awesome warrior, a master fighter, a conqueror and a man of valor. We're talking about a King when we talk about David. And he was a philanderer, a whore-monger, a womanizer, a Freaky Freddie, a rabble rouser, and...a lady's man! And he was a killer. David had a man murdered; first-degree homicide; conspiracy to commit murder; all behind chasing a skirt-tail. And yet the minute we find out a pastor has had one indiscretion we are ready to kick him out of the church. I'm all for getting crooks out of the church. I get upset with Benny Hinn, Kenneth Copeland and a lot of these other con men. Benny is a con. Why didn't Hinn (or Copeland) meet the ambulance (at Emory Hospital in Atlanta in August 2014) carrying the Ebola patient? And why didn't Benny touch the ambulance and heal him? Why doesn't Hinn go to West Africa and hold a healing service? A lot of those dudes like him and Copeland etc. have never even believed in God. They are simply hustlers. Hinn is Kevin Trudeau with a Bible…

But there are some men who have an anointing on their life. They can preach and teach. And they struggle with issues and with conflicts. And when men truly believe in God, and when God lifts them up in ministry, they struggle. They are often tormented. But when David messed up he didn't call somebody for counseling. He knew he couldn't afford to tell some of his secrets. But he knew exactly who to talk to. David went to God and said, "Against thee and thee (not people) only have I sinned." He would sing, pray and repent so vociferously that he moved the hand of God. But a lot of people teach us that we don't even need to repent. We're already forgiven etc. etc. But I believe in repenting. When I mess up…

David wept for seven days and nights but when he heard them whispering he perceived the baby was dead. He had mourned and wept unlike any man we'd ever seen in the Bible. Oh how he mourned; the mighty man of God, fasting and praying. But what happened after David perceived that the child was dead? …A father who is weeping, troubled and fallen because of his child.

But today we have an epidemic of absent fathers. Many fathers are in the same place that I'm in. And the new system of slavery understands clearly that the father is the head of the home. And if you can attack, attract, incarcerate (enslave) or destroy the father you'll destroy the home. Destroy the home, you destroy the family. Ruin the family and you'll destroy the neighborhood. And attack enough neighborhoods and you will cripple an entire generation of people. And the end results will be millions of men who can't vote, can't own a gun, can't get a job and are useless. And an unemployed man who feels unemployable will often resort to crime and drugs. And then we'll pass a three-strikes law and make it retroactive and we'll enslave you for life. And in the new slave system we use the "F" word much more than the "N" word. Once we call you "felon" it's almost always over. This system of slavery always begins with an attack on fathers. And if we men would go back and look at the mighty man of God, David; and look how he reacted to his child. It can be instructive for us.

We have to begin to strategize and organize around being "there" for our children. We take their bias and racism as a given. But if I love my child I need to be willing to weep for her and to fight for her. I need to be willing to do right for her… A greeting card company states that well over 90 percent of prison inmates buy Mother's Day cards. Yet, less than 20 percent of inmates buy Father's Day cards. Well over 82 percent of prisoners come from fatherless homes. How deep is that? If we could simply find a way to rectify that problem we would revolutionize our world. What can we do to get fathers back into homes? Why are we so angry with fathers?

I talked to inmate Cobb (aka "DoLow" and he's paroling in 18 days. He's a dope addict and an alcoholic. And unfortunately he'll be re-incarcerated in less than six months) the other day. And I told him I'd just hung up the telephone with my dad *James Scott Manning*. And Cobb stated, "I hate my pops. We never talk and we don't get along." In 2012 I interviewed 200 prison inmates and took a poll on their relationships with their fathers. 169 guys had not spoken with their fathers in well over five years. So guys who grow up in fatherless homes often go to prison. Then what do we expect to happen to the children of the 2.7 million of us who are in prison today? Some of us have 4 and 5 kids by different women. But if each of us has only 2 kids, that's almost 6 million kids who are at-risk by virtue of the fact that their dads are in prison. We need to wake up and change this.

Every American pastor ought to call a code-red on men. We need to preach and to teach about it. We need to read, to study and to pray about it. We need to develop think-tanks, committees and task forces whose sole focus is to keep our children out of prisons. This ought to be a priority for Mayors (especially black Mayors), city councilmen, Governors, State Senators, pastors, ex-cons and cons. I won't invite our do-nothing Congress. All that Congress seem capable of doing now is hating President Obama. Most of the older white men in Congress were affiliated with the White Citizen's Council and some were in the KKK. They hate President Obama's skin color. I know the media won't say this and President Obama can't say it. But 60 percent of Obama's problems in the Congress are due to racism…

We must engage in a *war on slavery*. And our chief aim must be to intervene, to rescue and to mentor the kids of prisoners. We have a vested interest in not letting them form gangs, get locked up and go to prison. I don't want my tax dollars to pay to raise their kids. Keep them out of prison. I don't want to pay to keep them in prisons.

I want to go home and hold symposiums at churches, colleges and at convention centers. We need to discuss the new Jim Crow and the new slave system. We need to discuss "Just Mercy." Perhaps I can get Russell Simmons, Bryan Stevenson, Master P, Magic Johnson and Steve Harvey etc. to help underwrite this project. We cannot wait until 2016 to begin organizing. I need ambassadors to start calling people right now and start talking about this book. Tell your pastor, your professor, your homeroom teacher, your coach, your girlfriend and your boyfriend about this book. We need to begin to prepare an assault on the media (and on the politicians) right now.

I need all hands on deck. I need Nick Prato, Dylan Marron, Melanie (or Natalie?) Delsendico, Alex Hayes, Jimbo Spalding, Tim Griffin, Jacob Goodin and Jakob Karr (contact them via email and tell them to get this book) to join us. We need ex-Bloods, Crips, AB, Skinheads etc. And we need you. Let's rescue our children today and build them up and make them strong. We will need Daniel Kovarbasich, Clayton Burnham and Justin Berry etc. We need people with experiential expertise to help us turn youngsters around. I'd like to find Curtis Sykes, Eugene Langford (in Atlanta), Frank Carter and John Garvin. I'd love to locate Scott Johnson (in Warner Robbins, GA) and have them to join us in "The Joseph Project." Our workshops, seminars and our symposiums etc…

David? The mighty man of God; the King of Israel. David? A man after God's own heart. He wept, he fasted and he lay upon his face for seven days and seven nights. And… If you listen to David in Psalm 55:4, 5, "My heart is sore pained within me, and the terrors of death have fallen upon me." This mighty man seemed almost suicidal. And in II Samuel 12:16 David pleaded with God for his child. Have you ever pleaded with God for your child? And what do you do when you pray and fast and God says no? What do you do when you know He can but He won't? In Genesis, Joseph did not want to go to prison for a sex crime which he did not commit. And I'm certain that Joseph fasted and he prayed but God didn't move. For 13 ½ years Joseph (I know what I'm talking about, intimately) had to listen to haters tell him, "Where is your God now? If you really didn't try to take her p-ssy how did she get your clothes? If you were a man of God why did He let you get convicted? And you've been here 13 years Joseph so why won't God get you out of prison?"…

David pleaded with God and he lay on the ground. So the elders arose and went to the mighty man of God to raise him up from the ground. But David would not get up. Have you ever gone through a storm when what normally lifts you won't lift you? Have you ever been in so much pain and sorrow that the stuff that normally would raise you up won't raise you? If you keep living long enough you may find yourself in a jam, in a situation or in a predicament. And the people who normally came to your rescue won't come. The people who normally bail you out won't come. But I believe that God will allow these kinds of situations to teach us to lean on Him. And I believe that these tortuous trials come to make us strong… But when David *perceived* that the child was dead he arose… He arose… David got up from the ground and he washed himself. And he anointed himself. And he changed his clothes and he went to the house of the Lord and he worshipped. Then afterward he went home and he ate…

"But now he is dead; why should I fast? Can I bring him back again? I shall go to him, but he shall not return to me." Then David comforted his wife and they had another baby. When you have done everything which you can do; when you've cried and fasted; when you've prayed and believed; and when God says no, you have to get up, wash yourself, anoint yourself. Don't go without the anointing. If you try to anoint a dirty face it won't work. And if you're clean but not anointed you will fail. You have to anoint yourself and change clothes. And then you have to get into the presence of God and to worship Him. Then you have to put the past behind you and move on. "David, when it's over wash your face and have another baby." But God let us see a man weep, lie on his face and pray for his child.

And I'm calling upon men who are willing to weep for our children. David is a sign to men in 2016, 2017, 2018 – 2024 (and beyond) that we must be willing to fight to save our children. Fight your way out of gangs. Fight your way into college. Fight for a job, a career or a promotion. We have been wimps when it comes to our children. How dare we quit or give up. I want a national revival to fight for our children. God can still do the almighty through the least likely. The last can be first and the first can be last.

But we must explore the new slave system. If you are a slave get out. Become a runaway. Read your way out. Pray your way out. Think your way out. The system is designed to make you think like a slave. And the dangers of the prisons lie in their ability to make you think, act, walk and talk like a slave. So to wash your face and change your clothes signals the changing of your mind. Learn how to talk like a free man (civilian). Learn how to live, think and act like a free man. Prison institutionalizes 87.3 percent of the inmates who spend 3 years or more inside. Prison also institutionalizes people who work in prisons. There is nothing worse than an incarcerated mind or a locked up spirit. We need to devise more programs which teach men to deinstitutionalize and deprogram themselves.

There is a certain way you have to walk, talk, live, think, eat and even sleep in a prison. Things that are acceptable or classy for men to do in civilian society will get a man punked, screwed (literally) or even killed in a prison. Prisons are not natural, normal or ordinary. We've become a society too willing to send too many people to prison, too quickly. And once they get locked up many of them will never be the same again. Don't take my word for it. Ask Judge Greg Mathis, Brian Banks, Lane Garrison and Jeff Deskovic. Prison can ruin you forever. And… What do you do when you get out if you didn't do it? That seems repetitive here. But the more I (personally) think about it the more I understand why so many of them get out and return…

If I get out in 2016 what will I do? Will Quincy Lavelle Carswell, Marcus D. Cosby, Paul Morton, James Henderson, James Morton or any pastor invite me to preach in their pulpit? I'll be a 43-year old ex-con who has to register. What, pray tell, can I offer anybody? Who can I call on? I'll admit it looks bleak. But I must tell you that I'll either have to believe that God really can do anything or not. I will have to believe that God really is who He is or not. And if God be for me I will get out. And if I get out I don't know where He will send me. I don't know what pastor He will move. But somebody will say, "*Manning* you can come preach for me. You don't have to impersonate Jasper Williams. You don't need to impersonate *Andrew Young* etc. Just come on over to so-and-so Baptist Church and you can preach for me Sunday morning." And I'll preach and I shall also lecture and speak at colleges and at universities as an expert in criminal justice, sociology and on crime and punishment. And I don't need to re-litigate my wrongful conviction at every church. If folks wanna know my conviction they can get this book.

I am wrongly convicted of raping a man. His name was Ricardo Calvario. He was a female impersonator. I did (indeed) sin. I had no need to pick up a hooker. I'm not an unattractive person. I've had a lot of women. I was being opportunistic and exploring L.A. I picked up who I thought was a woman. We drove to the back of his apartment building. When I discovered who it was (a man) I demanded that he get out of my car. He insisted that I should have known he was a man and I must pay him anyway. I reached under my seat and got a starter pistol (for sporting events) and said, "Get out of my car." Calvario went to a payphone and dialed 911 and reported that there was a man threatening people. He hung up…

A few minutes later he called 911 again and said, "He raped me." They took him to the hospital. The physician found no signs of rape. So why am I here? Because I had an all-white jury and *no lawyer*. And he "who represents himself in a court of law has a fool for a client." And when I get out I intend to prove that I was wrongly convicted. I pray that Brian Banks, Jeff Deskovic, Freddie Parrish and Justin Brooks etc. will help me. I don't know how but somehow… I'll get on YouTube and lecture on the internet. I'll do voice-over work wherever I can find it. I'll start my own podcast where we discuss politics, politricks, the criminal justice system (the *new slave system*), crime and punishment. As long as I have to "register" I'll only speak at high schools if I have a police officer with me...

I want Jake Tracy, Jacob Gabriel, Kyle Day, Jeff Allen Walker, Jason Voltaw, Christopher Wood, Brent Sehati, Zach Brown, Jarod Gaber, Justin Sech, Joel Carpenter, *Cody*, *Hayden* and Zack (Attack) to join us. I want Frankie Grande, Raider Runner, Eddie Cannon, Curtis Sykes and Alex Bernhardt to join us... We need to inspire a nation of youths to start back *reading*. Reading is the key to evolution. Real change does not transpire through revolution. But real change comes through evolution...

The *Joseph Crusade* will recruit Professors Stevenson and Alexander. And we will use the internet to educate, to enlighten and to uplift people. What we've been doing has not worked. With more black men in prison than there were in slavery? This is an emergency. We need all hands on deck. Even the hands (*especially* the hands) of the wrongly convicted. Even the hands of ex-cons who were rightly convicted. *Gang Bangers* For *God*[TM ShermanD.Manning] will connect with *Helping Educate At Risk Teens* (*HEART* [TM ShermanD.Manning] ) will connect with *NAPS*, will connect with *The Joseph Crusade* [TM ShermanD.Manning]. And we will ask college professors to pledge to mentor ex-cons as well as at-risk youths. We will ask pastors to mentor. We will ask entrepreneurs to mentor. I will ask ex-wardens like Tim Virga, Captain Rhonda Carter and Associate Warden Linda Johnson Dovey etc. to mentor youths. I know this sounds odd etc. but we've got to think outside the box if we want to end *the new slavery*...

There are ex-slaves who have been *branded* for life. And some have been branded for crimes which they (we) did not commit. I will be asking teams of lawyers, public officials and ex-judges etc. to help us to help those who have been branded... Opportunities can come wrapped in opposition... I will go and see Tom Mesereau, Justin Brooks and Robert Sheahen when I get home... Your weakness (proclivities and addictions etc.) creates a platform for other people to look big. They need you to be dysfunctional because it gives them a job and makes them look important.

...I want Joel Ward, Dan Remer, Jordan Robbins, Zach Everhart, Cole Simmons, Tim Urban, Mitch Grassi, Tyler Grady, Justin Sech, John Schreiber (in Davis), Ryan Coolley, Chris Holdsworth, Daniel Jensen, Kenton Shimozaki, Chris Godek, M. Hiscel (Stockton), Grant Shetz, Stephen Zinn, Christopher James, Caleb Light, Justin Tankersaey, Quinn Halleck, Kevin Sullivan and Noah Mathis etc. to read this book. I can't reach them. I need you to email them and tell them to get this book... My team wants Max Hodges, Steven Fabian, Peter O'Riordin and Adam Glynn to do the B.E.B. Challenge (pp 313) for $2500.00...

I will be calling on Ian Wallach, Ben Pavone or Ed Higginbotham etc. to help me. You can't convince me that I was chained to a hospital bed for 14 months with Valley Fever. And I was there at the behest of Mike Bunnell. And they could steal my appeals and lawsuit to manipulate the statute of limitations etc. And now I still have nightmares, depression and sporadic insomnia. I still wake up yelling, thinking I'm back in that hospital. And CDC refuses to treat PTSD. And they send this shade-tree psychologist Dr. Stabbe to make fun of my nightmares etc. If Ian Wallach is reading this we have to do something. I was treated worse than Nazis. The Nazis used the Geneva Convention to get themselves removed during World War II out of the Valley Fever spores in the Coalinga, CA area.

The United States Government removed Nazi prisoners of war because of the risk of Valley Fever spores. Yet, the State of California decided to put American prisoners in a prison, in the same place which was too dangerous for Nazis. And I was held in one of those prisons… Carol Leonard and Roberta Franklin warned me about Valley Fever. And… I was in the at-risk group(s). I'm black and I'm an asthmatic. And a corrupted, wicked and deadly Associate Warden (Mike Bunnell) became angry with me because I wrote about him in a book. And he told me he was transferring me to PVSP so I could "catch Valley Fever and write a book about that." And Carol, my team and I wrote to everybody up to and including the Governor. Yet, they forcefully transferred me to PVSP. And four months later I was nearly dead. I spent 14 months (I repeat) chained to a hospital bed. I got down to 96 pounds and my Valley Fever lawsuit is barred due to the statute of limitations. I met every statute. But Bunnell enlisted the Green Wall (aka CCPOA), Ryan Wenker, Joseph Stratton, Layton Johnson and others to delay, sabotage and steal mail to cause me to miss the time restraints… I'm still spending nights with no sleep. And when I do sleep I have nightmares (I repeat) about that hospital. I have severe flashbacks… If Bryan Stevenson, Michelle Alexander or Jason Feldman etc. are reading, there must be some way to sue these people for what they did to me…

Sgt. Joseph Stratton was angry with inmate Hernandez. And he retaliated against him by putting inmate Garcia (V23865) in the cell with Hernandez. It was actually in June 2012. And Garcia nearly killed him. And guards and supervisors are so poorly trained that it took them 1 hour and 42 minutes to get Hernandez out of the cell. He nearly died waiting. And I've seen Stratton, Konrad and Sharma (time and time again) spend nearly two hours trying (or at least acting like they are trying) to get bleeding and dying inmates out of cells… Hernandez tried to sue. Yet, the mailroom "lost" his appeal. And if you don't exhaust an appeal you can't file a lawsuit…

The stuff guards get away with in the United States. If that happened in other countries we'd be talking human rights violations. You know we don't "torture" terrorist suspects. But we do "torture" California inmates. We torture state and federal prisoners every day of the week. Why don't you hear about it? Well… Who is Marlene Pinnock? Why don't you remember her? Who is Caree Harper? You've forgotten them because the "media" has a short attention span. And they moved on. I want you to Google Marlene Pinnock and her attorney Caree Harper. Look at the video. Now you remember her? ... Remember "Bring Back The Girls?" Why have you forgotten them? James Wood? Who is he? You don't know? He was an American who was on that Malaysian plane which went missing. (Christopher Wood, are you reading? Here's to you Bro'… Send me a missive and let me know you read this).

…Yesterday in Ferguson, Missouri a teen black kid was gunned down by a white cop. The cop murdered him. Why don't you remember Ferguson? When I was a kid preacher in Atlanta, I led the prayer vigils and prayer march (alongside Mayor Maynard Jackson) for the *Missing* and *Murdered* Children of Atlanta. It was front page news. Yet, you don't know a damn thing about it. The American media gets paid to keep you from remembering it. Because "they that know not their history are destined to repeat it." The blessing in not growing up in the 20s, 30s – 50s is that a lot of youngsters (are not crippled, damaged or limited by the residue of racism) don't know what overt racism looks like. And the danger of not growing up during those times is that a lot of youngsters don't know what overt racism looks like. The same thing which is a blessing can also be a curse. If I don't recognize the nuances, hints, the nods and the winks of racism, I could be recaptured by a "master" and not even see it coming.

What alarms me about the gangs in Chicago, Los Angeles, Detroit and in Stockton etc. is that all of those gangbangers are killing each other off. And white people (certainly not all of them but the segment which is racist and often in power) sit back and laugh all the way to the banks (which they own). Many cops are white. Most prosecutors (as well as public defenders) are white. Most judges are white. The jail guards are white. The prison guards are mostly white. The prison wardens (in California) are all white. So…if I kill you and you are black, brown or (poor) white, then I've eliminated your existence. The racists no longer need to worry about you. You are gone. And since I murdered you, so am I. I'll get locked up by a white cop. I'll get prosecuted (and defended) by a white D.A. I'll get judged by a white brother (and if he's black he'll be whitewashed). I'll go to a jail run by a white sheriff. And I'll get sent to a prison run by white people. I could elucidate this semi-genocide by tribal warfare in so many ways. If I shoot you and you survive, you'll go to a hospital which is run by… What color do you think your surgeon will be? Most of your nurses will be Caucasian. And…lest you think I'm obsessed with "race" I tend to differ. The system is obsessed with race. The system is obsessed with class. And money can buy justice. The only reason Chris Brown (a black woman beater) is not in state prison right now is because money buys justice. The rich get richer and the poor get prison. Justice is never blind, deaf or mute…

My fear is that I may not be able to tell enough black, brown and white people what is really going on. Folks like Paul Ryan, Mitch McConnell, Ted Cruz (See my book "*Don't Mess With Texas*" on Amazon.com) know exactly what I'm writing about. There are (I repeat) people who get paid to prevent you from knowing the truth. I know a white guy who is 83 and worth $100 million. He told me that if the Governor announced he was pardoning every prisoner and he announced it in the newspaper, most prisoners would never know. A. Because prisoners don't read newspapers. B. Prisoners can't read newspapers. I was floored when a professor told me that penologists and criminologists look at third grade test scores to determine how many prisons they will have to build. Most kids who are doing poorly in school in third grade will end up spending time in prisons. See…when I hear a fact like this it makes me want to immediately set up programs which rescue 8-year old kids who are doing badly in school. But Bishop Flip Flop and Reverend Willie Wonder are doing nothing to change this. We need to intervene now. Many schools in Oakland, Detroit, Chicago, New York and Los Angeles etc. are pure dropout factories. And 87 percent of black boys and 84 percent of Hispanic boys who dropped out of high school (in L.A.) in 2004 did jail and/or prison time by 2010. The reason poor kids drop out is because we've not proven (to them) the connection between education and aspiration. Rich kids learn the connection between education and aspiration as toddlers. It's in their DNA.

…If you hang around 9 broke people you will become the 10$^{th}$. Nothing changes your life (except God or love) like moving your credit score a hundred and twenty points. We need to start teaching poor kids financial literacy. We've got to break the "broke" curse in Black America. Too many of our families have too much month at the end of their money. Poverty is a state of mind, first. I'd like to take financial literacy and make it a civil rights issue. If you deal with class you get race for free. There are tens of millions of poor whites (on welfare) in this country. 10 million households in America don't have a bank account. We need to start having "Shark Tank" for kids beginning in elementary school. We need to have classes that teach 25 businesses that kids can start for $500.00 or less…

     I would like to take a revival, a crusade or a campaign across this country which is a "curse breaking" crusade. I'd like to go to churches, colleges, companies, clubs, conventions and to unions. I'd like to motivate teachers, pastors, high school students, high school athletes, college frats, symphonies and orchestras etc. to begin to break the cycles of poverty; because poverty leads to prison. Eliminate poverty and solve the prison problem. Sell the American dream to Americans, and you won't need to cell Americans. If you teach a man to *sell* he won't need a *cell*. Teach him financial literacy and which stocks to buy, try or sell and he won't go to jail.

     …What is a money market account? Sadly (just between you and I) if you are a black male (between the ages of 16 – 29) without a college degree etc. there is an 85 percent chance you don't know. That is also heartbreaking. And we must rapidly change this. May I repeat? White judges, prosecutors, bankers, stock brokers and financiers etc. are glad that you don't know that a money market account is similar to a savings account. But a money market account pays a higher yield than a savings account. It invests in short-term investments etc. And it is insured for up to $250 grand. We have got to start teaching, preaching and speaking money. And I'm not talking about get-rich-quick schemes either. We need a crusade, not against gangs. I don't give a damn about Bloods, Crips Norténos or the AB. I want a crusade 'for' gang members to be taught money. Most of these dudes joined gangs for protection, family or money anyway. And many feel like a man being in a gang. Nothing says 'man' like 'paper' in the bank. Nothing says man like owning your own house and eating steaks and lobsters. You can be in a gang all day long but if you're still living in the projects there's not a lot you can tell me. You can be a 'killer' but if you're still living with your momma? You need to learn how to kill those bills. Let's *gang* up on poverty and kill off ignorance. I want to see a revolution. And real change comes from evolution and evolution leads to revolution. It's time to become thinkers. I wonder what would happen if people (in Ferguson, MO) could have figured out a way to withhold all funding from the police department until the cop who killed the boy was fired. When you pull and control the purse-strings, that's real power… I did not know that Donald has donated money to Storm Front! Storm Front?...

     I have an announcement: Donald Trump wants you to stay in his hotels (if you can afford it). Trump wants you to watch his television shows. But Trump has no interest in you joining the Billionaire's Boys Club. As quiet as it's kept there are many people who look like you (Jay Z., P. Diddy, Dr. Ben Carson etc.) who have no interest in seeing you join the middle class. If they did they'd be sounding the alarm in Zion. They'd be telling their fans etc. (at every concert) to get your ass back in school. Read joker read. If you want to join the middleclass you gotta mimic the middleclass. You must learn to think like they think. Read what they read. And even if you're in the ghetto you don't have to have a ghetto mentality. You can get up. But you must think up and see up before you can be up. If you can see it you can be it. The sons of dropouts often become dropouts. Just as the sons of physicians often become physicians. Education is passed down generationally. Just as gangs are passed down.

One problem with the ghetto is the only symbols of success kids see are from the drug dealers. Our kids need to see, touch and feel others who go to, are going to or have gone to college. If you take an English teacher and high school principal and they get married, there is a strong chance that their child will go to college. If you get a drug addict and a pimp and they have a kid, it might not go so well for the kid. Broken and angry people produce broken and angry kids. So the cycle or the curse must be broken. And it needs to be broken right now. This is an emergency. I want rich and educated kids to mentor poor students or students who are doing poorly. Each one has to reach and to teach one…

…Police departments have had a war on black people (around this country) since Nixon. Cops always have one kind of war or another against the poor. But you never, ever see a war on child molestation or a war on kiddie porn. Because who are the purveyors of child porn? All around this country there are police chiefs, successful attorneys, judges, bank presidents and chairmen of boards etc. who buy, sell, trade and love kiddie porn. Statistically? (There are surprisingly few statistics) 89.3 percent of America's pedophiles are white. Call your police chief, news station, newspaper or talk radio and ask, "When was the last time you all had a war on kiddie porn?" We have crackdowns on drunk driving, crackdowns on drugs, prostitution and pimping etc. But when will your police department enact a special task force to catch pedophiles? They will not because "class" and "money" buy "justice." And the judges, physicians and businessmen in your city who like kiddie porn have enough connections etc. that if arrested they'd… Cut off the money to the police department. Well-connected sexual deviants have so much clout that Dateline no longer does "How to Catch a Predator." It's gone…

I abhor anyone who would molest children! It is absolutely unspeakable (and if a person does that they need God, a shrink and a miracle). But in this country if you have enough money, you can be a known pedophile and not go to prison. There are police officers (every day in America) who are bribed into looking the other way; to ignore kiddie porn. You are a city cop who earns $52 grand per year. You can't even afford to send your daughter to college. And you stop Bryan Singer and you see kiddie porn on the seat of his Ferrari. And…"I'll give you $50 grand in cash to not arrest me. $50 G." You can get what it takes you 52 forty-hour weeks — right now. In cash… And you know the pedophile (with the illegal stash of kiddie porn) is not going to snitch you out for letting him bribe you.

By and large there are no rich people in prison. If a sheriff or any politician runs for office on a platform of "A war on rich pedophiles" (read my book *America's Richest Pedophiles*") or a "war on kiddie porn" he will lose. The media (I.E. Dale Schornack and Co.) will not cover him. And he will not get any money. Speak out against Jews (Mr. Farrakhan) and you'll get banned from coverage by ABC, CBS and NBC. Is America really a democracy. Corporate owned media cater to their corporations. Especially since (according to Mitt Romney) "Corporations are people"… Attack rich pedophiles from a large platform and you will lose your platform. A former Secret Service agent stated that kiddie porn is a $ trillion dollar (worldwide) business…

(I need readers to help me get this book to Tal Safron, Faisal Saleh, Daniel Jennings, Daniel Jensen, Charles Askew, Casey Askew, Andy Hines, Eugene Langford, Gabriel Herrington, Zachary Sampson, Cody Linley, Cody Simpson, Chris Godek, Caleb Light, Max (or Mike) Hiscel, Justin Hoop, Jared Gaber, Quinn Halleck, Aaron Hoover, Mark Buda, Trevor Buda, Alex King, Juan Pablo, Michael Tennant, Ari Shapiro, Joshua Peavy, Travis Ulerick, Kyle Pratt, Kyle Carr and Cody Baetge etc.)…

You all remember Trayvon Martin? He was murdered by George Zimmerman. And after all of the hooping and hollering, all the marches, vigils and protests etc., Zimmerman still got away with murder. The black life is devalued in the United States. We watched this black woman beat down (viciously) on a highway by the CHP. And then the CHP hid her in a hospital, under a false name because they didn't want her family to see or to photograph her bruises. And? We've already forgotten her black ass. She was "homeless anyway so who cares?" …

We clearly watched a NYPD cop choke a black man to death in June of 2014. The chokehold has been outlawed for 20 years. Yet, in close view of a camera the cop choked him to death. He yelled "I can't breathe" five times. And yet, the cop is still a cop! When the paramedics showed up they did not administer CPR. Why? The devaluation of black life in America… Now we have the Ferguson Police Department. They have 53 cops and only 3 of them are black. And if white cops can still declare "open season" on blacks while we have a black president and a black attorney general, what else do I need to tell you?

Remember Christopher Dorner? He went on a killing spree because he had been a LAPD officer and he'd reported a cop beating a citizen. And they fired him because he broke the code; the no-snitch rule among cops. And when the LAPD was looking for him they heard he was driving a blue truck. And cops saw a blue truck (with two female occupants) and without hesitation they lit the truck up with bullets. Never mind the tag number. The two women lived and the LAPD Police Chief offered a lukewarm apology and a new truck. To add insult to injury the chief tried to renege by giving the women a used truck… When the LAPD caught up with officer Chris Dorner they murdered him. They burned down the house to make certain that he was dead. He violated the code. He crossed the thin blue line…

Someone asked me what would happen if people followed the NYPD cop (who murdered the brother with a chokehold) home and burned his house down with him in it. I said if they killed that cop the NYPD would hunt them down as if they were Osama Bin Laden. If somebody killed the Ferguson, MO cop the cops would attack every black citizen in Ferguson. Cops would set the city on fire and then burn down the town. Most police departments (in 2016) are basically armed militias… The answer? Not another march or protest. But the answer is for every 4$^{th}$, 5$^{th}$ and 6$^{th}$ grade minority to begin to read business books; read books about money; become financially literate; and learn how to start, run and operate businesses. We must learn to buy banks, not Bentleys. We need to learn how the financial markets operate. Quit studying baseball, basketball and football. And study money and banking instead. I know guys in prison who know football as well as Tony Dungy. They are as strategically learned (in basketball) as Phil Jackson. But many will never in their life go to another basketball game. They have life sentences. They would be better served by studying economics and business etc. But we've been taught that 'business' is for white people…

This book will deal with Mr. Simpson in the next chapter. But the truth of the matter this book is more about the "*No J's*" than it is about O.J… The title of this book is wrong. It should not be titled "*The Truth About O.J. …*" It ought to be "*The Truth About No J.*" Trayvon was a *No J*. That's why Zimmerman murdered him and got away. The little black girl who was intoxicated and had a car wreck and was gunned down in Detroit when all she did was knock on a man's door. The jury convicted him but he will not receive a life sentence because the girl was a simple *No J*. The black college football player in North Carolina who wrecked his car, he got out and knocked on the door of a white lady's house and she called the cops. And a white police officer showed up and murdered him. Do you recall the black guy's name? It was *No J*…

In 2009 inmate Edwards was pepper-sprayed to death by Sgt. Joseph Stratton , Sgt. K. Porter and Officer Ryan Wenker. He was in restraints, in a spit mask and locked in a cage. They murdered him. When he yelled, "I can't breathe," Stratton stated, "If you are talking you are breathing," and they watched him die. And there was a conspiracy to cover it up. They got away with it because inmate Edwards was *No-J*… Back in 2002 before Stratton was a sergeant he conspired to murder inmate Salazar through his cell partner (Frank Christian). They murdered "Rocky" Salazar. And the media never mentioned it because Rocky was a "*No-J.*" "*No-J's*" get murdered by guards and cops inside and outside prisons every day. And this has been going on since slavery.

White men used to lynch black men for looking at white women. And all through the 70s, 80s, 90s and even into 2000 cops would lie and say, "That didn't happen." And there was no cellphone, video etc. And even I would sometimes doubt that an officer is just going to kill somebody. But how wrong was I? And how foolish was I! "The *Truth* About Mr. *No-J*" is that he is not considered a "mister" by police officers. They still devalue black life. They devalue the poor. And they disrespect people who have no clout. They know that "all they are going to do is protest and loot etc. They'll burn down their own neighborhoods and then we (the cops) will get overtime pay for dealing with them. And we will drive back out to the suburbs undisturbed.

That is sick and there must be a better way. I'm tired of watching us try to solve a smartphone problem with a payphone solution. We must embrace the 21$^{st}$ century… I'm not even worried about weapons of mass destruction. I'm more concerned about the weapons of self-destruction which we are still utilizing to numb, retard and to kill ourselves. My vantage point is very interesting because (again) I'm watching inmate Cobb who will be paroled, now, in less than a week. And he is still drinking hooch and snorting pills every day of the week. He is destroying himself… So if I need to encourage you to stop drinking booze, smoking dope or using crack etc. you are not ready. I will pray for you. I care about you. And I would like to see you get off of drugs. But since wishing is not a strategy, I can't help you.

But for the individual who is hungry or searching, there's help for you. If you can't see it you can't be it. The good book says that "without a vision the people perish." The worst man in the world is a man with no vision, no dream and no goal. If you find a man who has no dream you should run as fast as you can, as far as you can away from him…Joseph (in Genesis) had a gift (a coat of many colors) given to him as a boy. And he also had a dream. And his gift and his dream made him stand out. But standing out also created envy. His own biological (blood) brothers hated him. They hated him because he was their father's favorite son. So anytime you find favor with anybody ( a father, a mother, a CEO, a warden, a coach etc.) you will always be hated by somebody. Please, please, please get that understanding and get it now. They may not tell you that they hate you. They may not show you that they hate you. But somebody is going to hate you. And when you couple favor, or a gift etc. with a dream or a vision etc. they will hate you more.

So Joseph had this dream and he dreamed that his brothers were going to have to bow down to him. Now Joseph probably should not have told his brothers about this dream. He had found favor with his father. He was gifted and he had a dream. But he didn't have the wisdom to keep it to himself. That's one school of thought and I think we can learn from that. Yet, another theological view is that he had to tell them his dream. Because had he not told them his dream (Genesis 37) then the will of God would not have unfolded as it did…"and they hated him even more" (that's Genesis 37:5). And "even more" meant that they already hated him before he ever had the dream. In verse 8 he'd told them about another dream that he'd had. And in verse 8 the Bible says, "So they hated him even more." They hated him and they envied him for his "dreams" and for his "words." So you've heard that "misery loves company." Well if you want to be loved just be miserable. Do nothing and aspire to become nobody. Because if you dream and if you speak about your dream you will be hated and envied. And envy will cause people to mistreat you. Envy can cause people to set you up, lie on you, lie about you or even to murder you. Envy and hatred are powerful and deadly emotions…

Can I be extremely candid and authentic with you? I have learned more from the life of Joseph than I have from almost anything else I've read in my life. And I've probably read 12,000 books in my life. If you want to own a company, build a career, an empire or anything great, I say study the life of Joseph. He was a fascinating dude. He had a gift and a dream. Since he had a gift, a dream and was not a criminal how did he end up in a prison? After he told his brothers about his dream they conspired against him and later on they said, "Look, this dreamer is coming. Let us kill him," hide the body and then "we shall see what will become of his dreams." They plotted to kill Joseph and he didn't even know it. They lurked secretly and they plotted. The moment you begin to speak about your dream there will be haters, enemies and forces which come against you. And sometimes you won't even know that they are coming against you…

They wanted him dead but Reuben told them not to kill him. So they threw their own brother into a pit… Then they pulled him out of the pit and sold him into slavery. They'd already stripped him of his coat of many colors… Then the Midianites sold Joseph to Potiphar and Joseph found himself working in Potiphar's house. And there he was working when Potiphar's wife tried to seduce him. She ripped his clothes trying to get him to have sex with her. Now this was not on some TV drama etc. This is not "Fifty Shades of Gray." This is 66 books of the Bible. I'm not making this stuff up. It's in Genesis chapter 39… After Joseph refused to bed his master's wife she lied on him. She told Potiphar that "he tried to *rape* me." She falsely accused him of a sex crime. He was wrongly convicted and he went to prison. How does a gifted man with a dream go to prison? And how does he get convicted of a *sex crime*?

I can imagine that Joseph had some doubts, stress and even some arguments with God. "I have a dream! And yet I've been thrown into a pit?" Somebody reading this book has been going through some stumbling blocks, obstacles and some pitfalls in life. And you've started doubting yourself. "Maybe I don't have a dream? Maybe it was only a fantasy? Dreamers don't end up trapped in pits!" Can you imagine Joseph wondering in that pit "What about my gift? What about my dream?" Then life can get worse before it gets better. Some people actually give up on their dream while they are dropped in the pit.

And then the same people who put Joseph in the pit came and pulled him out of the pit. And I can imagine Joseph saying to himself that, "God has answered my prayer. I was beginning to think I might die in that pit. But a pit is not the place for a dreamer. They've changed their mind and come to pull me out of the pit." And yet when they pulled him out they sold him. Can you imagine how that troubled Joseph's spirit? Just when he'd convinced himself that his dream was not in vain. And he thought his brothers had a change of heart.

But they pulled him out of the state of captivity and then sold him into another state of captivity. Now Joseph had to contend with the reality of the fact that he was now a slave. And slaves are not dreamers he probably reasoned. And from slavery he went into another form of captivity. He was sold to Potiphar. And while he was a slave in Potiphar's house the Book says (in Genesis 39:2) that "The Lord was with Joseph and he was a successful man: And he was in the house of his master..." So don't tell me that today's judicial system and its prisons are not the *new slave system* because many black people are successful. We even have a black president. Yes — we do. But Joseph was successful and the Lord was with him and he was still a slave. I want black people to know that many of us are successful (Like O.J. Simpson was. And remember he was acquitted of a double homicide charge. And his lead lawyer was black and successful...). But still slaves; don't believe the hype...

Now after Joseph left the Midianite captivity he found himself in a new form of captivity. Then he got falsely accused of a sex crime. Then he got wrongly convicted and locked up in a prison. He left one form of captivity (where he was actually living well) and now he found himself in another form of captivity in a prison. Many of you reading are in captivity. You may be held captive by poverty, miseducation, addiction or affliction. But just because you are currently in some form of captivity does not mean you are not gifted. And it does not mean that your dream is invalid. God was showing us through Joseph that you can go from failure to failure. You can go from addiction to affliction, to jail and to prison. And you can be locked up more than one time and still be a dreamer. You can be locked up more than one time and still be anointed and be gifted...

While Joseph sat in that prison I guarantee you there were haters all around him. I can hear them ridiculing him: "Joseph, what happened to that coat of many colors you claimed you had? What happened to your dream? Joseph where is your God now? Why won't God get you out of prison?" And the Bible says the Lord was with Joseph in the prison and he found favor even in prison. But I can see the prisoner's telling him that "this little dream interpretation stuff you are doing is just luck. If God had his hand on your life why are you a rapo? Joseph you know you tried to take that p-ssy. If you were not raping her how did she get your clothes? Quit playing games man. You've been sitting in this (New Folsom State Prison?) prison for five years now."

I want you to know that a dreamer can be incarcerated. But don't allow life to incarcerate your dream. There is a difference in an incarcerated dream and a locked up man. If you allow their hatred, gossip and envy to cause you to stop trying to achieve your dream, your dream will get incarcerated. And if you are not careful your dream can get destroyed. There are a lot of frustrated dreamers and visionaries in this country. There are people who are 20, 30, or 40 years old. And you start thinking, "I'm 40 years old and I still don't have that degree, or that company, or that house. It may be too late now. Especially since I'm trapped in this trailer park." You've gotta remember that captivity does not negate your dream. Used properly, captivity can actually ignite your dream. They want you to give up on it. They want you to doubt yourself. They want you to settle.

What if Joseph had given up while he was in the pit? But he had to go through the pit to get to slavery. He had to go through slavery to get to the prison. And in that prison he sat for
13 ½ years. My question is how long have you been there? How long have you been in that pit, that house, that dead-end job, that prison or the prison of a low (or no) income? How long have you been there? Some of you have been stuck in poverty, in trailer parks, in ghettos and in prison for so long that you've quit. It's been so long since you've prayed about your dream, vision, business, future or freedom etc. that you have forgotten what you prayed. Some of you have been locked up in the prison of depression, mediocrity, addiction or a bad marriage etc. for so long that you don't even believe that you are gifted. "If I was really gifted why would God allow me to be wrongly convicted of rape? While I'm 3,000 miles away from home. And I'm convicted of raping a man (Ricardo Calvario)… Maybe the haters here are right. If I was really gifted, if I had the favor of God on my life, why am I still in the New Folsom State Prison?"…

Have you ever doubted yourself? Have you ever doubted your gift? Have you ever doubted your dream? Joseph… From a gift, a dream and a way with "words." To an attempt on his life by his own brothers. To a pit with no water. To slavery and a registered "sex offender." And I guarantee you that when you've had bad, after bad, after bad things to happen in your life people will start talking and they will start murmuring and complaining; and even folks who support you will start doubting. And that doubt can affect you… "Well, you know he said she lied on him. He says he did not try to rape her. But every lie has a kernel of truth in it. And they say where there's smoke there's fire. And the woman did have Joseph's clothes. And his DNA was on those clothes. And…"

"God has all power. You reap what you sow. Why would God keep letting Joseph have all these bad things to happen to him if he wasn't a rapist? God is gonna let his own brothers hate him? My brother doesn't hate me. My brother is my best friend. Blood is thicker than water. But what do his brothers know that we don't know? He did something to make them hate him. Maybe this wasn't his first rape? Maybe this is just the first time he got caught. Ain't no telling how many people Joseph has raped and gotten away with. I heard that his own father had to rebuke him. God let him get thrown into a pit, slavery and a prison. And he has the audacity to sit in that prison after being there all of these years and he thinks we are stupid enough to still believe that God has ordered his steps. Well why won't God order his steps out the prison?"

…When you hear that it's easy to say well "I don't remember trying to rape her. But maybe I…maybe the way I looked at her made her think I was getting ready to try to rape her. And… They've got a point… I've been sitting in this prison (*writing* and *studying*) interpreting dreams for 13 years now and I still have not gotten out. And if I actually got out tomorrow I'd have to register as a "sex offender." And who is going to hire a 43-year old ex-con from Atlanta, Georgia? Byron Allen, Tyler Perry, Steve Harvey, Tavis Smiley, Paul Morton and Bishop T.D. Jakes etc. are not going to hire me. Where can I lecture, preach and teach?... I was doing just fine working in Potiphar's house. I was successful. Why did God let this happen to me?"… Joseph looked back (no doubt) and said, "I would have been better off just staying in Potiphar's house and being his overseer. At least I was not in prison. And Potiphar trusted me with everything."…

But if God has placed a dream, a vision or a goal down inside of you, and if He has allowed you to be in a certain stage of your life, development or journey etc., when you get comfortable, you are in danger of settling. And God will snatch you out of that situation and disrupt you. God will shake, disrupt and interrupt your entire life because He is positioning you to give birth to your dream. Your dream may be locked up in your belly. You may have miscarried your dream. You may have had a still birth. Your dream may be locked up in your bowels. But God won't let you rest with that dream inside of you. So don't throw up your hands. Don't turn to drugs or alcohol. Don't say it's too late now. That frustration, test, trial and that loneliness are simply preparation for your destination. Now is the time to seek God like you've never sought Him before. And trust God to finish what He started in your belly.

It's difficult to believe in your dream when you have more revelation than you have situation. Joseph was frustrated in that prison. He'd been there 13 years and he may have *almost quit*. He had told a guy who was getting out to *"remember me"* when you go back to work for Pharaoh. And for a time it seemed that this guy had *forgotten Joseph just like all* the other *parolees* did… Genesis 40:14, "But remember me when it is well with you, and please show kindness to me; make mention of me to Pharaoh, and get me out of this house. For indeed I was stolen away from the land of the Hebrews; and also I have done nothing here that they should put me into the dungeon…"

…Verse 23? "Yet the chief butler did *not* remember Joseph, but forgot him"… Two years later Pharaoh had a dream… So Joseph had been in prison for 11 ½ years when he made the interpretation for the chief butler. And Joseph said, "Remember me?" Have you ever said to somebody "remember me?" When they are getting a new job, a new promotion, or a new company; when they've just signed an NBA or a NFL contract etc. "Remember me." And Joseph felt desperate. He probably felt like "I'm running out of time… I've got to manufacture a movement. I can't sit here and snort pills. I can't sit here and drink pruno. I've got to utilize my gift (writing?) of interpretation to get out of here. I'm a frustrated dreamer. I've been a dreamer who was lost; dreamer who was thrown into a pit; dreamer enslaved. Now I'm an incarcerated dreamer but I can't let my dream get incarcerated. I can't let the dream get enslaved. I had to dream in a pit, as a slave, in this prison and dream in panic. I'm locked up but gifted. I'm locked up and dreaming and now the one man I thought would help me forgot me. I interpreted his dream for free. And he got out and forgot about me."

Are there any desperate dreamers out there? Has anyone thought certain people would never abandon you but they left you? Has anyone ever told you they would help you but they left you? Has anybody ever forgotten you? DO you know what it feels like to see your dream look like a nightmare? What do you do when you pray and fast but God still won't move? The butler has been gone a full *year* now and Joseph has been dreaming, praying and hoping. And the Lord was with Joseph. And what do you do when God is with you but you still get forgotten? What do you do when God is with you but you still can't get out? What do you do when God is with you but the people around you still hate you?... It has been a total of 12 ½ years. And a full one year since the butler went home and Joseph is still in the prison…

I need readers to locate Kyle Day, Julian Loy, Justin Chirigotis, Dylan Wilson (in Huntington Beach), Kalok Geng, Jake Zoard, William Aisenberg, Caleb Riley, Paul James, Jacob Faulkender, Chance Mulligan, Ben Cornejo, Anthony Madrid (Stockton), A.J. Ali, Victor Smalley, Jason Slattery, Brent Sehati, Cody Williams, Jamieson Knopft, Josiah Wotila, Dominic Burrows, Cody Lloyd, Cody Hassler, Hasib Habibi, Kory Carico, Kasey Schutz, Chris Hues, Mergin Bajraliu, William Haskell, Brooks Buffington, Brody Jenner, Devin Dwyer, Stuart Campbell, Patrick Crowe, Matt Jacobs, Kyle Pratt and Max Marmer. Tell them to read this book. And tell them to drop me a line…

…Things which are planted as well as things which are dead both go into dirt. But just because you're buried (in a prison, in bills, in depression or in poverty etc.) does not mean you are dead. It might look like you're buried but God has planted you. And…sometimes God will move you to a jail, a prison, a new city etc. It may be that the soil is not ready for what your vision is. The soil where you are may not be able to handle what God wants to plant. But the 'PROMISE' is big enough that it justifies the preparation. The man who didn't do the prep and the man who did do the prep can face the same storm. But the man who did the prep will survive the storm. No matter how hard you pray you will face some floods and storms. But the struggle (of surviving the storm) will make you strong…

Joseph was still in that prison. And everyone reading this has a cage. David says we were born in captivity. You can have an incarcerated mentality… "I know you like to bring your kids and look at me and throw peanuts. But I've got to get out of this cage"… Follow your instincts and get out. Even when all of your experiences say "stay in the cage," get out. Freedom is scary. You can be sure that you don't want to go back. Yet feel strange about going forward. Don't allow your history to hinder you from your destiny. God asked Joseph's father (Jacob), "What is my name?" Who are you? Are you the one in the cage or are you the one in the wild?... You don't get to define my destiny based upon my history. God told Jacob thy name shall no longer be called Jacob. Your name shall no longer be called gangster, inmate or crook. You are not defined by where you came from. You are not who they say you are.

You might have done what they said you did. But you are not who they say you are. Your gate is open and your soul can escape…

They were calling Joseph all kind of names: liar, rapist, pervert, devil, crook, duplicitous and manipulative etc. because prisons are built like that. The prison subculture feeds on negativity and on gossip. And news in a prison travels faster than the speed of light. And there are always guys in a prison who build their entire lives around watching others. They study soap stars, singers, athletes etc. and they study the folks around them and they think they know your business better than you know your own business. So believe me, they were talking about Joseph in that prison. The fact that he found favor with the warden already put him on "front street" (sic) in the first place… Can you imagine what Trump or Ted Cruz would have said about Joseph? Especially since Donald is (allegedly) an undercover "rapist!"…

I remember when I would walk across the yard with Wardens Jimbo Walker and Tim Virga and fellow prisoners would become jealous. They would murmur, gossip and whisper. So I know the dynamics of the prison setting. I've conducted studies on guards, studies on nurses, studies on physicians and studies on prison food service as well as prison food servers. Suffice it to say that Warden Jimbo Walker told me, "You are definitely an expert on prisons." So I can assure you that Joseph was talked about in the prison. I've had prison guards (i.e. F. Wong, Garrison, Mansky, Breckenridge and Lebeck etc.) to complain that, "Manning you always run straight to the warden with your issues and you…" They are offended when they see an inmate talking to their supervisor. And whether I sell one book or 1 billion books, I am hated because I'm a *published author* and prisoners are not supposed to be writers; much less *published authors*.

So I guarantee you that Joseph stood out. And the things which can make a man stand out in prison you'd think other prisoners might look up to them: Absolutely, totally and completely incorrect. Someone on the outside looking in might find it admirable or commendable. But prisons are very complex. And if you are here and you have any influence or power etc. people will kiss-up to you if they think you'll benefit them in some way. But even those who kiss-up to you are gossiping behind your back. But if you don't smoke dope, drink pruno, snort pills or run with gangs etc. they will hate you in a prison. And when you have a gift in a prison it does draw attention to you. And when you shine amongst prisoners there will be some (inmates and guards alike) people who go out of their way to try to dull your shine.

And when you can interpret dreams like Joseph could it will create envy and jealousy. And jealous people look for dirt. And… "All of that dream interpreting that he's doing I wonder if he ever dreamed that he was gonna be hated by his brothers? Since he interprets dreams did he dream about that pit I heard he was put in? Did he dream that he was going to grow up and become a rapist? I'm not hating on the brother but I'm just saying. Regardless of how many dreams he interprets he still has a R (aka "rape," aka "restriction") in his jacket. So can he interpret that?" You can bet your bottom dollar that Joseph's prison mates hated him.

Prisons humiliate gifted men. And humiliations create humility. People don't applaud you in a prison. And I grew up being applauded. "Ladies and Gentlemen: *Rev. Sherman D.*

*Manning.*" And here comes the applause…prisoners don't applaud other prisoners; period. Humiliation can teach you. Joseph told his brothers about his dreams. He should have never told them. Joseph told them about his dream even knowing they hated him. Wisdom would have said, "Well they're already jealous because daddy gave me this coat. So it will only create more animosity if I tell them about a dream in which they appear to be subservient." But Joseph told them anyway; and even though that made them hate him more. Still he had another dream and did he say, "Well I saw how they reacted to my first dream so I'd be foolish to tell them about my second dream?" No! He told them and his daddy. Joseph talked too much. And I used to talk too much. I felt like I had a right to speak the truth. Talent or gift can teach you how to speak. But wisdom teaches you when to speak. And hatred, pits, slavery and prisons will teach you wisdom.

All the while Joseph was in that pit, in slavery, in Potiphar's house and even in the prison, you never, ever hear him tell anyone else about his dreams. Even after he interpreted the chief butler's dream and was lobbying with him to get him out, you never read where Joseph said, "Hey I've got a dream. And I'm going to be a prince. And…" Joseph learned how to shut up. And the Lord has taught me how to shut up. Don' t tell all your dreams to just anybody. The soil has to be ready to accept the seed. If you plant certain seeds in the wrong kind of dirt you'll lose the seeds. I'm in prison right now. And I can count the guys on one hand (and have several fingers left over) whom I've shown my books which I've written. I don't try to campaign in prison. And Joseph learned when and how to speak and when and what to say. While he was telling the guy, "Remember me," he never said, "Remember my dream." Joseph interpreted the butler's dream. But he never told the butler his own dream. Did you miss it? People want you to explain what their dreams mean. But sometimes they are not interested in hearing your dream.

So the lesson for salesmen, teachers, parents, leaders and mentors etc. is to always ask people to tell you their dream but be very careful and selective about who you tell your dream. Talk to them about what they want to do. And even be willing to advise them on how to do it. And people will remember you more for what you taught them about themselves (their visions and dreams) than they will about what you told them about you. Learn to be quiet. And when you do talk learn to be interested in the person you're talking to. Joseph had learned some lessons in that prison… "I've been in slavery and in a pit and now I'm in prison; all because I was stupid enough to tell my dream to folks who meant me no good. I should have chilled. I should have shut my mouth. I made rookie mistakes. If I ever get the chance to get out of this prison I'll keep my dream to myself. The key is not to *tell* my dream. The key is to *live* my dream. If I get out of here I'll just do it. Some stuff you have to keep to yourself." So Joseph did tell the butler that he had not committed a crime. But he didn't mention his own dream a single time. Not once…

One full year after the chief butler got out of prison he had forgotten about Joseph. Has anybody ever forgotten about you? Have you ever been in a pit, in a prison, in a problem or in a predicament? And you actually helped someone else even though you couldn't help yourself. And they promised to help you. And they promised not to forget you. And they said, "Lean on me when you're not strong. We all need somebody to lean on." And yet they left you. And yet they forgot you. It may hurt you but you gotta keep reading, keep studying, keep living and keep the faith. Tell yourself "God is not through with me yet. I don't know why God has allowed this to happen to me but I trust Him." …The lessons which Joseph learned in the pit prepared him for the prison. And many people don't survive prison but the pit had prepared him. The lesson Joseph learned in the prison prepared him for the palace.

People may forget about you until they need you again. But God can create a problem only you can solve. And if President Obama had a problem and somebody in the West Wing said, "Mr. President I know somebody who can solve this problem, but he's in prison." How long do you think it would take the President to arrange to get you out of prison? If he really needed you bad enough… Two full years after the chief butler got out of prison King Pharaoh started having dreams… Read Genesis Chapter 41. Pharaoh's spirit was troubled by these dreams. And guess who finally remembered inmate Joseph? Pharaoh got Joseph and brought him out of the prison and Pharaoh put him in the palace. Lord have mercy…

Joseph became the prince of Egypt. And his own brothers who tried to kill him; his own brothers who threw him in a pit; his own brothers who sold him into slavery. Those brothers who hated him ended up needing him. In Genesis 42:6 the same brothers who hated him came and bowed before him. They had no idea that it was Joseph. And verse 8 says clearly that Joseph recognized them but did not tell them. The pit and the prison had taught him not to tell everything. It's all about timing. Prison had taught Joseph so well to be so wise that his brothers (who did not recognize him) did not even know he spoke their language. Joseph was so bad that this brother spoke to them through an interpreter. And in his presence they began to speak in their language (thinking he could not understand). And they said, "This is happening to us because of what we did to our brother Joseph." And he turned himself from them and he wept.

Listening to them gave him flashbacks. The pain of the pit, the pain of slavery and the pain of that prison came back to him. And here he stood with the power to kill them. And yet, he walked away and he wept. In Genesis 43:30 Joseph "made haste and sought somewhere to weep. And he went into his chamber and wept" again. When you come out of your pit, your prison or your problem you may find yourself weeping over and over. But you may want to weep in private (if you can). But when you finish weeping, wash your face. All the way through Genesis 42 and 43 Joseph did not tell them who he was. And in Genesis Chapter 45 (when the time was right) Joseph revealed himself to his brothers. As much as I have studied the life of Joseph, as many times as I've read it, I still have to fight tears when I read where Joseph said; "Please come near me; I am Joseph your brother whom you sold into slavery…" I am *Sherman D. Manning* who used to preach at Salem Baptist Church (Atlanta, GA), Trinity Baptist Church (Richmond, VA), Mt. Pisgah (Chicago, IL) and Temple of Deliverance (Memphis, TN). And you forgot me.

"But now, do not therefore be grieved or angry with yourselves because you sold me here; for God sent me before you to preserve life." Stop! Wait! Joseph told them that "you sold me here…" He said "you sold me…" But right after the word "here" he says, "For God *sent* me…" Read Genesis 45:5… That revolutionized my life (recently). When I read that the words jumped off the page. And this very moment my pen is trembling in my hand. And

I want to get this message, book, word and wisdom to you so bad I can't see straight. Lord help me to *write* this *word*. It just hit me… All this time I've been wondering, why did God allow Ricardo Calvario, Mary Hanlon, Judge Robert Altman, Conrad Gamble etc. to *send* me here? Why did He let this happen? I've been saying Ricardo *sent*… But Ricardo *lied*. Mary Hanlon "sold" that lie to an all-white jury. But "*Sherman?*" "God *sent* me…"

I don't like it. This prison has been so painful, and it hurts so bad. And I'm so far away from home. "But God sent me…" And if God sent me He can bring me out. He can fix this thing for me.

Whatever you are in right now it might be time to forgive the people who you think put you there. You might have to weep like Joseph did. You might have to scream like Joseph did. You may have flashbacks like Joseph did. But you have to wash your face like Joseph did. You have to keep trusting like Joseph did. You have to grow up like Joseph did. You have to grow wise like Joseph did. You have to grow strong like Joseph did. You have to keep practicing your gifts like Joseph did. You have to work, *wait* and pray like Joseph did. 45:8 "So now it was not you who sent me here, but God"…Hallelujah… You did me wrong brothers. You hated on me. You envied my gifts. You conspired and connived against me. You tried to kill your own brother. You put me in a pit. You sold me into slavery. I ended up an inmate in a prison. I was a registered "sex" offender. But it "was not you who sent me here bur God; and He has *made* me…" Glory to God.

All the while I've been sitting in this prison convicted of a rape which I did not commit. All this time I've been sitting here longing to be in Atlanta. It is 2015 and I've lost so many loved ones while I sit here in California. I've ached so badly about loved ones who are in heaven… Loved ones I'm not even willing to write about yet because it is still too painful. I have a wound in my heart and in my spirit about somebody I love with all of my heart. And she went to heaven last year and… I can't write about it… Not yet!... I've been worried about how people are gonna look at me and… God sent me here? For what? "And he has *made* me…" Did you read that? I was gifted but conflicted. I was gifted but unwise. I was gifted but undisciplined. And…

I hate to go here but have you ever seen a person who was gifted but unwise? And/or gifted but undisciplined? Thank God I've never used drugs or drank a lot of alcohol. But when you are undisciplined and/or unwise you can fall into addictions. You can be the King of Pop but be so addicted that you pay a physician $150 grand per month to put you to sleep. When you are gifted but afflicted and conflicted you are restless. And I was a restless soul. I could sleep but I hated sleep. And you have to be a tortured soul to pay somebody to snort Propofol to make you sleep.

A lot of these young pop stars you see who keep speeding, getting busted with weed, fighting, throwing eggs and being idiots, they are gifted but undisciplined. A lot of them made a hundred million dollars in 2014. But if you catch 'em in 2024 they'll be broke as a joke. And some will still have some money but have no peace and no love. Ask Mike Tyson what it means to be gifted but unwise or undisciplined. He had $380 million and he ended up in prison for rape. Nobody with $400 million goes to prison for rape. Ask Kobé Bryant and

William *Kennedy* Smith. But Tyson went to prison. And… Tyson got hooked on drugs. And Tyson went completely broke… "There but for the grace of God go I."

I was gifted all along but God wanted to "make" me an author. He wanted to "make" me an expert on criminal justice. He wanted to "make" me an expert on race, class, justice, power, money and prisons. He wanted to "make" me an expert on prison guards and police corruption and brutality. And… "I can't *make* you unless I *send* you. I have to send you through a conspiracy, through a pit, to a prison and then I'll make you. The pain, the torture, the sorrow, the loneliness and the frustration will make you. I'll make you like I made Joseph. I'll make you like I made Paul. I never left Paul in a prison. I was with Joseph in the pit. I was with Joseph in the prison. I am with you in the prison. I'm hard to recognize in the middle of a storm. I'm hard to recognize through your tears. But *Sherman* I love you. And *Sherman* I'm making you. And when I get ready I'll let you live your dream." I said, "Lord but I've had it so hard in prison. I've encountered so much hatred and envy and duplicity in prison." And God said, but "I sent you. And now I'm 'making' you."

Have you ever been real hungry? And your momma had something in the oven. And you peeped in the oven and the corn bread (banana pudding, biscuits or whatever) looked done to you? But momma said it's not ready yet. And you feel like you are so hungry you're gonna faint... And (Palm27) "I would have fainted unless I believed that I would see the goodness of the Lord on the land of the living." It seemed to me like I was ready. 7 years ago. I looked ready. I felt ready. I sounded ready. And… A biscuit can look (smell and…) ready and if you are hungry it will look more ready. But if you bite down into a biscuit that is not fully done you'll know it's not ready. And when you've baked enough biscuits you know when they're ready. A good cook can time it. She'll tell you to put the stove on 450° and leave them in the oven for 16 minutes and thirty seconds etc. etc. And you can bank on a good cook to do it right. So I thought I was going to "faint" from my hunger. But God still has me in the oven. And "I would have (but I didn't) fainted if I did not believe that I would see the goodness of the Lord in the land of the living." So although I'm in this prison and I don't want to be here, I will see the goodness of the Lord in the land of the living…

It was "not you who sent me here but God… Ye thought evil against me but God meant it for good." How did Joseph find it within himself to save the very people who tried to kill him? God taught ("making" him) him compassion. When you sit in a prison for 13 ½ years for a rape you did not commit, you get bitter or better. When you keep hoping, praying and believing that somebody is gonna get you out, God can teach you compassion. Joseph, inmate Mandela, inmate Rubin "Hurricane" Carter and Brian Banks etc. they were never the same again after they got out of prison. Inmate Mandela waited 27 years in prison wrongly convicted of terrorism. Attorney Mandela became inmate Mandela. And he grew wise, strong, reserved and disciplined in that prison. The Attorney Mandela who went into that prison was transmogrified while he was inmate Mandela. His prison did something to him, with him, in him and through him that the university couldn't do. Prison did something to him that law school didn't do. And it was not "the" prison. It was how he opened himself up in the prison. Prison can get very lonely. In his book "*Long Walk To Freedom*" Mr. Mandela talks about being so lonely that he "initiated conversations with a cockroach." I hate to admit that I can relate to that kind of loneliness...

Mr. Mandela rose from the ashes of a prison in which people had left, abandoned and forgotten him. Yet he got out and he forgave his enemies. And he became the President of South Africa. He became the President of a country that he could not even vote in when he went to prison. And he went to the presidential palace and he began the famous (and transformative) "Truth and Reconciliation" committee. And he fascinated the world who wondered how a man who spent nearly 3 decades in a prison could be obsessed with forgiveness. The same God that had the power to "make" Joseph wise, compassionate and disciplined in a prison; that God could also "make" Mandela forgive those racist white people. Just as Joseph forgave his brothers. Just as Rubin "Hurricane" Carter forgave his enemies.

Hurricane spent 20 years in prison for murders which he didn't commit. Hurricane was a professional boxer when he went to prison. Joseph was a dreamer who was gifted. Mandela was a successful attorney. Hurricane was a pro boxer. *Sherman* was an orator and a preacher. All had achieved a level success... God sent. God made. God taught. And God released Joseph, Mandela and Hurricane. And all 3 men got out of prison and changed the world. And President Mandela wrote the foreword to Hurricane's last book. Hurricane died in 2013 and President Mandela died in 2013. Joseph was in prison 13 ½ years, Mandela 27 years and Hurricane 20 years. Three men spent a combined 60 years in prison... Lord have mercy. But they changed the world. Rubin "Hurricane" Carter said that, "when the prison is awake I will sleep. When they are asleep I will wake. I want nothing to do with the prison... We must transcend the prisons that hold us... When I picked up that pen I literally left that cell!"

And he was not lying. I have a pen in my hand right now (4:44 a.m. on a Thursday morning). I waited all day for the prison to go to sleep. And I'm in my bunker like J.D. Salinger. I'm in prison like Joseph, like Paul, like Mandela, like Hurricane, like Brian Banks and still I write. I had forgotten that I was in this cell. And... God is still on the throne. And I sit at the feet of Joseph, Paul, Mandela etc. And I'm learning. I wanna be able to take a pen, like Paul, and shake a city with a few strokes of my pen. I wanna write and write and write. I wanna tell the world that just because its dark right now does not mean you won't make it. I want to tell ex-cons, drop-outs etc. that you can drop-in. You still have a dream. You still have gifts and talents. There is still hope for you. No matter what you did do or how bad it was, you can get back up and live your dream. You are better than the worse thing you've ever done. This pain will subside. This hurt will get better. You're still important and we need you...

There are gifts, talents, skills and untapped treasures which are hidden inside of you. I know it is difficult to believe. You say, "I've been living with me for 20 years and I know me. And if I had another gift I would know it by now." Wrong. There are gifts buried inside of you and some of the stuff inside of you is latent. Joseph had dreams. And his dreams created envy. Actually his gift (coat of many colors) created jealousy. So he had a gift. And then his dreams exacerbated the envy. Yet, if you read Genesis you shall see that Joseph told his brothers about his dreams...

Genesis 37:5 states, "Now Joseph had a dream, and he 'told' it to his brothers." It did not say he 'interpreted' it to his brothers. So Joseph knew he had a gift. He also knew he had dreams. But it was not until 'after' they plotted to kill him, after they put him in the pit, after they sold him, and after he got into prison that he found another gift; the gift to interpret dreams. The gift to dream caused envy and basically put him in the prison. The gift to interpret what was dreamed got him out of prison. If you read Genesis 42:9 it says, "Then Joseph remembered the dreams which he had dreamed about them…" He remembered what he had dreamed. And now he understood why he had dreamed. You may know about your gift to sew. Perhaps you sew dresses or suits. And it may be after you go bankrupt, after you get out of rehab or after that divorce; you may 56 or 57 years old before you discover that you have the gift to 'design' suits. I have known house builders who went on to become architects. I've seen paramedics become physicians. I'm not certain when you'll discover it.

Some people will live their entire lives without ever discovering all of the stuff inside of them. You can have too many distractions to look within you. Many people are too doped up on cocaine, crack, speed, pills or booze etc. They are so busy running, partying, screwing and playing games etc. Then they get 70 and 80 years old and they still don't know what is inside of them. I certainly don't allege (nor do I advise) that you have to go to prison to discover yourself. I'm simply saying you have to go inside (of you) to discover yourself. And many people refuse to take the time that it takes etc. until or unless they get in trouble. But when you do get in a problem, a pit or a prison etc. sometime that will slow you down long enough to get to know you…

We (actually "they" because I'm not into this stuff) know Bieber can sing. And I think he is 21. And the problem is that he grew up poor and now he has well over a hundred million dollars. He is too young and too unwise to even understand how much money he has. And having that much money at 18 – 30 is like giving the keys to my Rolls Royce to an 8-year old boy. There is nothing wrong with the boy. There is nothing wrong with the car. It's just that the boy can't drive. He is too young, unwise and inexperienced to handle a Rolls. Give him the keys and he will either kill (or injure) himself or somebody else. He can't see it at 8. He thinks he can drive because he saw me drive. It can't be rocket science. He thinks he can drive. He drives cars all the time on video games. And he does well. He flies planes in a simulator. But if we put him in a real cockpit at 8-years old and at 35,000 feet, he would kill himself and everybody else. And knowledge is not enough. You have to add experience and age to knowledge.

There are many 30-year olds who can't fly a plane. They are no smarter than the 8-year old when it comes to flying planes. The difference is most (if not all) 30-year olds would have enough wisdom to decline an offer to try to land a plane. And most 8-year olds would try if you allow them. Bieber has been given the Lear jet of a life. And he's trying to fly solo. And he's lost. And the people he keeps around him are lost. The rappers who live with him are lost. And if you hang around 4 lost brothers you will be the 5$^{th}$. Association will cause assimilation. Birds of a feather. And Bieber might succeed and survive. But… I would not be surprised if he was dead before 40. I would not be shocked if he was broke before 40. Mike Tyson had 3 times as much as Bieber. And bad management, bad decisions, a lack of wisdom, drugs and riotous living drove him "*From the palace to the prison.*" Tyson was a tortured soul. And too many of us are tortured and don't know it. We can be tortured and won't admit it. And then we begin to try to tame, nurse or manage the demons with sex, drugs and alcohol.

And I don't have time to write about sex in this book. But more men (actually boys masquerading as men) have wasted more time (life, money, talent, resources and productivity) chasing, pursuing, seeking the 3-minute high, than anything I know. I can recall a weekend I spent in New York. I arrived at the airport at 1:47 a.m. on a Friday. I got to my hotel room at 3:00 p.m. I spoke at a convention for an hour. I probably spent 42 – 44 hours (from Friday – Sunday night) chasing sex. Chasing 3 (maybe 20) minutes of pleasure with a woman. Now I'm not anti-sex. It can be and is (when done appropriately and in a relationship) great. But I know too many men who spend almost fifty minutes per hour thinking about, planning, remembering or pursuing sex. And I'm not just talking about weirdos who flash people or go to sex shops etc. I am talking about more of "us" who consider ourselves normal.

If we could be a camera inside the mind of Bieber, I'll bet he spent over 80 percent of his waking hours (yesterday) thinking about or engaging in sex. I read a study which said the average man spends at least 9 minutes of every hour, thinking about s-e-x. If we reduced that by half and invested the time in reading, studying or strategizing etc. we'd all be considered brilliant. There are men who are serving hundreds of thousands or even millions (collectively) of years in prison for raping people (certainly some are wrongly convicted. Wrongful convictions happen every day). But how could a man give up 20 – 30 years of his life for two minutes of pleasure? (Not to mention how can you get pleasure while hurting someone else? How can you feel good by making someone else feel bad? It's absolutely sick.) I know guys doing life sentences for rape. They woke up one morning and decided to give up their freedom forever, for? "I want to put my penis inside of Taylor Swift's vagina. And I want it so badly that…" Even if you have no connection to her, you're willing to "take" it. You want to feel, touch and smell her so badly and… You are not able to think that "this will traumatize her for life. I may ruin her life. And this is not normal. And when I do this I will spend the rest of my life masturbating because I will go to prison for life."

Now that is the extreme. But what's sad is that what we call our "norms" are gone crazy. The glitz and the glamour of Hollywood can be dizzying. And…guys like Justin Bieber (Kanye West, Kim Kardashian etc.) have become addicted to partying. And they don't know who they are. They are on-the-run. I'd bet you $10 grand that Bieber, Kanye, Kim, Paris and Lohan have not read one book (combined) this year. They may have read "*Fifty Shades of Gray.*" They don't read. And…they don't know what they can do. They are lost in space. The space(s) of addiction and… Rather than envy or look up to them, you need to celebrate who you are. If you don't celebrate you nobody else will. You are somebody. You may never become famous. You may never meet President Obama. But that does not make or break you. You need to be President of Y-O-U. You are the CEO if "You Enterprises." Quit wishing you were somebody else. And find out what all God planted in you…

When the chief butler went home and left Joseph in prison, Joseph didn't envy him. And Joseph never said, "I wish I was you." Even though Joseph was a lowly prisoner locked up on a sex crime, he still loved himself (without being full of himself) and he didn't ask God to "please let me be like him." And thank God he didn't. Joseph ended up being a prince (not a butler). Joseph ended up being the Governor. Don't envy the butler while you are an inmate. Don't envy people who seem to have it going on. But instead of envying them you need to seek Him. Ask God to show you what is in you. "Show me what your plan is for my life. What did you plant inside me? Who am I? And what is your plan for my life?"

…I've written thousands of words about Joseph. And my primary focus has been on Joseph's perspective. But I want to take a moment to talk about the brothers. I know that most of "us" want to say that we are like Joseph. We all want to be a prince. And in certain ways we are all like princes and princesses in God's sight. But lest I be a snake-oil salesman I must admit that not everyone is going to be like Joseph. Fortunately, not everyone desires to be like Joseph. You will probably never become the President of these United States. And you probably don't desire to become the President of the USA. Many people reading this don't even want to be president of the willing-to-fry chicken committee. We all have different callings and giftings. But I want to acknowledge another perspective of Joseph's pedicament. I know you've never envied anyone. I know you've never been jealous of anyone else. No, not you! But for that other guy who is reading this book, for those of us who have felt intimidated, small, diminished and belittled before, I want to take a moment to look at the brothers…

"Now, Israel (who is Jacob) loved Joseph 'more' than all his children." Now can we keep it real? If your father loved your siblings more than you, and if your father made it no secret; if he gave your brother something that he didn't give you , how would you feel? If we are being honest we must admit that even a strong child would be intimidated. I still remember my daddy (James Scott Manning) buying my brother (Reggie Manning) and I two motorcycles for Christmas. I was 12 and Reggie was 13. He got us both Kawasaki 75's. Now if James had bought Reggie one and not bought me one I would have been hurt. And hurt unattended can fester into hatred. You are 11 and your brother is 12. Your father spends $300.00 on your brother's birthday and gives you a card for yours. Are you really telling me it would not bother you? A psychologist would probably argue that a "wise" father wouldn't have made it so obvious that he favored one child over another.

So, a lesson for fathers who don't want to raise children who are full of envy, and if you don't wanna watch the envy in your children turn to hatred and rage etc. don't show favoritism amongst your children. Go out of your way to appear evenhanded and fair to them. If you have a favorite don't 'show' it. Because the book said that when his brothers 'saw' their father loved him more they hated him. Have you ever hated or envied somebody? In Genesis 37:3 Jacob gave Joseph something that he did not give the other brothers. In the very next verse it says they hated him. Have you ever seen somebody get something that you didn't get and you hated them? Ever watch somebody come on your job and they haven't been there six months and they get a promotion you've been wanting for six years? Then Joseph told them about his dream and they hated him even more. So you show up on my job and get a promotion that I've been trying to get for years. Now you add insult to injury. You start telling me about a vision for our company that you have. And when you describe your vision to me you have yourself leading the company and I'm just a gofer. You are a quarterback and I'm just a water boy. So now my reaction is I'm intimidated and I can't stand you…

And the devil got a hold of these boys and they plotted to kill their brother. And then we know the story. But those conniving, plotting, scheming, jealous and hurt little boys are not alone. There are millions of "Joseph's brothers" in the world right now. Some of you don't even know when it was that you (too) became a hater. You have hated for so long that it seems normal to you. And I can relate to the fact that you feel small, because "I saw him get a gift and I got nothing." And "I heard him tell his dream and I don't have a dream." And since "Jacob loves him more than he loves me, I feel forsaken." Somebody should have gotten a hold of those brothers who felt abandoned and felt forsaken and told them this: "When my father and my mother forsake me then the Lord will take me up." And if the brothers didn't spend so much time looking at Joseph and their father they could have concentrated on themselves and said, "Who am I and what do I have?"

The danger we face when we get caught up in envy is that if I expend all of my energy, mad because of your gift, it leaves me no time to find, to cultivate, to polish or perfect my gift. I'm not gonna go to the gym and spend all of my time hating and mad at you. Jealous of your muscles. I'm gonna get up off my butt and workout my muscles. Rather than use you as an object of envy I'll use you as ammunition to propel me into my destiny. Jealousy, envy and hatred are time-consuming. They zap you of your energy, incarcerate your creativity and lockup your innovation. When you see someone with a gift you didn't get make it a habit to be happy for them. Admire their gift and even compliment them on it. And don't let it make you feel small. Let it drive you to work on you. Begin to look for your gifts, your dreams and your talents…

But after Joseph's brothers envied, hated, lied, enslaved and even tried to kill their own brother… In Genesis 45 after all the plotting, scheming and the mess those brothers did they still ended up in the palace with their brother. He forgave them and provided for them. That gives me hope that there is room at the cross for me. That lets me know that no matter how bad we may have messed up, no matter what kind of crime or sin we may have committed. Maybe you've been in the prison of jealousy, animosity and hatred for years. Maybe you've been secretly hating your own brother, sister or some other. But if you come clean and stop the hatred God will still bless you and He will forgive you. No matter how evil we have been God can still bless you. But…

I don't want to deceive you and just tell you what you want to hear. If you read Genesis 45:22 you will see that after the forgiving, weeping, making up and coming together. Joseph blessed (and forgave) all of his brothers. And he gave all of them clothing and money. But — he gave Benjamin more than his other brothers. Benjamin was his favorite brother. But when he gave Benjamin more than he gave the others they did not get jealous. They did not hate Benjamin because they had learned (what we must learn) that you can't measure your worth by the size of somebody else's bank account. And I'm so focused on the ten grand you gave me that I don't have time to figure out why you gave my brother $39 grand. I just want to say thank you. Reuben could have really gotten angry. "Hey man, when they were going to kill you I saved your life. I kept them from killing you. And you giving Benjamin more than me."

Why didn't that happen? The brothers had learned that our God is a "just" God. But that does not mean "fair." And favor is not fair. Be glad I gave you anything. And take what I did give you and "work that thang baby." Don't waste your time trying to figure out why God gave you one gift and me another. Take what He gave you and cultivate it…

Can I tell you that Jacob thought Joseph was dead? For years he thought his boy was dead. His sons told him he was dead. And all the while he had grieved and grown gray for a child that wasn't even dead. Don't believe every bad report somebody gives you. You might be weeping over a funeral that didn't happen. Joseph was not dead. His sons lied to him. A lie drove Joseph to a prison cell. And a lie almost drove Jacob to his grave. Don't beat your mind, body and spirit down simply based on what somebody told you; even if they bring you some bloody clothes. That was not Joseph's blood. It was a goat's blood. Somebody can send you some anthrax in the mail and you have a heart attack and die. The anthrax scared you that bad. And after you died we tested that white stuff. Guess what? It was powder. It was not anthrax. It could not have killed you. Be careful what you believe because belief becomes reality…

What do you do when you ask God to order your steps and today he orders trouble? Trouble can teach you how to handle blessings. You may wonder is there a way that I can be what I need to be without going through what I have to go through. Joseph had to go through a problem, a pit, slavery and a prison. But how bad do you wanna make it to that palace? Joseph left home… He lived with his brothers but he left. If you don't fit where you are don't stay where you are. Many times the universe will move you from where you are because you don't fit.

While you are being tried, prepared or trained (for what God has called you to do) you will see Him bless people. What do you do when God blesses somebody that you are angry with? Sometimes we get mad with God. And many men get mad with themselves. I've never met a man who became abusive and beat his wife and liked himself. You can get angry over what didn't work, angry over who succeeded while you were failing etc… Prison prepared Joseph for the palace. He must have watched others succeed while he was in prison. He probably heard about the successes of others while he was in prison. Wonder how Joseph felt when he heard that his brothers were succeeding while he was in prison?

The test is not what you do when you're the victim. The test is how you handle power. What do you do when you're on top? Prison taught Joseph and it prepared Mandela and Rubin "Hurricane" Carter and Malcolm X to handle power. Sometimes God will put you in a dead-end job and let you watch others get promotions which you should have gotten. He will let you experience all kinds of unfairness and injustice because God is preparing you to handle power…

President Mandela told Oprah that the one thing he missed about prison was the ability (and time) to sit down and think. When a man is alone he hunts himself. He becomes himself. He blames himself. He beats himself… Jesus found a man alone in the tomb and he was cutting himself. A man needs to confront his own rage. Wife beaters need to get alone. Murderers need to get alone. Churches need to start having altar calls for men who need to confront their own rage. That would not get the crowd because nobody wants to expose their dirt. I don't wanna be known as a woman beater. But if you don't confront that rage now you will end up at an altar call in prison ministry…

Whether you think O.J. Simpson committed those murders or not (and I'll deal with that in the next chapter) we know he beat his wife. And what if he had confronted that rage in 91, 92 or 93? He wouldn't be visiting a prison chapel right now. The most vicious struggle any man will ever have is the struggle he has with himself…

The best thing you can do to prevent yourself from becoming a "new slave" is to change your mind. And if you read this book and do everything else except change you have wasted your time. You want to change. We've got to get rid of that slave or ghetto mentality. I want to go around the country and inspire people to get their minds back. We have people wearing mink coats living in trailers. We have people owning Rolexes who live in the projects. We've got to change this… If it is on your ass it is not in the bank…

39,518 people committed suicide in 2013. More than 108 people will kill themselves today. We have more suicides in America than homicides. And we'll get out and march saying stop the violence. Some of us need to march saying stop killing yourselves. A man can have a great wife and a great life but still have a tortured soul. We have to teach people to love themselves. I want Brent Levin, Ryan Brophy, Lucas Culbertson, Kent Boyd, Jordan Goodin, Charles Lutz, Roger Walthorn, John Foraker, Joshua Simpson, Michael Strange, Tylor Murray Clark, David Proctor, Chad Sherman, Brian Devin Graham, Josh Brown (in Charlotte), Sam Pritchard, Alex Bernhart, Christopher Beck, Joseph Cox (Roseville, CA), Matt Jacobs, Max Steele and Bradley Standiferd to read this book. Let them know it is out…

…I never dreamed I was going to be in a prison. I'm a frustrated dreamer. I have to dream in a prison. I've learned to dream in a problem, a pit and in a prison. I've had to dream in a panic, in a hospital and even on life support… Don't give up on your dream. You may be disappointed with where you are. But God will allow you to be disappointed so that you'll remain humble when you get appointed…

O.J. Simpson had nearly $20 million in 1993-94. He had bought his way off the plantation. He was O.J… When he spent all of his money he re-signed the *slave contract*. He lost his "*free* agent" status. They that know not their history are destined to repeat it. You can get out of jail and get locked up again. O.J. got locked up again…


### *Did O.J. Simpson Commit Murder?*

We will get to Mr. Simpson very soon… But I want to remind you that God might just be preparing you for your greatest moment. If God ordered it then that means He will anoint you to get through it. It is only preparation… Don't let people judge you by where they met you. Peter cut a man's ear off. And Peter denied that he ever knew who Jesus was. If you had met Peter while he was cutting a man's ear off; if you had met Peter while he was lying and pretending not to know Christ, we would have talked about Peter like a dog. "He walked and talked with Jesus. And as soon as he got to the fire he turned his back on Him. He ain't nothing (sic) but an old hypocrite. How can he sleep at night, lying about the Son of God?" But this same cutting, cursing and lying hypocrite ended up preaching the first sermon in the Book of Acts. And when Peter preached, 3,000 souls came to Christ. No matter how bad a man sins, lies or denies, God can still call him back into service. And…

I want readers to help me get this book to Caleb Lamb, Caleb Butler, Maryann Finocchiaro, Brent Sehati, James Merryman, Anthony Madrid, Chance Mulligan and Ben Cornejo…

The question of the 20th century was did O.J. Simpson murder Nicole Brown Simpson and Ron Goldman? Obviously I've interviewed most of the living lawyers who were on the O.J. Simpson Dream Team. Prior to Johnnie Cochran's death he corresponded with me on a number of occasions as you can see from some of the missives we published in this book. I'm very close to Bob Blasier. Bob was a member of the "Dream Team." Bob's wife, Charlotte Blasier, is a distinguished private investigator. Charlotte was also on the "Dream Team." Bob and Charlotte know where the bodies are buried… I can only do written interviews. And I can do a limited number of telephone interviews for this book. So I would suggest that if you want to do a television or radio interview regarding O.J. Simpson etc. call Bob Blasier. Go to www.Blasier.com. As I said — Bob and Charlotte know where the bodies are buried…

I've learned not to give up my sources. So if anybody told me anything in confidence you'd never know. What I find fascinating about the O.J. Simpson saga is that he was acquitted of two murder charges that a lot of people felt he actually committed yet, he's now imprisoned on lesser charges of which many think he's innocent. Oh what a difference a day, a judge or a jury can make. No! Oh what a difference a $ million can make. I could lecture for weeks (at Morehouse, UC Davis, UC Berkeley, Stanford, McGeorge or at Princeton etc.) about how/why O.J. Simpson ended up in a prison. When O.J. was tried for murder he paid over $10 million for his defense. He had to sell his house. If he didn't have a football retirement plan which pays him $300 grand per year he would be destitute.

The problem for O.J. is/was Johnnie Cochran was dead when his new cases came up. And O.J. did not have a $1 million. O.J. went to prison as soon as he was reassigned to slave status. When he spent his money it was as good as signing up for the draft during a war. You know you will end up on the battlefield. When a black millionaire has been acquitted of murdering 2 white people and he loses his money — he loses his status, power and his class. He loses black exceptionalism. And he loses the right to get equal protection under the law. O.J. had to relearn what it was like to be black. $20 million will buy you the feeling of what it's like "to be white" in America. You can put a white woman on your arm and move to the white suburbs. But if you don't have the funds to retain a Gerry Spence, a William Gary or a Roy Black etc. and if you get into trouble, the judicial system will remind you of your blackness…

You know why O.J. is in prison today (if you don't know then Google it). Justice does not matter because justice is for sale. Ask Ethan Couch. At 16 he got into his truck drunk. He killed 4 people driving while drunk. His father bribed a Texas judge and Ethan Couch did not serve a day in jail. Ask Robert H. Richard. Robert admitted to molesting his 3-year old daughter. He molested her and he admitted to the molestation. And…he did not serve a single day in prison. This is not some antiquated case from the 70's or the 80's. This happened in

2014. The judge (the dishonorable Jane Jordan) stated that she didn't think Robert would "fare too well" in prison. So she gave the serial molester probation.

The back story? Irene… Irene who? Irene Dupont! Irene is an heir to the 'Dupont' fortune. And? Irene Dupont is the mother of Robert H. Richard. And she is a close friend of Robert's judge. I could name twenty more cases (off the top of my head) in which rich people (mostly white but not all…) received slaps on the wrists for the same exact crimes the poor are sent to prison for. I study these statistics daily.

…100 blacks are killed each year by white police officers. Black men are 6 times more likely to go to prison for the same crimes than whites. Black men receive 25 percent longer sentences (for the exact crimes) than whites. Poor people are 86 percent more likely to go to prison than the rich. Justin Bieber and Chris Brown should both be in prison right now. Justin would have entered as a 'tight end' and he'd exit prison as a 'wide receiver.' They ought to be in prison…

I've gotten extremely close to some of the participants in the O.J. Simpson saga. Shockingly (are you ready for this bomb?) I'm told that not only did O.J. Simpson murder Nicole and Ron but, he had help. Ever heard of Kato (some spell it Cato) Kaelin? He was with O.J. Simpson when the murder took place. O.J. murdered Nicole and Kato helped kill Ron. O.J. promised Cato $250 grand. He never paid him. That is why Cato's story has shifted over the years. But he can't tell-all because it would put him in jail. And once a man has been acquitted of murder he can't be retried. Pragmatically it makes absolutely no sense for Kato to "snitch." I'm 99.9 percent certain that this information is credible. It came to me from an extremely reliable source. And… Kim Kardashian's dad? Attorney Robert Kardashian (definitely) disposed of the murder weapon for "Juice." O.J. is a murderer. When the trial was over I shall admit that I cheered. I was not cheering for O.J. I was cheering Johnnie Cochran. The sheer brilliance, boldness and the tenacity of a black lawyer being able to do what the greats (Clarence Darrow, Bobby Lee Cook etc.) have done for clients for years. And the fact that the client was black was a bonus.

…Eventually I became very upset with O.J. Simpson… When O.J. was acquitted I thought he would be pragmatic. The first thing O.J. should have done was go on a speaking tour. He would have been welcome at every black mega-church in the country. He should have thanked black America for standing with him, supporting him and for praying for him. Since he'd exhausted all of his funds he could have made a good living. O.J. could have easily commanded $10 grand per speech in 1995. And then he should have gotten a black girlfriend. Call me Mr. Olivia Pope (or Mr. Crisis Management) but O.J. should have shown that he still respects, love and honors black women. I've dated white (Latina and Asian) women. I don't oppose interracial dating or marriage but if you've just gotten acquitted of murdering your ex-wife and her white friend etc. it is pragmatic to date a black woman for a while. But O.J. was a "fool." He was absolutely an idiot. He ran away from black people. He immediately got another white girlfriend and he moved to a white neighborhood in Florida. And he played golf (daily) with white people. He was 'in your face,' arrogant and unwise. And when you are unwise you tell yourself lies. And arrogance will cause you to dabble with other weapons of self-destruction…

All of my research, studies and the inside data to which I'm privy indicates that O.J. Simpson clearly and convincingly got away with murder. And that his live-in guest clearly aided and abetted him. His house guest was known to snort cocaine and run sexual trains with O.J. and he also helped 'Juice' commit two counts of double, first-degree murder. And Marcia Clark and Christopher Darden were too blinded by the O. in the J. to see that there was a "No J" who helped O.J. to murder those people. And Robert Kardashian disposed of the murder weapon…

I'm told that Carl Douglas, F. Lee Bailey and three other lawyers (whom I shan't name herein) are the only persons (other than O.J. and Kaelin) who know that O.J. got away with murder. Robert Shapiro was convinced from day-one that O.J. killed them. Yet, O.J. did not trust Shapiro well enough to tell him. A rift developed (between O.J. and Shapiro) when O.J. admitted to Cochran that he killed them. Shapiro wanted to plead him out. Then Cochran took over and led O.J. to a rapid trial. Shapiro became upset that Johnnie was getting all the press. Shapiro even insisted on sitting first chair. And he wanted to do the opening argument. Johnnie benched him. "This is my case, my client and my jury," Johnnie reportedly told Shapiro. "And Robert do you happen to recall that you have never (ever) tried a murder case in your entire career as a lawyer? And I refuse to allow you to use the Juice's case as practice. Sit down and be quiet please," Cochran told him. Carl Douglas was noticeably pleased by his boss putting Shapiro in his place…

Attorney Gerry Spence told me that "letting Shapiro lead the case would have been the worst mistake O.J. could have ever made."… Quite frankly it is probably. "Be not deceived God is not mocked; whatever a man sows that shall he also reap" which has O.J. in prison today. I talked with Leah Beverly (a beautiful African-American sister) who helped prosecute O.J. in Nevada. And I told Leah that it's hard to believe that O.J. trying to retrieve his sports memorabilia was armed robbery. And Leah said, "*Sherman*: O.J. probably deserved probation for what he did but this case was not about sports memorabilia. It was about a black man who used to be a celebrity; who got away with killing two Caucasians." Leah told me that, "The judge was out for blood. We (in the DA's office) were gonna reduce the charges to misdemeanors but the judge said, 'No!' She told us that O.J. was going to prison. And if she had her way he would die in prison."

O.J. was able to buy his way out of slavery. He went nearly broke. He's lucky some hillbilly Klansman did not shoot him. He was to white folks what George Zimmerman is to blacks. When he went nearly broke he had to be black again. And the injustice he received in Nevada is a kind of karmic collision. Do I have sympathy for O.J.? Not really. I can say that Bob Blasier always speaks highly of O.J.…

As I write this Ferguson, Missouri has exploded. By the time you read this you may say, "Ferguson what?" Black men are in trouble in America. Anytime the woman is distracted and the man is discouraged; that's when the enemy destroys… Men are screaming although our lips don't open. And the worst part of the masculine scream is that the feminine ear cannot hear our frequency. We need help. But if God brought you to it He'll get you through it. When you don't change the "it" that you are looking at change how you look at it. God will teach you how to change your perspective when you can't change your problem. "Joseph I'm not going to get you out of New Folsom State Prison yet. I know you didn't rape anybody but I'm teaching you; right in the darkness of your prison cell. The strongest steel comes out of the hottest fire. I am purifying you through the mother fire of suffering. You can't be (in the palace) what I want you to be unless you go through (the prison) what I'm taking you through. But keep the faith. I'm the God of the day and of the night. And I will get you through this night season."

...I want Max Hodges, Dave Bernal, Nathaniel Mullenix, Izzy Gardon, Keenan Harris, Matthew Wendt, Joseph Latham, Tyler Straub, Michael Snowden, Max Wiseltier and Jacob Gabriel to get this book. Help me get it to Alex Bernhart, Josh Zwick, Mike Corsetto, Chris Colfer, Daniel Coverston, Dillon Banionis, Nicholas Pelham, Daniel Bugriyev, Mark Kashiretts and Cody Baetge. Tell them the book is out. Tell Maxwell Hanger, Steven Fabian, Jeremy Hudson and Jerry Wines...

Ferguson, Missouri? I want the young people in Ferguson to be careful. All youngsters seem to be more willing to pick up a gun than they are willing to pick up a book. They know all the words to rap songs but they haven't read a book this year. Youngsters in Ferguson, Chicago, Detroit and in other inner cities feel persecuted by the police. Phillip (in the book of Acts) was a man driven by his own persecutions into the destiny of God. Many times the people who persecute us are the agents of God. Many times we receive directions through persecution to direct us into His next move. That's why Joseph told his brothers that, "You sold me but God sent me." And he said, "You thought evil upon me but God meant it for good." It does not matter who God uses to usher us into His next move as long as you make it. If God allowed me (or you) to go through this it must be for your (or my) good. He would not withhold any good thing from me.

To all of you brothers (Mexican, black, white and Asian) who feel like you are under attack etc., I want to remind you that one man is important. One man can turn a city upside down. One anointed man can revolutionize your city. When God got ready to deliver the children of Israel He used one man named Moses — who says go down there and tell Pharaoh to let my people go. When God gets ready to feed the Israelite people he uses one-man named Joseph and says if I can get Joseph out — Joseph will deliver everybody else out. For I have prepared Joseph for this problem. When God gets ready to let Jerusalem know His heart is broken he uses one-man named Jeremiah the weeping prophet.

One-man. When the devil finds out one man is coming he'll send out all of his abortionists trying to kill every male child in the city. He's not after the masses. He's trying to kill one-man. But he's willing to kill countless male children trying to find that one-man. Because the devil knows that if you ever get loose, everything connected to you is gonna get loosed too. That's why he keeps you tied up in violence, drugs, guns and poverty. That's why he wants you to join a gang and to drop out of school. He knows you're one-man. He knows you're one-man. I know what I'm talking about because I'm one of the ones. That's why the devil's been fighting you and me. All of our lives. Because I'm (you) one of the ones. I'm a jailhouse wrecker, a mountain mover, I'm a giant slayer and I'm anointed to slay the enemy. And that's why the devil's been attacking you (and me) all of our lives. He killed your brothers, he killed your friends, he killed your family, he killed your neighborhood. But he was looking for you.

I still remember the murdered and missing children of Atlanta scandal. Young black boys who were my age were being kidnapped and killed. Since I was a boy preacher and I led the prayer vigils for the "missing and murdered children." I was given police protection at school. Looking back — the devil was after me. He came into Atlanta trying to kill me. And it very well may be that he has come into your city, your group or your neighborhood and he is trying to kill you. But don't let the enemy win brothers. Pull them pants back up and go back to school. Put that gun down and pick up a book. I need you young men to go down into your hoods and tell the dope dealers, the pimps and gang leaders to let my people go. I'm on a mission and my assignment is to find some Phillips and some Josephs. And I want you to recognize why you are under attack. And we need to begin to strategically and methodically respond to the attacks upon our people. And if we use our minds we can solve these problems.

Let O.J. Simpson be a lesson to learn from. I try to learn from every situation. Even Ferguson is a lesson for me. I see Ferguson every day. Many prisoners are black but we have all-white administrations because the white folks in C.D.C. don't want African-Americans in their good ole boy's network. New Folsom State Prison has an all-white club: Warden (Jeff Macomber), 4 Associate Wardens and 6 Captains. All-white. Fifteen or twenty Lieutenants? One black…

I need to raise up some men… I want Stephen Zinn (in L.A.), Dawson Jope, Christopher Wood and Kyle Pratt (in Sacto) to read this book. I need readers to tell them about it…

How you confront obstacles determines how your story ends. …Stop weeping over who left you. They did what they were supposed to do. They provoked you to change. That is the message I want to carry to churches, schools, colleges and to juveniles etc. I want to get me some fellas… And to go on a crusade across this country and plant the seeds of Joseph…

I saw Jason Riley (widely considered an Uncle Tom) on Meet The Press criticizing black people. Riley was livid that Rev. Al Sharpton was in Ferguson, Missouri and in Chicago. Riley felt obligated to get on white TV and criticize black people. He's a sick brother. I do not always agree with Rev. Sharpton and Rev. Jesse Jackson etc. but you will not see me on TV criticizing them. I'd like to point out that Riley was neither in Chicago nor in Ferguson. He was instead at a table full of white people while he criticized blacks. I want to go to Greater Grace Baptist Church (in Ferguson), Glide Memorial (Rev. Cecil Williams) and to St. Sabina in Chicago. I'd like to go to New Greater Saint Stephens Full Gospel Church and to teach textbook 'Joseph.'… What is the recovery plan for Ferguson, Detroit and for Chicago? Now that the media has moved on to the next tragedy.

…"We've learned to swim the seas as fish. We've learned to fly the air like birds. But we've still not learned to live together as brothers and sisters." And we must "learn (in Ferguson, in Chicago etc.) to live together as brothers and sisters or we shall perish apart as fools." We must teach youngsters the way of peace and nonviolence. We must tune out racists like Heather MacDonald at the Manhattan Institute. We must change the way we think. You are where you are because of what you think. I must tell young men (especially young men of color) that this too shall pass. You cannot be (I repeat) what you're supposed to be without going through what you have to go through. You can't get a great testimony baby boy, without a great test.

...And words are spirits and words are life. And words shape how you see yourself... I want Richard Hansen (grad student in Reno, NV) to join us. I will be asking Pastor Steve Green and Pastor Paul Morton etc. to mentor me and to pray for me. I want to be the Michael Jordan of book writing. I want Jonathan Cheben , Nick Pelham and *Andy* (the volunteer at Homeboy Industries) to join our campaign. We need to teach lessons learned in the pit, lessons learned in the problem and in the prison. We have got to manufacture a movement. Y'all help me to find Christopher Bird (and Tammie Counts), Joshua Stipp, Juster Brewer and Cory Laymen... Let's roll... Once you exit slavery O.J. don't try to be white. Just be right and be free. I want Daniel Jennings and Daniel Jensen to join me. I want to meet Captain Ron Johnson, Chris James, Stefan Hornaday, Dr. Cornel West and Dr. Charles Ogletree etc. and form think tanks and networks. Maybe the Hidden Hands are running the world. But I want to deal with the hands (Ted Cruz, Ryan, McConnell, etc.) which we can see...

Don't forget the past. We have sanitized Dr. Martin Luther King, Jr. and he is now a media darling. The media (the Schornacks, the Williams and the N.Y. Times) now love the King. But when he was alive they hated him. Before Dr. King died he had a 79 percent disapproval rate (maybe that's why President Obama is not too worried about polls). The media love to anoint and to 'saint' a leader. And they love (even the more) to tear leaders down. I'm looking for some thinkers, some dreamers and some visionaries who don't allow the media to select or reject their leader. Al Sharpton did work with the FBI once but Riley works for them now. Jesse Jackson did have a baby out of wedlock but Jesse did not kill Uriah. The Bible is clear that David had a sex demon that he couldn't get rid of. And David also had an anointing. I know Jesse Jackson personally, and I know Jesse has an anointing...

When you own the media you can control the narrative. When you own the airwaves you have the power. I am fascinated by the power which a person can acquire when they own the media. I keep seeing all of these people in Ferguson, Missouri protesting and I'm well cognizant that when this book publishes most will have forgotten Ferguson. And I want to motivate, inspire and encourage all of those who were in Ferguson to get organized and to get money. I have to be candid. The best way to check a police department or a power is with money. Get enough money and we can demilitarize our police. I just saw Mayor Dan Wolk (in Davis, CA) explaining that Davis did not need the new $700,000 armored vehicle given to them by the Pentagon. When you give police weapons of warfare they will invent reasons to use them. I say get on Facebook, Change.org and Kickstarter etc. and raise money. And when you raise money contact politicians etc. They always want money...

I hope Cathy Jenkins (at Cathy's Kitchen in Ferguson) will get this book and share it with her customers. I hope Zack Askew, Jakob Karr, Jerrod Biscus, John Garvin, James Nesmith, Harvey Lashler, David Joyner, Joshua Scannell, Ricky Lebarron, Ronald Wright, Jason Sutherland, Ryan Fehr, Tyler Fehr, Nolan Wong, Frank Carter, Cody Hassler and Cody Baetge etc. will hear about this book and read it...

Yes: O.J. did it plain and simple. What else do you need to know about O.J.? He had enough money to get the best trial, scientific and medical minds etc. He out-lawyered the State. Justice is for sale. And if you've got enough money you won't go to jail; period…

**Did O.J. Simpson Bribe The Jury?**

Perhaps you've read John Grisham?… I'll get back to O.J. in a moment… "Kill every male child"… But they hid Moses (in Exodus) in a Hebrew slave's house. God hid Moses. He had nothing around him but opposition… He floated through some stuff that should have killed him. And all the while Moses floated God protected and hid him. And God let the right lady, be in the right place and find Moses, at the right time… Pharaoh said kill every male child. That was in Exodus.

…Now (in 2015, 2016, 2018 and 2022 etc.) they kill the male children with crack, speed and booze. Now the gang-warfare kills the male children. And what the street gangs don't kill the prison gangs kill. And if the prison gangs don't kill every male child the police officers will kill. We have millions of police officers who see no problem with shooting (and murdering) an unarmed man 20 times. They have no problem killing deranged men who wield pocket knives. Time and again we see the lone assailant with a small pocket knife. And there are 13 police officers around him. And all 13 will shoot him. So you end up with 40 bullets in a man. And he's dead because all 13 of these poorly trained officers claimed that they were "fearing for their life." There seems to be a renewed order to "kill every male child." And boys have got to seek God, power, inspiration and education so we can reverse this curse. I want to be a part of a new trend which will *reverse the curse* of that death order which hangs above our heads.

I can't play games. I'm not a holy man. If I get home I'll probably hve a drink of alcohol from time-to-time. I'll probably be the exact opposite of celibate. I won't be nice, correct and polite all the time. I have issues, struggles and I have conflicts. I am nowhere near a perfect man. But I will do my best to reverse the curse. I want every male (and female) child to live life and to live abundantly. Jails, prisons, racist cops, poverty and injustice etc. "kills" male children. We say reverse this curse. So I want to go on a crusade across this country and I want to elucidate the story of Joseph. I want to explain to men and women that we don't have to kill every male child. We don't need to jail every male child.

I will ask Michael Struening, Joey Grissett and Scott Czeda etc. to join this crusade. I'll call Brian Banks, Christopher Bird, Ryan Ferguson, Jerry Wines, Ronald Cotton, Marcus Dixon, Justin Cash, Jacob Gabriel and Daniel Kovarbasich. I shall call upon Alex King, Eugene Langford and Kyle Pratt. Maybe Russell Simmons, Tyler Perry, Steve Harvey, Stedman Graham and John Hope Bryant etc. will help us underwrite the crusades.

But we will do this. Not as a youth ministry etc. but we're going after all the "male children" whom the enemy seeks to kill. We will reach them and teach them in schools, colleges, old folks homes or churches. We will catch them at the club and try to transmogrify them. I need you to pray for us. Ask God to get me ready to do my part. Ask Him to expedite my release and to prepare me. Ask God to give me the divine connections I need to make this work. I need help. I'll be an ex-con with no help. But God can do exceedingly and abundantly above all I may ask or think…

I believe that if Ryan Ferguson gets this book he will be moved and inspired by it. I need to meet Ryan Ferguson. I followed his case so closely on TV that I felt like I know him. I wept (don't tell anybody) when Ryan was released. Google Ryan Ferguson and read about his wrongful conviction. I want to meet Christopher Bird. I sensed an anointing on Chris. He was on the Ricki Lake show. He was falsely accused… And you (the reader) can help right now. You can go online and locate Ferguson and Bird on Facebook. Tell them you've just read about them in this book and ask them to email Hallopeter@sunrise.ch.

We can do this. We can have an international speaking tour. It will be speaker-mania. We will have tag-team speakers (Banks, Dixon, Ferguson, Quindt, Bird and I etc.). And we can go to Harvard, UC Berkeley, Princeton, Morehouse, Howard, Grinnell and to Stanford etc. And we can address students and professors. We can talk about injustice, prisons, jails, juveniles, lawyers, public defenders, prosecutorial misconduct, judicial bias, juror misconduct, false accusations and wrongful convictions…

O.J. Simpson did not bribe Judge Lance Ito. Nor did he bribe the jury. Johnnie Cochran "owned" that jury. And whenever you can get a jury to fall in love with the defense lawyer or his client, they will never convict someone they love. When you find a jury in love with the judge, the judge owns that jury. And they will vote exactly the way he wants them to vote… To Robert Shapiro's credit (inside sources have told me) he put together the team of brilliant lawyers who would secure O.J.'s freedom. One O.J. lawyer told me, "We were not the Dream Team. We should have been called the *nightmare* team. We hated each other and we did not get along. Lee Bailey was a shell of himself and he came to court drunk."

…I keep talking about the "*Joseph Project*"(™) and the "*Joseph Crusade*"(™). Hell maybe we should call it the "O.J. Simpson" project. What better way to teach men how not to live than to use O.J. as an example. Here is a brother who had it all. He had enough money that even white people (in the 80's) would pretend to like him and rich black men (in the 80's) could purchase white women. Not 'that' way. Stated differently, many white folk would pretend to be cool with their daughter etc. dating a black as long as he was rich and famous. He had it all… But he snorted cocaine (I hope he doesn't sue me) and he battled inner demons. And he also beat women. And the cocaine abuser who became a woman beater, went from a superstar to a prison cookie thief.

We live in an extremely materialistic society. What better way to show men a man who had it all. But he had no character. And he compromised his own integrity. As I think about me I can tell you that my gift opened doors for me. My gift took me places that my character couldn't keep me. I was gifted all-the-way down to my toenails. But I did not have the patience, the integrity and the character to stay where I went. Your gift may take you before Kings and Queens. But… It's like having a woman with the kind of looks and body that makes men go crazy. She might bed a great man. But with no character, integrity and class she won't keep him. She might have a lot of one-night stands. I had a lot of one-day successes. But the quality of my relationships did not sustain me. But I thank God that I didn't die in the nest. Sometimes if you follow God you can rest in the nest. I don't want to make a career out of something that should be a hobby. I can't keep lying to myself. I am not supposed to stay here. I was supposed to *start* here. But I can't *stay* here…

This is the mess*age* which can come out of my mess. I'll let Jack Van Impe and others condemn gays and lesbians to hell. I don't have a heaven or a hell to send anybody to. But I want to make a difference in the lives of folks who feel like they have hell on earth. Ryan Ferguson, Brian Banks, Pete Rose, Christopher Bird, Ronald Cotton, Eric Gilbert and I can do this. Look at all that world out there. And here I sit laying in my excuses. Laying in your cage. Laying in the prison of poverty; the prison of illiteracy. This is too small. You've got to get up from there. I've got to get out of this. We can do better. You may not be all-the-way out of the hood or the trailer park yet. You may have one foot in and one foot out. But you're crossing over… Get out of there. People may say I forgot where I came from? I'm trying to and I wish you would. I can't go back. I'll pull you out if you need me but I refuse to go back…

I wish I could find Brandon Scott (in Auburn, CA), Jullian Gonzalez, Caleb Butler, Jacob Goodin, Jordan Simon, Steve Mara, Luke Otterstad, Conner McKenzie, Dillon McKenzie, Jay Davies, Jay Davis, Justin Berry, Ryan Hreljac, Maxwell Hanger, Cody (from Big Brother 2014), Hayden and Zack. I wish I could reach Jerry Wines, Jacob Gabriel, Daniel Job and Joseph Latham.

We can turn this thing around. We need to be relentless in our pursuit of change. Call this our "*Truth and Reconciliation Campaign*" (TM), "*The Joseph Project*" (TMShermanDManning), "*Let Us Make Man*" (TM) and "*Creating Monsters*" seminars, workshops, clinics and crusades. Call this "The O.J. Simpson" project. Whatever you wanna call it. But I need you to join us. We want to save, transform and rescue the "male child" that the enemy seeks to kill. We can read, teach, educate and elucidate our way out of this. Prison is too small for us. We've got to get up and we must get out.

…Holly Williams? Have you seen Holly Williams? That lady is bad. She is a CBS reporter. And she has body with a capital "B." Good golly Miss Holly. And… Okay I'll get back to O.J. No he did not bribe the judge…


**Hands Up: Don't Shoot:**

…I want readers to find Joe Breen (he went to Yale), Eric Bulrice, Will Stabler (he went to Kenyon), Kevin Johnson (he went to law school but worked as a waiter in New York), Roger Walthorn, Charles Lutz (Rossville, MN), Steve Mara, Shawn Selby, Marcus Filly, Ben Honeycutt, Jeff Dinosh, Ryan Hamsitengel, Anthony Carbojal, Alan Rafferty, John Foraker, Colton Dixon, Aaron Kelly, Daniil Turitsyn, Robert James Carlson, Jimbo Spalding, Alec Torres, Alec Hamlin, Abdiel Flores Torres, Zack Torres, Solomon Gomez (Imperial, CA), Zac Sunderland, Mike Crowder, Casey Neistat, Jason Kaseman, Jonathon Phillips, Jeremy Caldwell (cosumnes oaks), John Caudell, Kory Carico, Scott Czeda and Maxwell Hanger. Tell them to get this book and to drop me a line. I have an assignment for them. I need to reach Lane Garrison, Angus T. Jones, Cody Linley, Elijah Wood, Brian Glasscock, Sam Pritchard and Vincent Thomas (Vincent is an actor who lives in Los Angeles)…

"*Hands Up = Don't Shoot*" was the chant of August 2014… We've witnessed the militarization of America's police officers. It's a long way from "officer the friendly." And I call upon President Barack Obama and the Attorney General to retrieve all of the armored military vehicles which were given to American police departments. President Obama has not shut down Guantanamo Bay; as he said he would. He needs to demilitarize our police. We should never have to look at our T.V.s again and confuse Baghdad with an American suburb. And you will never see these military tanks in Beverly Hills or in Buckhead. They will only be used in the hoods.

Any psychologist can explain that the more weapons you give police the more they will create reasons to use them. Give them military weapons and they will view the community as a "war" zone. And they will see the citizens as "enemies." And they will continue to gun down black men. And there is already a war on black men. And even poor and the mentally ill, whites and Mexicans are being murdered by police. And I will remind you (tautology) that when the New York cop used an illegal choke hold to murder a black citizen (whose only crimes were being black and selling cigarettes) when the paramedics showed up they refused to try CPR. And he'd only been dead for 2 minutes. So the cops will shoot us. And the paramedics won't treat us. This war has triangulated… Jesse Potash, Freddie Escanilla and Andrew Wetzel are you reading?...

I'm telling young people (white, black, Mexican and Asian) to put your "hands-up" when you get near a cop, a gun, drugs or alcohol. But when you get near books = hands down. Be more willing to grab a book than a gun. The more books you read the fewer guns you'll need. I want a few good men and women to get this book (in 2016, 2018 – 2028 etc.) and decide to change. And change is contagious. And you can build up strong networks in your school, city, club or church. And you all can run the world. You have got to be able to see the invisible; so you can do the impossible. If you can see it you can be it. I'd rather see a sermon than to hear a sermon…

Cops are willing to kill you. And they will usually get away with it. And if they don't kill you they will kill your destiny. They will kill your future. Don't find yourself locked up in some racist prison like where I am. Just today Sergeant Joseph Stratton made a threatening and derogatory statement to me. On 8/21/14 he threatened to pull a "Darren Wilson" on me. It was at 12:01. I could report it but they will cover for him. He already has Associate Warden Ross Meiers threatening to transfer me. And… (He actually did transfer me in January 2015!).

The CCPOA is a gang. It is the Green Wall and taxpayers pay to defend them when they are accused of abusing us. And guys like Stratton cost California taxpayers $millions per year. He costs them in legal fees lawsuits and settlements. But Dale Schornack and other local media never see fit to do a story on how much money rogue guards (like Stratton) cost taxpayers. A prison Lieutenant told me Stratton has been arrested for DUI and other assorted crimes. He's gained 60 pounds within the last two years. "I heard Stratton has a lot of problems" the Lieutenant stated... I hope Dawson Jope, Matt Stuart, Daniel Jensen, Daniel Jennings, J-Si Chavez and Bradley McClain are reading this...

Prisons manufacture madness. And they "create monsters" (see my seminal book: "*Creating Monsters*"). Prisons are not only deadly places in the physical sense. They are deadly in the psychological sense. It is extremely rare to see anyone come out of a prison who is not psychologically damaged. Likewise most people who work in prisons are also abnormal. They may have been close to normal when they got here. But you can't work in this much darkness, deadliness and evil (long term) without it rubbing off on you. Evil is contagious. And Regional demons lord over prisons. Just as inmates become institutionalized; guards also become institutionalized. Yet, they reside amongst *you*...

...I'm more excited about this book publishing than I've ever been about any of my books. I can't wait... I want Robert Lopez (Univ. of FL, Gainesville), Greg Pugh (Richmond, VA), Tim Combs, Daniel Marsh, Brenton Thwaites, Joshua Simpson, Taylor Budowich, Matthew Stern, Tim McBride, David House, Stuart Watkins, Larry Rudolph, Drew Troller, Seth Loewe (in Fairfield), Alan Rafferty, Jeff Dinosa, Anthony Carbajal, Austin Adams, Austin Moore, Trevor Sanford, Austin Hatch, Josh Brown (Raleigh, NC), Josh Scannell, Erica Snipes, Tef Poe, Piaget Crenshaw, Trevor Leja, Peter Wohl, Joe Freedberg, Jonah Miller, Chaz Wolcott, Luke Kelly, Jamieson Knopf, Travis Shaw, Dylan Wilson (Huntington, IN), Jacob Faulkender, Ari Shapiro, David Isgur, Charles Costello, Jais Malcolm, Dawson Sturino, Sam Fuick, Mike Wilkerson, Billy York (Cummings, GA), Andrew Hines, Kevin Sullivan (Isla Vista, CA), Kyle Russell, Ricky Sweet and Eddie Cannon to get this book. I want John Mandern and Aaron Jackson (in Delaware, OH) to get it. I want Donald Dusk (*not* the author. Donald is in Akron, OH) to get this book. I need *you* to help me by letting them know this book is out. Do tell, do tell...

I can't wait for this book to publish. I feel like I'm in Ferguson (aka Folsom) Missouri. I have to see "The Green Wall" (aka 723 aka CCPOA) as the Ferguson Police Department. And everybody believes guards over inmates; just as they do police over suspects. Let me tell you about Joseph Stratton. On 8/21/14 he told me to "write that N-gger Eric Holder. Write that N-gger President Obama. We would kill both of them (sic) N-ggers in Folsom." And he told me the "fix" was in. They (C.O. Ryan Patrick Wenker, Layton Johnson, C.O. B. Humphries and Aron Ralls etc.) stole my "Valley Fever" lawsuit to circumvent the statute of limitations. They've selectively stolen, hidden, delayed and sabotaged my regular mail. And they make it next to impossible to sue prison guards. And when we do sue we end up out-lawyered by the CCPOA. I had Attorney Jeff Kravitz (of Carmichael, CA). He should be disbarred. Kravitz is a lousy lawyer as well as a meth addict. And he is intimidated by the CCPOA...

And I'll admit that they are dangerous. Stratton claims they've already bribed judges to make certain my lawsuit will get dismissed. He claims my judge is a black Republican who despises inmate lawsuits. Stratton alleges they bribed Judge Morrison England. And... He says Associate Warden Ross Meiers is very close to his father (Chief Deputy Warden George Stratton who is retired). And he says Meiers is developing a pretext to transfer me to another prison (and they did).

Stratton has participated in the murders of at least two (Rocky Salazar and inmate Edwards) inmates. There were civil rights violations. But C.D.C. covers for the guards. And… When we sue them you (American taxpayers) pay for their lawyers. Attorney Kristina Gruenberg and Kellie Hammond have billed taxpayers over $100 grand (to date) to represent these thugs. Google Ryan Patrick Wenker. Call KCRA-TV and ask reporter Sharokina Shams to send you the stories she did on Wenker. And taxpayers pay for his lawyers…

"*Hands Up: Don't Shoot*?" Perhaps I could have titled this chapter: "*I Can't Breathe*." That is what Mr. Garner (RIP: I hope Ellisha Garner, and Erica Snipes know that this book is out!) yelled to the New York cops who murdered him. The last 3 words he uttered on this earth were "I can't breathe"… Inmate Williams was standing in a prison dog cage. He had on a spit mask (similar to ones used at Abu Ghraib). He was in handcuffs and he was locked (totally confined) in a cage. There was absolutely no reason to pepper-spray Edwards. But Sergeant K. Porter, guard Joseph Stratton, and Ryan Patrick Wenker all emptied 3 cans of pepper-spray on Edwards while he was in the cage. And he was a heart patient. And his last three words uttered? "*I can't breathe*." When he yelled that he could not breathe Joe Stratton yelled "If you can talk you can breathe." Joe Stratton, K. Porter and Ryan Wenker murdered this guy. A black, sick and mentally ill prisoner. And they got away with it. They should be in prison as inmates right now. He could not breathe… Kametra Barbour was mistreated (she's black) by white cops in Forny, Texas. I hope she sues them…

(I need readers to locate Brian Sobocinski, Andrew Shah, Less Simmons, Gabe Barajus, Scott Vincent-Borba, Tyler Zhou, Mitchell Thorp, Trevor Law, Trevor Loflin, Creighton Baird, Nolan Wong, Jaron Brandon, Chance Fidler, Chad Newman, Richard Kenneth Chandler, Christopher Rousche, Ben Aaron, Jericka Duncan, Nick Pelham, Chessah Fox, Tim Quinn, Justin Bassett, Shephard Ferry, Larry Rudolph, Chris Biele, Doran Smestad, John Garvin, Gary Browning, Scott Coffman (Floyd, IL) and Steve Coffman. I need you to locate them and tell them to get this book. Please don't just read the names. Reach them…)

Guard Joe Stratton carries a baton, a flashlight, handcuffs, a knife, an alarm and a can of pepper-spray in the prison. He carries a "murder starter kit." Several prison guards are even afraid of him. C.O. Zerr does not trust him. Captain Rhonda Carter (a black Captain) told me to look up "evil" and "corrupt" in the dictionary. And she stated I'd find pictures of George and Joe Stratton (respectively). Captain Carter is a woman who loves God. And she told me that "God can use you when you get out, to go across this country and tell the world about the Wenkers and the Strattons who threaten and disrupt rehabilitation." Captain Carter is the first black (female) captain at New Folsom. And Stratton hates her. I was in her office one day when she sent him an email ordering him to move his car out of her parking space. Every time Stratton passes her office and sees me talking to her he rolls his eyes like a little girl. He is one of the most racist, evil, corrupted criminals to have ever worked in a prison. I'm told that if they gave him a drug test tomorrow "he would fail."

When ISIS beheaded James Foley guard Joseph Stratton stated "I wish it was that N-gger Obama who they beheaded. If I could get my hands on him I would literally kill him." Guard Ryan Wenker was notorious for threatening to kill President Obama if he ever met him. When you listen to some of these prison guards talk you'll think we're back in the 1950's.

You'll think you're in Ferguson (aka Folsom?) Missouri. 53 cops with 3 blacks? So less than 2 percent of the cops in Ferguson are black. Yet nearly 70 percent of the residents are black? At Folsom State Prison… (Exclude Captain Rhonda Carter). We have a warden, a chief deputy, 4 associate wardens, 4 captains and 10 administrators who are all white. Not a single black. And 75 percent of the inmates are black. Ferguson State Prison? And when an inmate argues the race issue or ruffles feathers etc. they will invent a reason to transfer him. And A.W. Ross Meiers just notified me that they will be putting me up for transfer. (By the time you read this they've probably given me a celly who may try to set-me-up. If I complain they will simply lock me in Ad-Seg and transfer me… CCII Janice Mayfield made it clear that I should be on single cell status. And I concur)…

The Department of Corrections in California should be renamed the Department of Corruption and a photo of Joseph Stratton should be the guard mascot… Inmates don't stand a chance against him or any member of the CCPOA. They're like the Mafia. They are lawyered to the hilt. And the courts (perhaps some of this due to Bill Clinton) refuse to intervene… I recall being threatened with Ad-Seg, A dismissal of my lawsuit and a transfer from Stratton. I informed Sacramento Federal Court about his threat. And the court responded by conducting what they called an inquiry. The inquiry consisted of asking Stratton, "Did you threaten *Manning*?" And Stratton's lawyer replied with seven pages of bullshit. So it's that simple; just ask "Did you do it?" And once the person says "No" through their lawyer: case closed! That's not justice; that is bias…

"Women are a crystalizing example of people that we put in prison that we did not – 30 years ago" stated Piper Kernan. Piper explains that not all Americans are policed the same. We are not all prosecuted the same. We are not all sentenced the same. There is no equal justice under the law. If I were inmate Bill Gates and Gerry Spence or Roy Black ran to Judge Allison Claire with my allegations etc. Joe Stratton would be on a trash truck right now… "Orange" is the new black? Green is the new white. California guards say they bleed green not red. Green refers to the color of their uniform. And "green before blue." Inmate garb is blue…

Solitary confinement is another weapon prison officials utilize in a Ferguson, MO-like manner. I've been thrown into solitary confinement many times. And it will break down the mind. And I was in solitary confinement with no TV, no radio, no clothes, no mattress, no sheets, no toilet paper and no running water. All of which is illegal to the tune of constitutional violations. You say, "Why don't you sue?" I'm glad you asked. Because I did sue. But guards stole the lawsuit. And when we report to the court that a lawsuit has been stolen etc. the court responds with disdain. It is as if Stratton was right when he said, "The fix is in." The court will dismiss an inmate's lawsuit faster than you can say "Why?" And the prison grievance system is a complete and utter fraud. When you file a complaint (i.e.) on Stratton it goes to the appeals office. The person who screens the appeal is Stratton's next door neighbor. The person in charge of the appeals office used to work for Stratton's father. It is a complete fraud, a sham and a scam. And the courts refuse to intervene…

You all pray for me please because God is bigger than "The Green Wall." God is bigger than the court. And while I'm talking about God I wanna tell the Garner family and

Michael Brown's family etc. to keep the faith. I know there is a lot of pain involved but keep the faith. God is with you. I'm not telling you all to kick back. I'm not saying don't litigate. I want you to organize, galvanize and to litigate. But beside all of that you keep the faith. If someone you love dies just keep the faith. If you lose your kidney just keep the faith. If you feel alone, like giving up or like quitting you keep the faith. At this stage in my life I feel like I'm an expert on loneliness. I'm probably an expert on pain and hurt etc. Not because of what I learned in an institution of higher learning. Not because of a lecture or a sermon. But because of life. The life that I'm living right now. I am 3,000 miles away from home. I'm in prison with gangbangers, vicious and cruel guards etc. And I'm alone… And yet I've had to somehow keep the faith…

Prison guards (Mike Bunnell) retaliated against me because of what I wrote about them in books. And Bunnell told me, "I'm transferring you to Pleasant Valley so you can catch Valley Fever and write a book about that." And I wrote to everybody trying to stop that transfer. But CDC is vicious and they sent me anyway. And I actually caught Valley Fever and it nearly killed me. I'm the longest hospitalized Valley Fever patient. I spent 14 months chained to a hospital bed. My family thought I was dead because CDC did not have the decency to call them. I got no mail, no telephone calls, no visits, no TV and no Bible. And… I was down to 96 pounds. And my family was still not called…

I sued Bunnell. But when you sue a corrupted guard it is guards who process the mail. It's like filing a complaint against a gang member. And you have to mail the complaint through a gang member. And the gang member holds the complaint to make you miss the statute of limitations. And when you stand before the Honorable Allison Claire she seems tone deaf. What happened to tempering justice with mercy? Where are the Thurgood Marshalls? Claire dismissed my lawsuit out of hand. I'm still suffering today. I have Valley Fever but I also now have the aftereffects. I can't sleep. I have nightmares about the hospital. When I do sleep I have flashbacks. I…tremble just writing about Valley Fever…

But… It may be "Good for me that I was afflicted. If I had not been afflicted I would not know God like I know Him. All things work together for good. All things don't feel good. All things don't look or seem good. But if God let me (or you) go through it it's going to work together for good. It may feel bad or hurt. But good is going to come out of it. If you will just hold on and trust God even when it hurts. Something good is going to come out of this. Something good is going to come out of you. Put your hand on your stomach (right now) and say (out loud), "Something good is going to come out of me."

… (I want yall to take a break and help me to get this book into some hands. I can't do book tours or speaking tours yet. So I must rely upon readers to promote. Cut on your computer and find John Jody Bear in Richmond, VA. Find John Caudell Richmond. Find Joshua Orapello, Johnny Goh, Corbin Gomez, Dillon Banionis, *Collin Stark* (in Laguna Niguel, CA we have a check for Collin), Kameron Koop, Kevin Lynn, Eric Sarnello, Derrick Sweeney, Lloyd Chen, Cody Lloyd, Keenan Harris, Joshua Stipp, Josh Ogle, Greg Pugh in Chesterfield, VA, Angus McCloud, Jacen Lankow, Sean Aiken, Desmond Schipper, Zach Kachmar, Karl Sadkowski, Neil Davidson, Gary Jiang, Gary Silvi, Tyler Yagley, Ari Shapiro and Daniel Jensen. Find Nathaniel Mullennix in Atlanta. Eugene Langford and Frank Carter in Atlanta. Find Ralph Cannon and Danny Horton etc. and tell them to get this book today!)

…What Stratton convinced A.W. Meiers to do was an elaborate pretext to transfer me. But pray for me. If I can just make it out of prison alive. If I get out of here, I will fight with every fiber of my being to expose this fraud of a criminal justice system. I will look for Jonathan Jackson (he was a publicist) and ask him to join our team. I will call Christopher Bird, Ryan Ferguson, Alexander Berki, Max Hodges, Adam Glynn, David Quindt and David Joyner. And I'll ask them to join me. But If you don't wanna go don't hinder me. I will go if I have to go alone. This can be a one-man crusade. But I will be an "uncommon man" on a mission. You can't lay chained to a hospital bed for one year and two months and not be changed. When you fight the kinds of uphill battles I've fought. It transforms you. This prison has been preparation for destination. Prison prepared Joseph for the palace. Prison prepared Mandela for the presidency. Prison prepared Rubin "Hurricane" Carter for the fight to expose wrongful convictions. It has prepared me to do battle.

I'll be calling Senator Corey Booker, Michael Nutter, Russell Simmons and I'll call Steve Harvey etc. and ask them to just give me 15 minutes so I can tell them my story. And if I don't convince them in 15 minutes I'll leave and never return. I'm a new me. I was wrongly convicted of this crime but make no mistake I did a lot of wrong things. I wronged my own mentor. My own booster, confidante and friend; Ambassador Andrew Young was my personal friend and I committed a sin against him. I called Don King and pretended to be Andy. I swindled $15 grand out of Don King and Andy knew nothing about it. I will pay Don King his money back. I apologize to Ambassador Andrew Young. I apologize to Don King. I was wrong plain and simple…

The prison system (especially corrupted guards like Joe Stratton and Ryan Patrick Wenker etc.) thrives on a currency of secrets and a conspiracy of silence. Guards get away with murder because they know the CCPOA stands ready and willing to defend their every deadly act. Prisoners such as me are thorns in the sides. We are locked in prisons and locked outside the system. God birthed a King in a barn. He births great things in strange and obscure places. He can birth something great in a prison. I won't let my circumstances intimidate me. I will get outside the system. The system is locked up so tight that God can't enter. And if He entered we would not recognize Him because Jack Van Impe has you looking for blonde hair and blue eyes. Prison has forced certain lessons upon me. And one such lesson is to work outside the system and redefine history. Nobody hated Jesus like church folks. Don't forget it was church folk who tried to kill Jesus. He died outside of the gates of Jerusalem. He was put in a barn so you could reach Him. I can't reach Him in a palace but I can get to Him in a hog pen…

I will work outside the system and let the system catch up with me later. Nobody wants to give you anything in the barn (prison). But when you get in the palace anybody will give you anything. Quite frankly I want to thank you for rejecting me. Because if you helped me in the prison you could say you made me who I am; when I get to the palace I used to cry about being rejected. But the rejection has taught me how to master working outside of the system.

Nobody wants to help you, to love you or to write to you when you are in the prison. But thank you…

I'm gonna call Jeff Deskovich, Bryan Stevenson and Brian Banks. I'll call Tyler Perry, Ryan Ferguson, Christopher Bird and David Quindt if I get home. I will ask them to work with me. But if they ignore me or say no at least I won't quit. I will not give up on my dream to use the errors of my past to teach the future. I want to work with Kyle Day, Grant Arnette, Colin Pilcher, Brandon "Brand" Olino, Jeff Dinosa, Zach Torres, John Stapleton, Dillon Banionis, Dillon Miller (Valencia, CA), Daniel Coverston, Tanner Franklin, Jared Gaber, Jack Meyer, Daniel Jennings (Tiburon, CA) and Tim Quinn etc. and I have to ask you (the readers) to email these people and tell them about this book. Because I'm in the barn I must work outside the system. I need Chris Hues, Kasey Schultz, Robert Krybyla, David Holycross, Mitchell Thorp and Keenan Harris to join us. Use social media to promote this book… Anybody watch America's Next Top Model (2014)? Romero (Salinas, CA), Danny (Staten Island, NY), Ben (Waverly, IA), Will (Nederland, TX), Franco Locasto, Lenox (Newnan, GA) and Yu Tsai. I need you to tell them to email me (Hallopeter@Sunrise.ch) asap…

I saw State Senator Holly Mitchell on TV talking about Michael Brown. She talked about racist police and racism in criminal justice etc. and I wanted to scream because I have personally written Holly Mitchell 3 missives (with my own pen) regarding racism within the prison system. And golly — Senator Holly has never replied to me. Yet, the moment she found a camera (and a national spotlight) suddenly she is interested in racism in criminal justice. I'm not singling out Senator Mitchell (she is certainly not the only one). But one of the reasons the criminal justice system as well as our police departments remain so racist is because of do-nothing politicians. These are politicians who don't read or respond to mail unless a campaign contribution is enclosed. But the minute a tragedy occurs and the cameras show up they're ubiquitous…

I'm reminded of Ted Cruz (see my book "*Don't Mess With Texas*") shutting down the government. I recall a reporter who was on the House floor saying she could smell strong alcohol on the breath of many stumbling legislators; as they left the House floor. I thought, my God, we have old, racist, perverted and "drunk" white men running our country. They are voting on the House floor while intoxicated… In California recently we had a State Senator arrested for DUI. He came from a party at the State Capitol drunk. Come to find out that in California there are no rules against drinking inside the State Capitol. News media could not find a single legislator who was willing to discuss the lack of rules on camera. Whenever a politician runs away from a camera something in the milk is not clean. So we have a state full of legislators who are DUI. They are *Deliberating Under* the *Influence*. Do you still wonder why Joe Stratton, Ryan Wenker and Layton Johnson etc. can steal my Valley Fever lawsuit and get away with it? You still wonder how Wenker remained a guard at New Folsom State Prison even after he served 45 days in Sacramento County Jail?

I'm told that Mitch McConnell, McCain, Ted Cruz and John Boehner rarely ever cast a vote while sober. One reporter told me that if you could see McConnell, Boehner and many others (like Joe Wilson) sitting around (behind closed doors) calling President Obama and A.G. Holder the "N" word and "monkeys" etc. it would make you think this was the 1950's all over again. And yet we wonder why they vote against Obama on everything? Because they are racist drunkards… (help me reach Katie Bicek, Susan Sarandon, Jordan Spaschak, Oliver Mikkelson, William Crouch, Brian Boykin (Richmond, VA), Mark Wuergler, Matt Siler, Joshua White, Nicholas Jeffrey, Nick Symmonds, Lacey Hipps and Daniel Wallace. I am serious about reaching those people. This is guerilla promoting. I need *you* to reach them for me.

Find Austin Ho, Loic Hostetter, Paul Tassi, Joshua Thibodeaux, Shohn Huckabee, Richard Allen (UC Berkeley), Spence Palmer, DJ Carpenter, Christopher Cox (Napa Valley), Justin Hoop, Cody Williams, Sharon Walker (Watts), Alex Lambertson, Nicholas Taxera, Jacob Faulkender, Tyler Kolb, Alex Sutaru, Kris Beall, Grant Silow, Timothy Goebbels, Jeremy Hudson and Curtis Sykes. Find Jesse Helt and Eddie Olsen. (Go online and tell them all to get this book. Do it now…)

This book is dedicated to *Michael Brown Jr.* (as well as Mr. Garner in New York etc.)… I told them not to put it on the cover of the book because I don't want the family to feel anyone is exploiting his name. I dedicate this book to all 100 black men who were murdered by white cops in 2014… The protests and demonstrations are over. Now we need legislation. We must enact laws which criminalize police killings. We must better train officers. I'd heard the cop shot Brown 6 times. Now I'm hearing he may have shot him eleven times. This has got to stop. *"Hands Up Don't Shoot"*… When I look at how quickly cops are to kill a black man dead it goes back to that $3/5^{ths}$ of a human being lie. We won't settle for $3/5^{th}$ justice. We must demand *equal* justice under the law.

…And I love President Obama. He has done a tremendous job as President. But he needs to recall those military vehicles (I repeat) that the Pentagon gave to local cops. We don't need a review, a relook etc. We need a recall. Take those military vehicles back. Ferguson looked like Baghdad… I'll betcha they would not roll (I repeat) a tank through Beverly Hills chasing the son of a banker. We have to stop allowing cops to go to lower class neighborhoods and police as if they were in Iraq. There is a police war on the poor. And we cannot stand for it. Cops need to police like it's the $21^{st}$ century; not the $19^{th}$ century… We have to address this backwoods, underhanded type treatment by cops. There are a lot of Lester Maddox and Bull Connor type cops on our streets and they will continue as long as we allow it. Want to know "How to get away with murder?" Be rich or be a cop. If you have enough money you can kill people and get away with it. Money buys justice. Money buys judges. If you are a police officer (deputy or prison guard) you can also kill people and not go to prison; every day of the week. A speech won't change this. A press conference will not change this. And I assure you that looting will not change this. Looting is the most foolish thing a people can do…

We will need to bring together people like Stuart Watkins, Tyler Stanley, Kai Dunn, Zach Hilberlin, Aaron Wangler and Eddie Cannon. If we bring Christopher Bird, Brian Banks and Ryan Ferguson etc. together we can develop a "recovery plan." What I keep seeing happen is cops kill people (usually black, Mexican or poor white) and folks get mad and loud. And they'll call in a noted speaker to fan the flames. And some Uncle Tom like Jason Riley will go on Meet the Press and criticize the speaker. While Riley sits in a studio wearing makeup.

And 6 months later the media has moved on to the next fire. And unfortunately so has the preacher they flew in to speak. People move on. But if you want to change a system there must be some people (who have a vested interest) who organize a sustained effort. Perhaps somebody in Ferguson (or in a prison, a jail or a juvenile etc.) should start an official blog called "*Hands Up Don't Shoot*." And maybe a group of youngsters can go across the country and invite police, citizens and leaders to churches etc. and have seminars and workshops. I think Cheryl Dorsey (a retired Sergeant with the LAPD) could be a consultant. Then… We need a group of lawyers ready and willing to sue police officers who are corrupt, abusive, racist, classist or bias.

CNN reporter Don Lemon was pushed by a cop who was later suspended. He was suspended because they found video of him saying he's killed a lot of people and he can kill more. "Get in front of me if you want to get killed." And he made racist comments about President Obama. The St. Louis police officer is Dan Page. He ought to be fired. And if I were an attorney I'd look at every case he's been a part of…

I'm looking for Kenton Shimozaki, Tim Griffin, Jimbo Spalding and Vitalii Sediuk. I want Gladiators (aka Shermanators). I want some people who will work behind the scenes (even if they want to work in secret and help to buildup movements etc.) I want guys like Devin Dwyer, Eric Lotke, Daid Begnaud, Chris Biele, Will Frampton, Jeff Maher, Ben Tracy and Bubba Franks. I want Steven Fabian, Peter O'Riordin and Adam Glynn to help us expose and promote "*Gang Bangers For God*" and "*NAPS.*" Just tell at-risk people, ex-cons, pre-cons, criminal justice professors, law professors and pastors etc. about us. I could see Max Hodges or Racquel Harper saying, "Yo it's a dude named *Sherman* and he's written 25 or 30 books. He did time for rape. He say (sic) he didn't do it. He don't (sic) look or act like a rapist. But anyway he is a real smart dude. And he lectures about corrupt guards, police brutality, violence in prisons and all of that… Anyway you ought to get him to speak at your graduation, church or convention etc."… I need folks to do that. Perhaps I need a publicist? Well I've been looking for Jonathan Jackson (he was an LA publicist?) for the longest. I'm in jail, so if I get Jackson you'll have to find him. It's all about promotion. If you tell your friends, colleagues, principal, students, professors, classmates etc. to read this book: You're a "*Shermannator*." If you tell your bookstore to order it you are a *Shermannator*…

I want to bring the "*Joseph Project*" (TM – aka the "*Joseph* Crusade") to your university, your church, your club, company or association. I want to bring innovative, creative, unique and "out of the box" seminars, clinics and workshops etc. to your organization. I'll come to the Peace Corps, basketball teams, Future Farmers of America etc. If you call (in 2016) I'll come. I want to teach the lessons I've learned in a problem. I'd like to share the lessons I learned in a pit. I want to share the lessons which I've learned in a prison. I can use my past to teach the future. I want to make a difference because "A charge to keep I have… To serve this present age, my calling to fulfill. Oh may it all my powers engage to do my master's will…" I wanna work the works of Him that sent me… I still have a future, God's not through with me. I still have a tomorrow; just you wait and see… You have to speak to yourself. You've got to stand up to life. Because life can beat you down. But don't give up on your dream…

## Advice I Would've Given O.J. Simpson

If I had been advising O.J. after his acquittals, this is what I would've told O.J. — Get yo (sic) black ass out of this country. Move to Switzerland, France or to Spain for six months. I spent a lot of time in Switzerland. It is a beautiful country with beautiful people. Last time I was there I was supposed to stay 14 days. I stayed 31 days. You could go there and just disappear into thin air. Then after six months you can return to America. You sign up with a speaker's bureau. And you begin to speak at large black churches and at colleges etc. You also want to speak at events for defense lawyers etc. You wanna call Bob Blasier, Carl Douglas, Johnnie Cochran and Gerry Spence etc. You ask them to tell all of the organizations and associations with which they are affiliated etc. that you are available to speak…

Get a black girlfriend for at least a year. If you have a problem (one lawyer tells me that O.J. does have a problem with black women. He can't get erect with a black woman anymore. A Harvard educated psychiatrist explained to me that black men who have been molested, beat or emotionally abused by black women have this problem. When asked how it is that O.J. fathered children with a black woman the shrink explained that it often does not show up until a guy is over 25 or 30.) with black women then you can have a snow bunny on the side. But for a year every time you go to a party or a club I want you with a black woman. I want you to speak about justice, injustice, racism and police brutality etc. But…do not talk about your trial or acquittal for 2 years. Then, after 2 years you'll write a book and agree to do Oprah. I want you speaking in churches every Sunday…

We'll hire you a publicist and a speaking coach. On a very, very personal level I'd advise you to get right with God. For some reason God has allowed you to literally get away with murder. You are not the first person (and won't be the last) to get away with murder. But you are one of the few black men to get away with murdering two white people in this country. There are black men in prison and some even on death row who are going to die because they were wrongly convicted of killing white people. So you are a rare species. If you did not have $10 million (plus) your ass would be on death row bro. If you believe in God you ought to repent, repent, repent. O.J. it's never too late to get right with God. I'm a strong believer that we are all better than the worse thing we've ever done. Just because you did "it" does not mean you have to be "it!" You don't have to be what they think you are. Nor do you need to live down to their stereotypes etc. There are tens of thousands of young men around this country who would love to meet you. Let's go on a campaign to get boys back in school. We can fight this drop-out epidemic. We can fight illiteracy. There is a lot of work to be done. So I'm super excited about the work which you (O.J.) can do…

That is what I would have told O.J. right after his acquittal. If I'd been advising O.J. right after his conviction in Nevada, I would have told him "Hey Juice: hang yourself! Either that or slit your throat!" I'm kidding. But I would have had to say "O.J. welcome to slavery. Now you'll see what it's like to walk through the *gates of hell*. Prison is hell. It is absolute slavery. You are about to learn what it's like to live on a plantation. Juice you're going a long, long way from Brentwood…"

## Where Do We Go From Here?

I've been able to successfully predict a lot of things. Sometimes I get this spooky feeling like "AM I a psychic?" For example: About a week ago I started thinking about Ethan Couch and how he got away with murder. He was on my mind all day. And… that self-same night I saw where Ethan's dad (Fred Couch) had impersonated a police officer and gotten arrested… But I would have never predicted that in 2014, with a black president, black attorney general, etc. etc. we would still be talking about the difference between black and white justice, police brutality and prison guard corruption etc. Institutional racism is rampant. And…as far as we have come; but oh how far we must still go. Police officers in full military gear in Ferguson, Missouri. I'd rather see Bull Connor and the dogs… Police have been beating, assaulting and murdering black men since the beginning. Prison guards do also. The only difference in then and now, are cell phone cameras. Deputy Sam Burnette (a Butte County deputy in California) kicked a mentally ill black guy in the head (it was captured on cell phone camera) in August of 2014. Instead of calling it excessive force the police are covering it up. "The camera does not show what happened before the kick." So what…

If a camera shows me shooting an unarmed man in the face, while he sits etc. does it matter what he did before? It always fascinates me how the police are always willing to justify, mitigate and ameliorate these killings. And the mitigating circumstances are "only" applicable to them. They do the same thing in the prisons. I remember when video showed six juvenile prison guards (of course in California) beating down two youth wards. They had the wards handcuffed, face down and lying on the floor. And yet, guards continuously pepper-sprayed, punched and kicked them. First they denied the beatings. When they found out a camera was rolling they changed their story. "If you'd seen what these guys did before we beat them you'd see it was justified." Narcisco Morales' nose was even broken. Narcisco sued these prison guards and won $3 million. All six were fired but… The CCPOA (California Correctional Peace Officers Association aka CA "thugs" union) sued to get their jobs back. All 6 guards were rehired and promoted. All built, rehired and promoted on a "If you'd seen what these kids did to us at first you'd understand why we beat the hell out of them" platform…

Deputy Burnette (white cop) knew his black victim (Michael Collins) and he even knew about Michael's mental health problems. I would not have predicted that we'd still be talking about police brutality. I can recall being with civil rights legend (he was one of my mentors) Rev. Hosea Williams in Atlanta. When a black man had been killed by cops in Atlanta, Rev. Williams said that it was "open season on black people." I was only 15 or 16 years old (I'm now 42) when he was leading a movement against police brutality. Over 26 years later and we're still dealing with this? I happened upon PBS the other day and they were airing some of Dr. King's "I Have A Dream" speech. And they were showing parts of the speech that most media never show. And as I stood there spellbound (this was in August 2014) I could not believe my ears: "We can never be satisfied as long as the Negro is the victim of the horrors of *police brutality*… (this was in the 1960's). No we are not satisfied and we will never be satisfied until justice rolls down like waters and righteousness like a mighty stream."

Fifty-two years after Dr. King complained about police brutality we are still being beat, hurt, set-up and killed by "killer cops." We need to focus like a laser beam on cleaning up our police departments nationwide. We need to insist that all cops wear cameras at all times. And until they get those cameras we must make sure that we film cops when they come to our neighborhood. We have Neighborhood Watch? We need Neighborhood Cop Watch… And neighbors should take turns filming cops every time they come to the neighborhood because police patrol much differently in trailer parks than they do in the suburbs.

…(I want readers to contact Jesse Helt, Cody Harlton, Nick Dannenberger, Michael Cody, Dan DeFilippi, Daniil Turitsyn, Daniel Tingen, Dylan Heath, Travis Wall, Spencer Liff, Daniel Malinovsky, Desmond Schipper, David Roddy, "Chris" who was on Inside Edition on 3/8/12 from Memphis, Neil Davidson, Jason Ravenscroft, Iman Taha Hassane, Sebastian Demers, Reis Kloeckener, Ian MaGruder, Blaire Casey, Nate Zavaleta, Patrick Yurick, Anthony Baker, Greg Baker, Kevin Poindexter, Akim Williams, Kevin Shoop, Peter Knegt, and John Johnson (in Lemoore, CA), Michael Wilkerson and Christopher Durbin in Dalton, GA and tell them about this book. And tell them to send me an email…).

I'd like to see Cheryl Dorsey and some other ex-cops make a video telling kids what to do (and what not to do) when stopped by cops. And just as Dr. King, Rev. Hosea Williams, Jesse Jackson etc. held "non-violence" workshops etc. The 21$^{st}$ century may be calling upon us to hold "How to deal with the police" clinics… Dr. Martin Luther King, Jr. was a magnificent leader. I honor, elevate, applaud and salute him. He's gone now. He's not coming back. He *told us what to do*. We're it; do it. That is where we go from here. If we want chaos there is a way. If we want community here's the way. We must come together as "brothers and sisters" or we shall "perish apart as fools."

Some of the basic solutions to man's problems have not changed. If you are shot you must find the wound. When you find the wound you must stop the bleeding. When you stop the bleeding you treat (key word being "treat") the wound. You may have to remove (surgically) the bullet. Some surgeons may elect to leave the bullet in the body… Many of our great civil rights leaders (Dr. King, Rev. Andrew Young, Rev. Hosea Williams, Rev. Joseph Lowery and Rev. Jesse Jackson etc.) decided to leave some of the bullets in the "body" of the black American community. And those bullets have begun to move in 2014 and in 2015. And when you see people looting in the streets etc. that's the bullet moving. And we get in an uproar because we've not seen that bullet in so long that we thought it was gone. We forgot about it. If we'd called Uncle Andy Young, Rev. Lowery or Rev. Jackson (in 12, 13, 14, 15 or 2016 etc.) they would have told us that the bullets are not gone.

And the wounds have not fully healed. Some of the wounds have become infected. But "we'll" get so caught up in a black president and a black this-or-that, that Generation X, Gen-Y and the Millennials all convinced ourselves that "the bullets are gone and the wounds are well." But just as what goes up must come down. What goes in is still in if it has not come out. So the words of Dr. King are still applicable: "No we are not satisfied and we will never be satisfied until justice rolls down like waters and righteousness like a mighty stream."

Dr. King's words are applicable in 2016 just as they were in 1965. The Bible is a very, very old book but we still apply it to our lives now. Dr. King (too) was a prophet just like

Jeremiah, Ezekiel, Daniel, Hosea and like Joel. It's difficult for some to believe that but if you believe God you must believe it. If David could be anointed, appointed and a man of God; yet, he was also a hypocrite, a philanderer and a killer. And God still used David? I guess we need to forgive Jesse Jackson, Sr. He did impregnate a woman who was not his wife (and so did King David!). The only difference is Jesse didn't kill anybody. But we can forgive David because he's dead and in the Bible. But every time certain people see Rev. Jesse Jackson all they can do is call him a hypocrite. He's more than that. He is a flawed, great, powerful, anointed human being. And I salute him…

Ya'll have no problem believing that Joseph sat in prison (for 13 ½ years) for an attempted *rape* that he did not commit. And God used the prison to prepare Joseph. And Joseph is dead and in the Bible. But "I don't know about *Manning*. He must have done something. *Manning* is not Joseph." Joseph is dead and he is not coming back. He told us what to do. We're (you and me) it. Let's do it. King David is dead. King David is dead and he's not coming back. We're it… He told us what to do. We are the kings, queens, anointed (and appointed) men and women of God. We are gonna screw up (sometimes) just like David did. Preachers are gonna trip up and have babies out of wedlock. There are going to be issues with preachers, teachers and leaders. But "we" must continue to worship God and not man. We must live the message and not the messenger. And don't get distracted or obsessed with somebody else's mistakes. Stay focused on the man in your mirror because if you live long enough you (too) are going to screw up. You are going to need mercy and grace. Just keep living…

There are things which a prophet sees which can draw him to his knees. Dr. King preached a sermon about being called at midnight. And he preached about being drawn to his knees. Habakkuk was also drawn to his knees by the hardheartedness of his countrymen… Dr. King told us about his dream…he told us what to do… HABAKKUK (2:2 and 3) "Write the vision and make it plain on tablets, that he may run who reads it. For the vision is yet for an appointed time; but at the end it will speak, and it will not lie. Though it tarries, wait for it; because it will surely come, it will not tarry…" They told us what to do. What shall we do? We'd better take those iPhones and use them to change the world. We'd better modernize and sophisticate our educational and developmental infrastructure. We can't use a payphone method to solve a smartphone problem. We can't solve the problems of the $21^{st}$ century with a $20^{th}$ century methodology. But we can utilize the wisdom of the past to predict and interpret the future. We can study history so that we won't repeat history. Never underestimate the power of history to help shape, predict and interpret destiny…

In LA Danny Bakewell has the Brotherhood Crusade. And if you give me a few good men (Jimbo Spalding, Alex Hayes, Dalton Graston and Jared Graber etc.) and we can begin a national brotherhood (and sisterhood) crusade across this country. I don't know if I can even write it with enough emphasis for you to feel my emotions. You can't see the tears coming down my cheeks so I have to make this book cry for me. I've had to turn my prison cell into a war room and to do literary warfare with this pen. I trained myself to take this pen and to put on a clinic about injustice. I've come to believe that the Allison Claires of life cannot see how foolish their rulings are. And perhaps a lot of this happened to me to show me how to survive as an utter and complete underdog. Allison Claire and many judges in this country are illiterate. Their illiteracy about the structural racism by whites causes them to accuse me of mere "histrionics." The illiteracy the media have perpetrated about structural racism causes a Dale Schornack to see no problem with glorifying Jeremy Meeks as a potential "model." Yet refusing to mention a prisoner author. There is an implicit bias in the courts, in the media and in general against blacks, Latinos, the accused etc. This is why I pray that I can get out of here.

And I want to ally my passion with Christopher Bird. Chris has been wrongly accused. Chris knows what it feels like to know that "I" did "not" do this. All the while the media are referring to you as a "rapist," a "sex offender," a "murderer" or as a "predator" and to know you did not do it. As I studied the life of President Nelson Mandela and I read that his prison C-file refers to him as "manipulative" (my prison file continually accuses me of being highly manipulative. I've learned that "manipulative" is a code word used by white staff whenever they encounter an intelligent black prisoner.) and as a "terrorist." I began to get the illiteracy of structural racism elucidated to me. As I read my C-file if I were not me I'd fear the Manning in my C-file. A "predator," a "rapist," and a… They've taught me that you can make *paperwork say* anything. And you can make a lion look like a lamb in *writing*. And that no matter how much evidence you provide to a judge (i.e. Mrs. Claire) you will not convince them to go against their government. That would require too much courage…

Sitting in my cell alone I've learned not to inhale the poison. And there is poison in the oxygen in a prison. Suffering makes true storytelling a written sound track to my everyday reality… I've been broken. But it is the *breaking* of life which produces the *blessing* of life. Never give up in the breaking process. Out of the cracks and crevices of life etc. that's where the blessing comes from. If anybody reading my words feels lonely, stressed, depressed or oppressed, I tell you to keep going. Hug yourself and love yourself. Out of your cracks will come your comeback. God can create a need that your suffering can serve. And if you survive it (whatever your "it" may be) then you can tell me how-to "survive" it too. There have been many (even as recently as 2014) times in my life where I've wondered if I would survive that moment. I've been so broken that I did not think I could ever pick up the pieces. And one day I said to myself that as messed up as my life is, as hopeless as it looks for me, as desperate as my situation looks, If? If (by chance, by destiny or by certainty etc.) I just so happen to survive this and actually come back from it. And if I can come out of this half-way sane, normal and positive, what can't I do? All I need to do is figure out how to stay sane.

And…when you keep losing people you love. And you keep hearing about who died. And you keep going to bed at night broken. And you wake up tired because you are so broken. And you are constantly reminded that on top of what you are going through (Joseph, Brian Banks and *Sherman* etc.) that everybody thinks you are a "rapo" anyway. This (I promise you even if you believe nothing else I write) is a lonely road. But Joseph did survive being wrongfully convicted of a sex crime. And because he survived and somebody wrote about it in a book (the Bible = Genesis) Joseph is able (even in death) to teach Brian Banks, Christopher Bird, Marcus Dixon and me etc. how to survive this kind of torture. And if I survive it? And if I write about it?...

O.J. Simpson? The great O.J. is now a No J. and if Kanye West, Chris Brown and some of those others are wise they will look at O.J. and use him as a lesson. O.J. should teach rich blacks to not become a No J. He can teach them how not to forget where you came from. Use O.J. as a motivator to help to educate, inspire and to enlighten the No J's… Simpson can teach us how and why not to become arrogant. No matter how much money you get (Kanye? Jay-Z? etc.) you need to be humble. If you are humble and pragmatic you will grow… I was very worried about my future. And then all the judicial (and the courts are merely an arm of the Corrections Department. They virtually work together.) chatter and innuendoes regarding me etc. and I said, "How can I ever make a comeback with people saying this kind of mess about me?" But people get remembered for what they build. Not by what people say about them. So I decided to build. From Folsom State Prison I built what you are holding in your hand. I built it (with a lot of help from Peter Andrist and the team in Switzerland) and it will still exist even after I'm in heaven… I repeat: Call Attorney Bob Blasier, Barry Scheck, Peter Neufeld etc. to talk about O.J. Bob Blasier knows where the bodies (no pun intended) are buried…

**Truth and Reconciliation (TMSherman D. Manning) Tour**

In a moment I shall explain with specifics what this campaign shall do, when and where. I hope Christopher Bird, Barry Gibbs, Brian Banks, Marty Tankleff and Lane Garrison etc. will participate in these campaigns. We will wage a desperate campaign to reach families who can't afford to sit on the couches of Dr. Phil or of Dr. Drew Pinsky etc… More on that in a moment. But first I'd like to address a literary elephant in the room. I'm probably going to lose my lawsuit against these thugs in C.D.C. They (Joseph Stratton, Ryan Couch, Ryan Wenker, Bunnell and Aron Ralls etc.) are like the *ISIS* of C.D.C. They are absolutely wicked. But my focus has now shifted to the judiciary. These judges… I used to wonder why the famed lawyer Gerry Spence gave judges so much hell in his books and speeches. Now I have the experiential expertise to attest to Gerry's accuracy. Judges act like gods but they are narcissistic, bribe-taking, biased politicians.

I recall when I bragged to veteran lawyer Ellen Dove on how great I thought my judge (Allison Claire) would be. I explained that she's a liberal, lesbian, democrat. And "she was a federal public defender" and… Ellen told me not to get my hopes up. "*Sherman* I have a liberal judge right now that I had faith in. But if you saw the bias he's shown in this trial you'd think he's Mitch McConnell. It's something about them that just makes them side with the police, prison guards and with the state. They put on blinders when it comes to guard malfeasance and police brutality etc." Judge Allison Claire has ruled against me and even mocked me in her rulings. If I tell her Joseph Stratton is a thug and he did this or that, she replies, "You make baseless allegations without witnesses." I say, 'read this.' And Anthony Torres writes directly to the court stating that he was my celly for 4 years and he was coerced by guards (Stratton and Couch etc.) to lie on me. When he refused A.W. Meiers and Dave Roth put him up for transfer to the worst prison in the state (High DeSeet State Prison). I had to get Warden Tim Virga to go against his own staff and cancel the transfer. Claire dismisses

Anthony out of hand. I got a Christian, C.D.C. employee (a facility captain) willing to tell Claire some of the stuff Stratton has done to me. A totally credible, authentic and a high-level CDC supervisor... When Claire dismissed that out of hand she acted as if the captain were a fantasy. Lawyer after lawyer told me no fair judge would release Attorney Jeff Kravitz from my case.

Kravitz was arrested in 2011 for cocaine possession. And police found a sexual bondage kit in the trunk of his car. Kravitz is one of the most deceptive lawyers in Sacramento. He sold me out to Kelli Hammond and Kristina Gruenberg. He left because he did not agree with something I wrote in a book about Gruenberg. And the great Allison Claire decided that "whatever" (she claims she didn't know what I wrote) Kravitz was upset about was good enough for him to be allowed to abandon me and tank my case. And Claire simply will not give me another lawyer. But she "fights for the little people?" Stratton told me the CCPOA bribed Claire. I have no proof of that. And Stratton is a known liar. But there is an obvious bias against me by this judge. I spent 14 months chained to a hospital bed with Valley Fever. I filed every document on time. But Claire quickly dismissed (in spite of the continuing violation doctrine. In spite of laws which state if they interfere with my medication it reopens the statute etc.) my Valley Fever lawsuit and never looked back...

If Allison Claire cares about plaintiff inmates — I own the Los Angeles Lakers. She will not give me justice. But...perhaps I can go around the country talking and conferring with law students and professors etc. Perhaps I can convince a few law students etc. not to turn their backs on the "little people." Perhaps the egregious manner in which I was mistreated by prison guards, lawyers and even judges etc. shall serve as a platform from which I can engage in literary as well as *oratorical warfare*. I will never, ever forget the lump in my throat and the pain I get in my stomach each time I read a letter from Allison Claire. When I open the envelope I already know its bad news. Because? I'm black, outspoken, a "felon" and I dare to voice my opinion...

Stratton (in September 2014) threatened me into never (ever) taking my itraconazole (Valley Fever meds) again. He told me they were too expensive. And that Bunnell wants me to die from it. And if I stop then my mail (regular and legal) will stop being stolen. So my physician (Dr. Sidiqqui) says not taking it can kill me. But on 8/28 and 8/29/14 Stratton made certain I did not get the meds... And I got them restarted again (because in 2012 Dr. Sidiqqui told me that an order had been written to discontinue my itraconazole. Nurse Suma also saw this order. When I filed to get it, Records refused to give it to me. Sidiqqui reordered the meds...). ...But on 9/14/14 I returned all my Valley Fever meds to Nursing. I believe Stratton can do exactly what he threatened and I'll take no chances. My hope is that I can live a year or two (without the meds) long enough to get out of here.

Justice is not indivisible. It is too often for sale to the highest bidder. And an Allison Claire basically says, "I agree with the defendant's view of your case. But even though I'm with Bunnell, Stratton, Wenker and Kravitz etc. against you I am fair. And you need to shut up." Well... We told Judge Claire about a guard (C.C.) rapist. This dude was told by Wenker, Layton, Ralls etc. to *steal* an inmate's mail and to *rape* that inmate. When we built up the nerve to tell Claire about the guard and the "inmate" he raped, and we complained that Jeff Kravitz had dropped this guard from my case (against my orders) — Claire dismissed it out of hand. Well now I resort to (the unthinkable) the *nuclear* option. Never has this been done in the history of book writing. No prisoner author (in history) has ever published a book in which he publishes *photos* of a prison guard (who is still guarding and in the CCPOA *right now*) in his *underwear*. And how did I get them? They are not on the internet. I have no cell phone and I take this unprecedented step because a federal judge called the claim of a rapist guard being told (by guards) to steal my Valley Fever lawsuit and mail etc. mere "ramblings" and histrionics."

I challenge readers to send this page to Attorney General Eric Holder and to the F.B.I. because they have the technology to authenticate these photos within 90 seconds! And the F.B.I. can even identify him! And… We have emails which this guard sent (under the signature of John Doe) to a person and the guard requested male nude photos. I'd tell the F.B.I. this face-to-face. And it is a federal crime to lie to a federal agent. The guard sent emails to a friend of an inmate (in June – 2011). And the F.B.I. could trace the emails to an IP address. What's more? The guard wrote missives (in his handwriting) to his rape victim. And when he built up the nerve to report all of this to C.D.C. Internal Affairs etc. in August of 2014? Lieutenant Ferris and Lieutenant John Mayhew both said they knew the guard and dismissed it out of hand. Even the prisoner inspector general ignored it. The question is why would a judge (Allison Claire) totally ignore an inmate's claim that this guard "raped me? And when I reported his rapes to Lieutenant Nielsen and Dr. Laura Martinez in 2012, Lieutenant Nielsen shredded my 602 (guess he learned from Bunnell?) and searched my cell and threatened me not to talk about it."

Why would Claire ignore this? The victim was threatened with another retaliatory transfer. And they said they'd use the guard's dad as an excuse (pretext) to transfer him again (although I can vouch that his dad is a good man. And it is highly unlikely he'd throw away his 29 year career by retaliating…). Why would Claire ignore this? Easy answer: Because if they acknowledge the possibility of the existence of a conspiracy (by white guards) to have an undercover bi-sexual (who is married with a child) guard to retaliate against a black inmate; and violate his civil rights; and to steal his mail (for Wenker, Layton and Bunnell etc.); and to rape him etc. If they open that can of worms by addressing it? It would blow *my* lawsuit wide open. And attract a Ben Pavone, Stewart Katz or a Geri Green etc. to take my lawsuit. So instead they call the claim "rambling histrionics." Well here's to Allison Claire, Kelli Hammond and to Kristina Gruenberg. Here is one for the history books. And (although the guard is named in my lawsuit by name and internal affairs and Judge Claire know his name! When I talked about C.C. in court Judge Claire ordered his name to be put under seal. I am not bound in a book by such order. Yet, I've elected not to name the guard out of respect for his wife, dad, daughter and his family…) I hope somebody does two things: A. Ask the F.B.I. (And A.G. Loretta Lynch) to identify the man (nearly nude) in those pictures (Why would he give them to an inmate? Why did Ferris and Mayhew sweep it under the rug?). And B. Ask his *wife* if this is him in the photos (certainly Allison Claire could have asked. But she did not even ask him because inmates are just 'liars')?

…This is the "nuclear" option (publishing photos of a rapist guard's body in a book on justice. Criminal justice professors, law professors, students and journalists etc. will have a field day with this one. Go on to Reddit, Gawker, blogs, etc. and talk about this *history*-making feat). Look at the photos below:

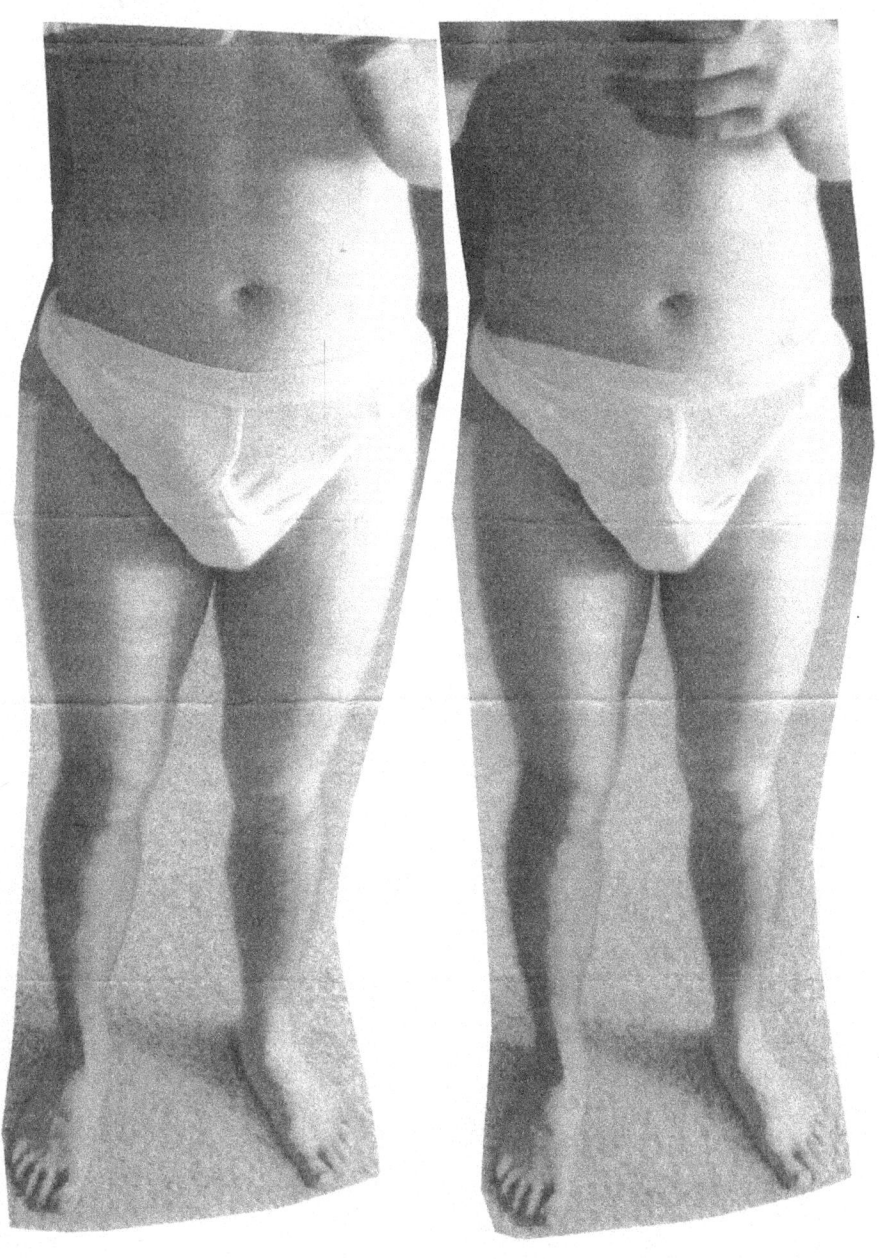

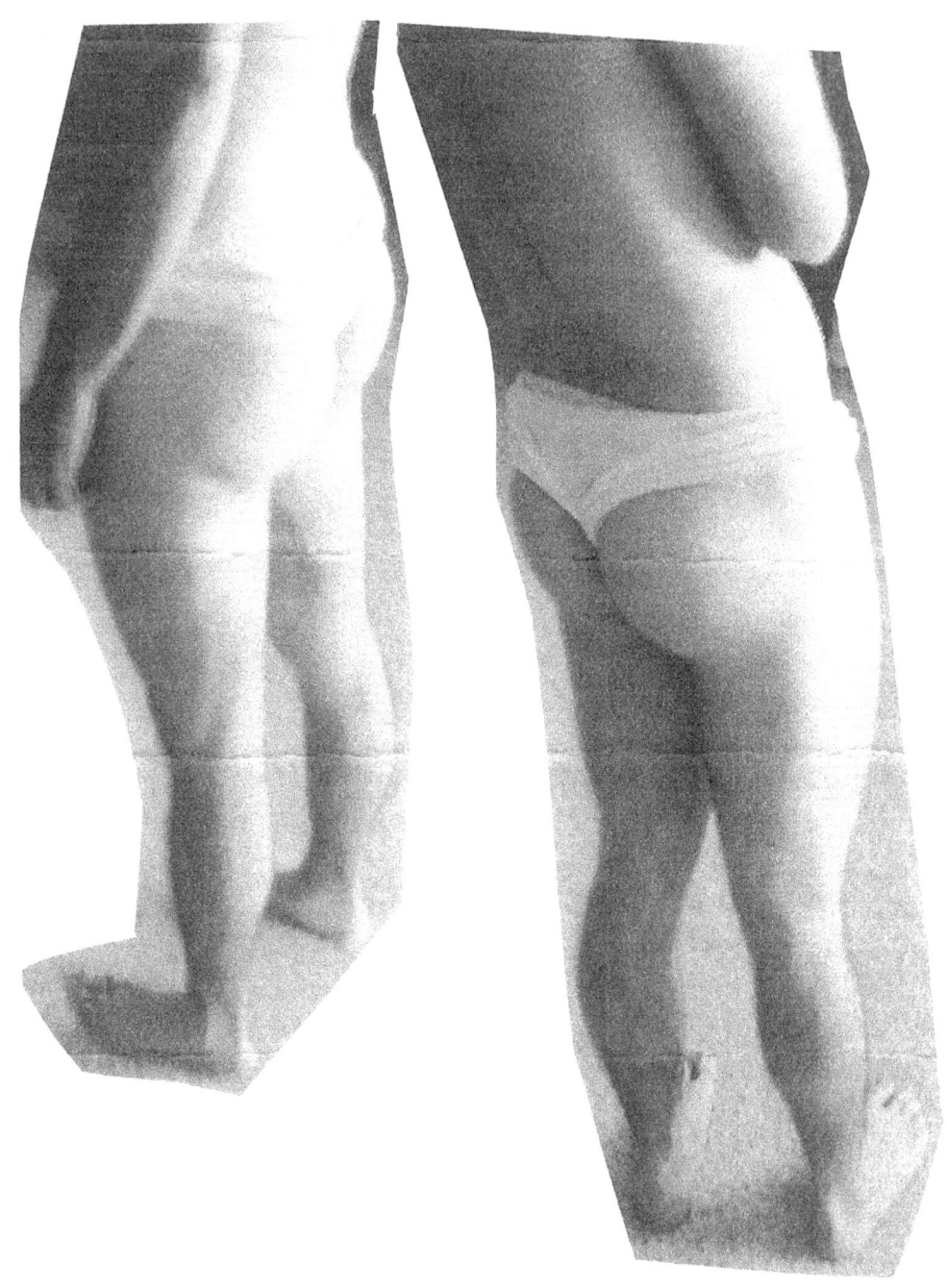

Well, there you have it. That is history. I affirm under penalty of perjury that the photos (above) are a current CCPOA member and a California prison guard. And he personally gave the photos to one of his rape victims. Why did he give them to his victim? That is a question we will only answer to the Feds or to a court. And you would think that a Deputy Attorney General for the State of California (Madame Kelli Hammond… Kelli.Hammond@doj.ca.gov) would want to know if those photos are actually pictures of a guard. A guard who (not to mention) Hammond actually represented until Kravitz, Claire and Hammond dismissed C.C. (I wonder why?) from my lawsuit. But Hammond does not want justice. It is not within her job description to want justice. Hammond wants (and Claire shall deliver) summary judgment to get rid of this lawsuit… Will Meiers and Stratton etc. use these photos as a pretext to transfer me again? Only time will tell. But do tell reporters etc. that this is perhaps the only book *in the world* with actual (authentic) photos of a current prison guard (in underwear) in a book. There you have it… Let it explode… I hope that the Dirty.com will publish them also. We are willing to give websites his name…

…Back to the campaign: I intend to go back to my roots. I'm going back home. I'll go to Antioch Baptist Church in McDonough, GA (Rev. F. L. Harris was the pastor. He also pastored County Line Baptist Church), Lamb of God Baptist Church, New St. John (in Atlanta – Rev. James Henderson was the pastor), Dixie Hills Baptist Church, to Rev. Dennis V. Lyons' church in Louisville, KY and to Greater 14th Street Baptist Church in Bessemer, AL etc. and I'll tell the pastors the truth: "I understand if you don't wanna let an ex-con preacher preach etc. But please pray on this one thing: Will you give me 12 minutes to address (not to preach) your congregation about a seminar we're having. We'll do a seminar for young men (and their fathers, mothers, siblings and girlfriends etc.) and I want to talk with them (in the seminar) about rebuilding our neighborhoods, our schools, our churches, our cities and our (i.e. "black") businesses by rebuilding our men and… our families."

Where did all of the young black men go? It's like a generation of young men have all been exported out of our urban cities (churches, schools and communities) and where have they gone? I can answer that question better than any professor, mayor or even a president. My entire platform is built upon answering the question: Where have all our boys gone since they left home? They have been exported back to the new slave plantation. In some kind of an amazing seismic, cosmic force (the chickens have come home to roost?) the *No J's* as well as the O.J. have both gone back to the plantation. At the behest of (often well-meaning) white people such as Bill Clinton (as well as Richard Nixon and Ronald Reagan). We wouldn't be here were it not for Clinton's AEDPA. And Claire would have to be fair were it not for Clinton's PLRA.

And I want to talk to churches, colleges, schools, teachers' unions, clubs and associations etc. about the cost of exporting our kids to prisons. Our churches will be empty at this rate in 20 years. Black men are far and few between in church, in college, in school and in business because we got shipped to the plantation (by design). And my approach is not to spend all day blaming whitey. Forget whitey. Often when you put blacks in charge of other blacks (i.e. Fulton County Jail in Atlanta) "we" will treat each other as bad as "they" treat us…

I wanna start in these little country towns (where I got my start preaching) like Winder, GA, Monroe, GA, in Macon, GA, Augusta, GA, Griffin, GA etc. and I want to talk about solutions.

I have an expert grasp of the internal dynamics inside gangs, jails and prisons. And… I know how prisons retard, dement and destroy mental, psychological and the social infrastructure of boys and men. And 95 percent of us leave prison in worse shape than we went in. And the cycle must be broken. We have to break this cycle. If it takes a village to raise a child it also takes a village to destroy that child. And our kids are in trouble. And I am a living, breathing in-the-flesh testimony of how prisons can divert a gifted human. I want to take "Just Mercy," "The New Jim Crow," *The Truth About O.J. Simpson*" and "*Kids Killing Kids*" with me. And I want to use "Just Mercy" and "The New Jim Crow" (other people's books) as well as my books as my *Bibles*. And I want to challenge every member, pastor, student, teacher, executive, paramedic, fireman, police officer, ex-con, gangs and… I want to challenge mayors, professors and professors etc. to join *NAPS*, *HEART* (Helping Educate At Risk Teens) and *Gang Bangers* for *God*, "My Brother's Keeper" and local ministries etc. and "Save Our Families."

I wanna visit every local radio show in every small town and talk about this new Gang (G.B.G.) aimed at ganging up against exporting our boys back to the plantations. I want us to be authentic. And the most unusual but effective and empowering way to begin this movement is by reconciling our families through the truth. We've got to confess our wrongs one to another. Apologize and to change. These secrets which we keep hiding and suppressing are killing us… I'll open men up by telling my story… I was thinking (again) today about how presumptuous of "us" (and me) to act like the only person I can relate to in Genesis 38, 39 and 40 etc. is Joseph. That's a lie. I can also relate to Jacob. And…to Joseph's brothers. I've wronged people too. I did not rape Ricardo Calvario period. I am wrongly convicted and it must be overturned. But I've been no saint. I've lied, cheated and deceived. I'm not just Joseph but I'm his enemies too. Plotting and scheming and hating. I did some stuff that when I look back I can't believe I did it. I hurt some people and stepped over some people and how did I disrespect people who were good to me? And I disrespected Ambassador Andrew Young (my most historical mentor), Jasper Williams and others.

Woe is me for I am undone. I'll call Don King and apologize to him. I must apologize to the folks I've wronged. Get the weight of the guilt and the shame off of me. And I'll tell folks in seminars etc. that we may not want to amplify everything. There's some apologies that son needs to make to his sister, or mother, or brother or lover alone. And that might not be enough to solve it. But if we get out of denial the only way we can get anywhere in the neighborhood of healing is if we confront those unspoken elephants and wounds in our families. Why did you leave me? Why did you molest, fondle, beat, abuse or rape me? Why did you give up on me? Why didn't you love me? Why didn't you help me? Why do you beat me? If you hit me one more time I promise I will leave you. I will not live with a man (or woman?) who beats me. You are angry with yourself. And I'm the closest thing to you that you can beat without feeling the pain. I don't want a spouse who can't love themself. If you don't get some help now I will leave you. I'm not gonna stay for the kids etc. It hurts kids to see their father beat their mother. You can't molest my daughter and then make love to me. I won't stand for this...

And we must get our kids out of these gangs by any and every means necessary. We will pray them out. We will preach, teach, reach, love school, educate and inspire them out. The gangs are an expressway into the prison system. Drugs and guns are wheels on the car. I'm going to ask Rev. Michael Pfleger, Rev. Joseph Lowery, Rev. Sharpton, Dr. Cornel West, Dr. Michael Eric Dyson, Charles Ogletree and Eric Holder etc. to be my advisors and my mentors. I'll ask Tyler Perry, Peter B. Lewis, Denzel Washington and Mark Zuckerberg etc. to underwrite this campaign. I'll go into a city and do a seminar with as few as 8 people. I'll look for ex-cons, lost boys, disgruntled students, stressed-out mothers and fathers etc. And I'll ask them to join us and let's take our families out of bondage, out of debt, out of the dungeon etc. Let's vaccinate and innoculate the coming children against the prison industrial complex. Our campaign is for whites, blacks, Asians, Indians and all Mexicans etc.

But there will be some special emphasis and focus. We will focus on the "Fergusons" of Atlanta, New York, Detroit, Sacramento and Chicago etc. We will focus on what the Ferguson(s) (i.e. the various police departments, local sheriffs, biased prosecutors and judges etc.) have contributed to the demise of black families. I'm not looking to organize a protest or a demonstration. I'm looking to pragmatically attack the *New Slave System* and to begin to degrade, demolish and to destroy it. It's good "for me that I've been afflicted (incarcerated) because I would have never known..."

Joseph could not have learned some of the unmentionables and "What they don't teach you at Morehouse" had he not gone to prison. The great President Mandela was prepared for the presidency by the prison. If you ever master the politics of the prison you are qualified (literally) to lead a nation. On that backdrop I intend to play a small part in helping to lead our nation away from Selma, AL, away from Cummings, GA, away from Ferguson, MO and away from the psychological residue of slavery. I'll say to pastors to come together and "Let us make man." I'll tell them to please let me tell your congregants why not to go to prison. Why not to let your child go there. And... I can speak to the fear of getting out. I am an expert on what goes through your mind when you say, "I'll be a 43-year old ex-con. Why would a T.D. Jakes, a Charles Blake or a Noel Jones etc. want to hear anything I gotta say? What the hell am I gonna do? I don't even have a suit? How am I gonna get home? How will I survive?"...

And we must set up teams to reintegrate ex-cons back into the church, the community and the job market. I'll ask Mayor Nutter, Senator Corey Booker and Congressman John Lewis etc. to help us. Not just by speechifying etc. but by educating. Let's teach our boys the power of reading, the power of articulation, meditation etc. We must teach leadership skills to our youths. We can model it on the JROTC program. We must (right here right now) begin to develop the trick to putting the unquenchable thirst for knowledge into the DNA of our kids. We must figure out meaningful ways to tie aspiration to education. I want teams of ex-cons reading newspapers out loud. Let's get together and teach public speaking, pronunciation and enunciation etc. We need to teach transformational creativity. We have to teach computer literacy and financial literacy. We...

(I need some guerilla "*Shermannators*" to go online and find William Zander, Mike Corsetto, Christopher Lyon, Keenan Harris and James Merryman etc. and tell them to get this book. And to send me an email. If we need to pay you to locate these people we will try to do so. Just let us know how we can help you. I don't mind paying a youngster $100.00 to search, locate and email Steven Fabian, Max Hodges, Malcolm Harris etc. I.E. There was a store clerk who was slapped by Katt Williams. And the clerk was fired. I don't even know his name. Find him and we can pay you. Find Raymond Flores, Chris Hues and Robert Krybyla etc. and we will pay you what we can…).

There needs to be a connection between the 'celebrity justice' which we see on TV and the aspiration of the masses to get equal justice. We need to use Ferguson, Trayvon Martin, and even Ethan Couch etc. as motivation to not just have a "moment." But let's develop a movement. This book really never was about O.J. the football player. It was/is about the No J in Atlanta, Cleveland, in Detroit, New York and in Miami. I wanted No J Hong (Ju), No J Hill (Timothy), No J Krybyla (Robert), No J Hues (Chris) and No J Bird (Christopher) to know that the only way you can get the kind of justice that Simpson got (in his murder trial) and that William Kennedy Smith got is you have to buy it. So you have to either 'not' commit crimes (the preferred route) or to generate a lot of wealth. Otherwise you will get No J (Joseph), No J (Mandela), No J (Hurricane Carter), No J (Ryan Ferguson) or No J Banks (Brian) *justice*. And No J justice will send a man to prison for life for a crime he did *not* do.

And Allison Claire and judges like Robert Altman etc. have no problem sleeping at night knowing that you are in prison and you did not do it. And the Claires of the judiciary are okay with your keepers (Stratton, Wenker, Bunnell etc.) stealing your manuscript, mail or money etc. as long as you can't get the media interested… Who cares?... I thought about my case the other day. It hurts you so bad that you can go years not thinking about it… All through my trial I kept saying that Ricardo Calvario was a prostitute and a female impersonator. And when a client discovered he was a man and got angry etc. Calvario would rob him. Ricardo was a speed freak.

And… Prosecutor Mary Hanlon and Judge Altman pretended to be baffled. They put on one helluva show. "Mr. Manning if I get any evidence that Calvario was actually a prostitute I'll dismiss this case," stated Robert Altman. And…(you can't make this stuff up) during my trial I stumbled upon another prostitute in the county jail. "What you got against gay guys?" he asked me…he went on to explain that he was a prostitute. Long story short I asked, "Do you know Ricardo?" He said, "Yes, I used to live with *her*. If she picks up a trick she'll try to give him a blow job only. Many men have done Ricard*a* never knowing she was a *he*." My heart stopped beating… This guy clearly described Ricardo Calvario. He told me Ricardo would lie, cheat, steal and rob. He said they prostituted together. But he had not seen Ricardo in 8 months or so. I bolted to the telephone. The self-same day a private investigator interviewed this guy. "He's credible and …there goes your ticket out of jail," he told me.

We informed Judge Altman as well as Prosecutor Mary Hanlon (this goes back to my lawsuit against Bunnell. I sued him for Valley Fever. He controls my mail and my movement. He simply stole the lawsuit. Claire? She simply dismissed my lawsuit. I'm suing Joseph Stratton aka Joseph Goebbels. And he controls my mail. And… I have to depend upon the people I'm suing to get my mail to witnesses against them. I'll never get justice when the courts and Corrections are intertwined). So Hanlon was responsible for having my witness brought to court to testify against Calvario. And... Hanlon had a D.A. investigator to come and interview my witness. And? He did not show up for court. Why? He got out at 2:00 a.m. Did he suddenly make bail? Absolutely not! Hanlon had all charges against *Bret Nelson* dismissed. And he was given (by Hanlon's office) a bus ticket to Oregon. And told to never come back to California. And... It took me a very long time to realize that both Hanlon and Altman knew that Bret Nelson's testimony would have sent me back to Atlanta, GA. And they were going to do whatever it took to send me to prison; period.

Ipso Facto, I'm convinced that Judge Allison Claire (in Sacramento Federal Court) definitely knows that credible lawyers like *Bob Blasier* and Douglas Oden were not lying in my case. Bob did not just wake up one morning and claim that my Valley Fever lawsuit was stolen. No? But Claire knows that one "Valley Fever" inmate was awarded $425 grand after a 6-week hospitalization. Well what do you think 14 months was worth? So Claire is not going to allow a guy with a 'voice' like mine to get a $2 million award... *"Sherman D. Manning* is a king. He does not wear a velvet robe. But he has a velvet voice and a velvet pen. And his keepers want him "silenced" stated a Swiss entrepreneur...

But what I can do is "tell" preachers, teachers, students, classes and the masses what happened to me. I can make "telling" this story of the No J justice the cause of my life. Why did I happen to meet Bob Blasier (the O.J. connection)? Why has my life played out the way that it has? And... I had almost given up. I had almost started to believe that I was who they said I was. Be careful whose voice you listen to. If they are sent to destroy you they will call you names long enough that you will begin to answer to the names they call you. *Words* are *spirits* and *words* have *power*. And you can *speak* a thing or even a person into reality. *Words* are *life* and they shape how you see yourself. Be careful who you listen to.

I found myself laying here about to give up. I said (to myself) "What will I do in February 2016? How can I leave a prison at 43 years of age with a rape conviction and succeed? What will I do? I am an orator, speaker and preacher. All I know is public speaking and preaching. But T.D. Jakes is not going to invite me to preach at The Potter's House in 2016. He does not know me. And I was convicted of rape. And...to add insult to injury I did not leave the preachers whom I know in good standing anyway. I used to call pastors (i.e. A. Lincoln James, Joseph Wells) and impersonate Jasper Williams in order to secure speaking engagements. So I won't be able to go to Salem and preach. I was an evangelist. But where will I preach? What will I do at 43 when I get out?"...

I had begun to doubt the destiny that had been spoken over me. I began to believe the critics. I began to believe the cynics. And... I wrote missives (in 2014) to 20 pastors and asked them to pray for me. And I asked them what they would advise me to do. "I'll be home in 2016. And I'll have nothing. And all I know is preaching. What would you advise me to do pastor?" And out of twenty (I wrote bulk letters to preachers at various times in 2014 etc.). I...even small-time pastors who I "knew" would at least write me a "form" letter, did not reply. "What am I going to do?" I asked myself (in August 2014). "Should I quit?" I won't even be able to preach. And what good is a medical license if no hospital will allow you to practice medicine? But…something told me not to quit. "Go to a third world country and you can practice medicine even without a license" a voice told me. And I thought about Ebola. And…I'll betcha "any" doctor will be welcomed "over there" I thought. Because if the need is bad enough people will forget what they "heard" about you. And if I'm starving bad enough I'll (take a chance) accept a meal from my enemy. If you get in enough trouble you will accept help from anybody.

And I began to think about the murder rate in Chicago. I thought about "Hands Up: Don't Shoot." I thought about the Bloods, the Crips the Northerners, Southerners, Nuestra Familia, the AB and the… All these prison gangs (with whom I reside at Folsom State Prison) that are running the streets. They run the guns and the drugs. And mothers are losing their children to gangs, the penitentiary and the cemetery. And nobody is reaching them. Nobody is dedicating their life, their creativity and their full energy to reaching the No J's. And the inner cities are all messed up. And boys (especially black boys) will still pick up a gun faster than they'll pick up a damn book. And we have these "boys" who are 18, 28, 48 and they have men's bodies but a boy's mentality. And they can't read, write and count. And the ignorance amongst many (not "all") of these young men is metastasizing throughout inner cities. And they're dropping out of schools and into gangs like flies. And we have an intellectual ISIL in these hoods. We have an educational ISIS right in *No J America*.

Our schools have been beheaded. We build jails and prisons in America. But we don't build schools and libraries anymore. And the poor (black and white alike) are as mad as hell. They watch banksters steal $10 billion and get away with a "fine." And they go and steal $10 dollars and have to do time. And once they are caught in this system they'll never get out. The rich get 'ACCESS' and they get to write a letter. And nobody gives a damn about them. And I've sat here and watched the *economic waterboarding* of the poor. I've watched Wall Street get away with murder. And I keep seeing petty thieves come here to prison. And I say well… If I have to get a bullhorn and stand on a street corner I'll preach (and I've never liked street preaching! Just keeping it real… If I have to do that I will not have a cup for people to throw money into!!). If I have to go to a pastor's house and hold up a sign that says "Please let me speak to your congregation for ten minutes on Sunday. I want to tell them why not to go to prison. I want to tell them why it's so important to read!!..." I'll stand in front of Bishop so-and-so's house 30 days straight if I have to. And I won't leave until that pastor at least allows me to tell "him" my *Joseph Manning* story. I will go to Ferguson if I have to. But I can't die until God's plan for my life comes to past. And so…

It was September 6th, 2014 at about 11:00 a.m. My cell door opened and they said, "Come to the office you received a book." And I went and signed for a large manila envelope. And as I walked back towards the cell I looked at the envelope because it did not feel like a book. And they'd just told me on the telephone the day before that they were going to order me a CD by T.D. Jakes. But this could not be that, yet it felt like CD's. So I lifted up the envelope and looked at the return address. And I saw "Bishop Paul Morton" Atlanta, GA. And it had to be a mistake because I'd just written Bishop Morton in New Orleans a couple of weeks earlier. And why would Morton be in my home city when he's from New Orleans? And I'd just hung up the telephone with a friend in Atlanta earlier talking about what church will I attend (in Atlanta) when I get home? My pastor (Rev. Moses Lee Raglin) is dead. I wronged Jasper Williams! And none of the Atlanta pastors I'd written had written me back. And now I have an envelope in my hand from one of the 20 preachers who did "not" write back. But Bishop Morton was in my city? I said, "Oh, maybe they do his marketing out of Atlanta because I know Paul is in New Orleans. His brother James is in Atlanta."

And I had always loved to hear Paul sing. I'd never met him. But he sings that song (almost universally known) "We Offer Christ to You." Paul can sang. I'd never heard him preach. But I saw him on TV and I heard his testimony about Hurricane Katrina and how he ended up losing… And then he got cancer. And I'd wept… Because (believe it or not) Hurricane Katrina had changed my life. And I was in jail when it happened. But I internalized it to the point that I ended up going into a serious depression. When I saw the No J's stranded on rooftops; and I saw a little girl talk about watching her momma die; and I saw a black guy (I think he ended up moving to Atlanta) talk about holding his wife in his hands as tight as he could. But Katrina took her from him and he watched the love of his life die. And…

I listened to the Bev Smith radio show. And people who were trapped on rooftops called Bev crying. They called Bev to ask her… While they were trapped I'm listening to them on the radio. And Bush wouldn't help them and I couldn't. All I could do was listen and pray… "These women are weeping! They are *weeping*," I heard Bev say…and…I was depressed for months… So when I heard Paul on TV testifying (6 or 7 years later) it really moved me… So in August of 2014 I decided waste 48¢ on a letter to Bishop Morton. And I would have bet you (literally) $5 grand that I would get zero response. And if I did get a response it would simply be a "form" letter asking for a donation. And…

It is 11:05 a.m. and I walk back into that cell and I rip this gold envelope open. And it contains not one, not two, not four or five, but six CD's by Bishop Morton. One is singing and five are preaching. I listen to "We Offer Christ to You." Then I put on a sermon by Paul called "So That." I had the light off and the cell was dark. And I was alone and I listened… Midway through the sermon I was absolutely weeping. I could not stop the tears. Paul Morton was actually in my hometown preaching. So a pastor born in Canada, who built his mega-church in New Orleans, was now in my hometown, ministering to me while I was in a cave in California. And the message he was preaching was "my" message. I can't even hardly write this. It was surreal. God used a pastor I've never met to preach me up out of the belly of a whale. This man preached me up out of my fear, my loneliness and my doubt. And…

Thank you Jesus. I couldn't believe they wrote me back. I could not believe they sent me 6 CD's and did not ask for one red cent. And… Lord have mercy. This is so much bigger than "pay it forward" and all that stuff. Listen to me today. God touched "somebody" in New Orleans and got them to "touch" somebody at Paul Morton Ministries. And He directed them on which CD's (specifically) to send to me. I believe that with everything that is inside of me. And Paul can preach. And his wife can also preach. And I lay there in the dark cell weeping. And I got up and sat at the edge of my bunk and I could not believe it… And…

(Yes) I certainly do hope and pray that I can "preach" for Paul. God just might instruct Paul to let me preach for him my first Sunday home (and He might not). But either way I will go to Paul's church when I get home. And I hope to travel and preach (across the country) every Sunday. But…my tithes will go to Paul's church until the day I die. That's crazy but I mean that. I write hundreds of letters (all over the world) every month. And the only preacher who responded with some "word" which was "life support" for a preacher who had been asking God, "Who? Where? When?"… I have never met Paul Morton. But he happens to be in the city where I'm going (in less than ten months). And this word got me up. And you think I'm not going to his church when I'm home? You are out of your mind. I'll probably only have one suit when I get there but I'm on my way…

Truly the Lord God Almighty revealed Himself to me (through the preached word) on September 6, 2014. I got touched by heaven; the preaching, the organ, the style of preaching etc. took me home… Preachers if you want to build your church you ought to do like Paul did and not forsake the prisoners. Why do you think Muslims were so strong in prisons? Because they were the only ones who would reach out to a Malcolm X while he was in prison. And too often the church refuses to reach men at their worst. But because Muslims reached Malcolm in the prison, he transmogrified his whole life. He read the entire dictionary in his cell. And…when he did go home he went straight to a Muslim temple. How could I not go to Paul's church? God I wish churches would reach out to guys in prison (period). And especially to the ones who are getting out. But when they get out they are "branded," *broke*, busted and *disgusted*. And how can they come to "your" church when they don't have a pair of dress shoes?...

…I will talk about the militarization of local police and prison guards (California prison guards also received military weapons from the Pentagon). I will call Narcisco Morales (you can Google him and tell him to email me now please), Kory Carico, Brenton Thwaites, Angus T. Jones, Brandon Cryderman, Mat Herman, Brandon Brockhouse (Natomas), Brad Alexander and Justin Brewer etc. and I will ask them to join me on a campaign. I will ask Jake Bartlett, Zoard Janko and Brian Radut etc. to just join me as I take a crusade across this country. I want to lead a war on illiteracy. A war on dropping out of school. A war on joining gangs. A war on using drugs. I have an internal expertise on the inner demons that lead to prisons. I know how "not" to become a slave. And it is going to take a "village" to save our nation's "lost boys." I'm embedded at "ground zero" for the destination for high school dropouts. I know every road that leads to a prison. And I'm going home to simply *elucidate* that roadmap to my people. We will have clinics, seminars, digi-tours, workshops and rallies. We will wake up the neighborhood. I will do my master's will… I need *Kyle Dickey* to join us…

Because I had to go through this I can tell you about it. Nothing happens in our lives by accident. Bishop Paul Morton reminded me (on September $6^{th}$) that God has a divine plan for my life. God allowed me to go to prison and to come through all of this "so that" I could become an expert on police brutality, an expert on gangs, and an expert on criminals, Corrections and on the prison Industrial Complex. My purpose is in the "that." I had to deal with this "that" in my life. I look back to Joseph. Prison is like being in hell. And now that I'll get out it'll be like the rich man in the Bible who said, "Please let Lazarus come down with a drop of water to cool my scorching tongue." He asked for *witnesses* to go tell his family that they "don't want to come down here where I am in Hades." I'll be back from Hades. And I'll go to colleges, schools and to churches and give my book reports. "Here's my book *report* on

Hades. And here is why you don't want to go there"... You have got to purchase the CD by Paul Morton called "So That." I encourage every person to call 888-424-2643 and order his sermon "So That"...

My test has been long and it has been difficult. But this test will be transformed into a *testimony* that will take me to Harvard, to Stanford and to Yale etc... "The storms that you are dealing with in your life; God is about to turn it around." Paul told me on 9/6/14... "But I want you to know, brethren, that the things which *happened* to me have actually turned out for the *furtherance* of the *gospel*!" You must understand that Ricardo Calvario lying on me has actually furthered the gospel. Are you reading "this" book? There would be no "this book" if Ricardo had not lied on me. No wrongful conviction for me and I would not have joined this fellowship with Joseph. "So that it has become evident to the whole palace guard, and to all the rest, that *my chains* are in Christ. And most of the brethren in the Lord, having become confident by my *chains*, are much more bold to speak the word without fear" (Philippians 1:12-14). Did you read what Paul said (I'm not talking Morton now but the apostle Paul in Philippians)? He's talking to you and me. But I want you to know brothers that the things (my *wrongful conviction*, all the racism I endured at Folsom State Prison) which *happened* in my life have actually turned out for the furtherance of the gospel. So I've not been wasting away. I've not been forgotten about. God knows exactly where I am and how long I've been here. He knows what I did *not* do. And He knows how dark these days have been and what I've lost. And He sent Paul Morton (on September 6th) to preach to me about Paul (in Philippians 1:12-14) to tell me it was *about* to *turn* around. My parole date is 2/14/16 but I believe God is going to get me home before 2016. They (the parole board) have told me no, over and over. But I believe...

I thought this was gonna bring me down. But Paul Morton says God can use this *wrongful* conviction to *bring me up*... The strongest steel comes out of the hottest fire. And I am in the fire right now... The brothers (in colleges, in churches, in the streets and in the juveniles etc.) will become more "confident by my chains"... "So that"... "My bonds in Christ are manifest in all the power and in all other places." Paul Morton said that God is getting ready to put me in some places (a special place) that I would have never been in my life *because* I was lied on. Don't give me a pity party because God is not sleep. He allowed this for a reason. I know my purpose and I know what I've been called to do. And I'm reminded of a song: "Sometimes, I have to remind myself of what I've been called to do. When I bow down that's how I remember what He anointed me to do. I anoint myself." So God sent Paul to "remind" me of what I've been "called" to do. "And you become followers of us and of the Lord, having received the word of God in much affliction, with joy of the Holy Spirit. So that you were examples to all that believe" (1 Thessalonians 1:6-7)...

Somebody is watching me. And when I get out they will say that if Joseph could make it; if *Sherman* can make it with all of that stuff they say about him. Then if *Sherman* can get out of prison and preach, teach lecture, write and elucidate, then I'm gonna press my way out of this gang. I'm gonna put this gun down and pick up a book. I'm gonna go back to school and get my diploma or degree. If *Sherman* can still hold his head up after all the mess I heard about him. They told me Sherman had a "life" sentence in prison. They told me he was not a preacher anymore. I even heard he was dead. But I just saw him on Tavis Smiley, on Steve Harvey and… I heard on the radio that he has a podcast. He's reading books on CD and preaching… If *Sherman D. Manning* can rise up over a "rape" conviction. Then I will survive this ghetto. I can get up out of this hood. I can get out of this gang and become one of those "*Gang Bangers* for *God*"… Somebody will look at my life after all of this. And my life will become an example that God can still "turn it around for you"… Now you may have to lose so that you can get get…

When I listened to Paul on 9/6/14 he talked about it. He had 10,000 members at Greater St. Stephens in New Orleans. And when the hurricane came he lost his church. He lost his cars. He lost his house. Jobs lost… And what pastor do you know of loses 10,000 members in a day? His members were scattered in 32 different states. Who even fathoms a story like this? This is movie-making material. Paul lost it all and he was rebuilding… But God told him to go to Atlanta and start a church… I can't get past pastoring a church with 10,000 members and losing them in one day. Members are scattered to 32 different states. And you are a pastor. How do you come back from that? And then Paul got colon cancer. And… I lost my church, my house, my cars, my friends and now here comes cancer… But God will turn your situation around. But God will give you something better. When it looks like your back is up against the wall here comes God. But Paul said God told him "I know you lost everything. But do you *trust* me?" And Paul said yes. Well your latter days shall be greater than your former days. Morton said think about something that makes you sad. And give that to Jesus. He can handle that. Christ can handle that. Listen to me. I listened to Paul and his wife for ten hours on September 6, 2014. Then I ended up writing all night. I lay down at 6:00 a.m. I could not stop…

Paul said he had folks *laughing* at him. They said Paul Morton it's over for you. You are finished… I can hear Stratton, Wenker, Bunnell and prison guards telling me it's over. But… They thought I was gonna die when I got Valley Fever. When I was down to weighing only 96 pounds. When I spent 14 months in a hospital. When prison guards refused to even call my family and tell them if I were dead-or-alive. With no mail and no telephone calls. They thought if Valley Fever didn't kill me the loneliness would. But God had it in his hands. And… Paul said that he used to get very upset every time he thought (or talked) about Hurricane Katrina. Paul said, "But thank you Katrina (*prison*)! That 'that' got me to where I am." I started weeping as Paul preached that word. His "Katrina" was my "*prison*." And my prison might be "your" something "else." But Paul preached! The brother said, "Thank you cancer because I learned a little bit better. 'He was wounded for our transgressions. He was bruised for our iniquities. The chastisement of our peace was upon His shoulders. With His stripes we're healed.' Lord, you've been good. Thank you Katrina. You got me to where I am right now!... Lord have mercy.

…In another message Paul talked about the six winged angels. Only two wings were used for flying. The other 4 wings were used to "cover" themselves in the presence of God. "Cover your eyes!" I had all kind of talent. I was a gifted preacher. But I was using my gift as if it were "mine." And my gift would take me places that my character wouldn't keep me. I was focusing too much on gift and talent. But I need to cover my eyes. And let God do the work. And just like I was sitting in a cell on September 6th. God can touch Debra in New Orleans. He can have her to touch Paul in Atlanta. And what started for me in Atlanta might be "finished" because of what was preached to me on September 6th. God reached Paul and Paul reached me. And now God is reaching you right now. It's not over for you. That's what I want to do with conferences, seminars and clinics. I want to reach *broken brothers* and reassure them that there's still some blessings down inside of them. And my job will be to wake up that blessing that sleeps inside of them. I must encourage them and inspire them. I must use the "*messes* of my life as a *message*"... Have you ever heard of Greenbriar Parkway in Atlanta? I have and it used to be my stomping ground. And that's what I saw on that gold envelope on September 6th. God was moving through Paul Morton. And if you had any idea how close I've come to quitting; if you knew how frustrated, hurt and disappointed I was; if you could have seen me on September 6th at the side of my bunk; and if you could've seen me weeping at that word. You would know that God is an awesome God.

    I never thought I'd be able to say it but "Thank you *prison*!" Thank you Stratton, Wenker and... Y'all got me to where I am now. And... Even though you tried to kill me, thank you *Valley Fever*. If it wasn't for Valley Fever I wouldn't really believe that it was good for me that I've been afflicted. If I'd not been afflicted I couldn't know God like I know Him. So I prophesy that this prison is a steppingstone. God may even take me to the White House to meet Barack Obama. And I wanna see what Bunnell, Stratton and Wenker will think when they see that "Ex-con, prolific author and criminal justice consultant *Rev. Sherman D. Manning* met with President Obama today!" Wouldn't that be awesome? But whether I make it to the White House or not is not nearly as important as making it to the church house. I just wanna get back to church. I'm gonna take my "*Let Us Make Man*™," "*Creating Monsters*™" and the "*Truth and Reconciliation*™" tours all over this country. Call my tour whatever you want. You can say I'll be on "The Chittlin Circuit" if you want. But I wanna get Corey Thomas, Joshua Stipp, Tyler Hadziki, Maxwell Hanger and Jesse Potash. I want to get Jason Sutherland, Tim Goebbel, Kevin Lynn, Kory Carico and Tim Fox to go with us. I want to get Alexander Dugdale, Dillon Banionis, Chris Butts, Brad Alexander (Sacto), Daniel Bugriyev, Mark Kashirets, Joseph Latham (in Oregon) and Brian Glasscock etc. and go change the world. If we can find James Merryman, David Joyner, Billy York, Eddie Cannon and... Scott Johnson (in Warner Robins, GA) we can revolutionize our communities. I am an example. Thank you prison... And now 21 books (in prison) later? Thank you prison. Thank you Valley Fever. I know what God can do now...

    It is 4:11 a.m. right now. And I can't stop the *pen* from *moving*. Thank you Jesus. I know what God can do. I can't stop this now. I want to reach that homeless man, the prostitute, the whoremonger and the crack addict. I want them to know that *it's me* too. I know exactly what it feels like to wonder do I still count? Do I matter? Will I *ever* get out of this? And the only reason I now know the answer is because I went *through* this. If you had to climb a mountain alone and it took you 16 years to climb it. People you love are gonna die while you are trying to climb that mountain. You will lose a lot of stuff while you're climbing it... But if you make it to the top you'll thank God for it. And all the while you were climbing God was doing, growing and building stuff up in you that you didn't even think about. All that pain in your legs, calves and triceps. And now 16 years later you get a mirror and you can't even believe it's you. Where did all this back arm come from and whose calves are these? But see you were alone and it has its benefits as well as disadvantages. You don't have a sparring partner… But you don't have time to "flex" and play "boys" games. You in too much pain to play. And you have no idea after 15 years and 11 months that you are about to walk right into your miracle. It's right around the corner. And when you come down off that mountain your very *presence* is a *testimony*. And all you need to do is tell us what you did. And your telling will teach us how to climb our mountain(s). And I wanna go back home and testify. I don't wanna pastor I want to testify. I want to clear my name. I want to apologize to the people I actually did "wrong." I want to apologize to Rev. Andrew Young, Rev. Jasper Williams and to Stella Bryant. And I want to teach… If you pray for me I'll get there.

  I want to find "Andy" the volunteer who used to be with Homeboy Industries (can you find him?). I want to reach Jacob Gabriel, Justin Brewer, Tal Safron and Max Wiseltier. I want Keenan Harris, John Jody Bear, Mike Crowder, Chad Sherman and… I want to reach the lead singer for the group "Before We Exit." I have a job for Tim Urban, Michael Castro and Charles Askew. I have a job for Alex Lambert and Tyler Grady. Help us to reach them. I want to reach Alex Mueller, Joshua Orapello, Aaron Wangler and Dustin Sisco. I want to reach Alec Loorz so I can tell him that Ryan Couch lied on me. Alec Loorz is a great dude. And we were going to work together. But a prison guard thug (Ryan Couch) called Alec Loorz and "lied" viciously on me. I want to talk to Alec and to work with him. I want to reach Jacob Goodin, Austin Ho, Nathan Peterson, Scott Czeda and Jeff Gerber. I want to reach Roger Walthorn and Charles Lutz (in MN) and Brandon Scott (Auburn). And if we get Chris Hues, Lane Garrison, Neil Davidson and *Robert James Carlson* to join our campaign, we can change the world…

  I don't know what your Hurricane Katrina is. I don't know how old you'll be when you run into your "Valley Fever." But I do know that you can make it. I do know that you may be broken… Dreams *broken*. Vision broken. Marriage or job broken. Your criminal record might be *broken*. But *blessings* come from the *breaking*. You can get back up again. Even if a *man* claims you raped him. You can get up. You can rise above any obstacle. But… Get back in school. Get back to reading and studying… I need some successful guys (like Jake Silberman, Van Harris, Gary Browning and James Nesmith etc.) to help us motivate dudes to read, to study to think and to learn… I'm searching for Raymond Flores, Johnny Keyser, Iman Taha Hassane, Eugene Langford and Austin Whalen etc. And I need their help. There's life after this and life after that. There's life after dope and life after crack. But we must believe. You can if you think you can. Your storm won't last always…

  …I will go home and I'll call pastors, professors, lawyers, city council persons and I'll call mayors. And I will ask them (i.e. Mayor Michael Nutter and Kasim Reed etc.) to tell us what they think we can do to get better. What can be done to help ex-cons get jobs and housing? What support groups can churches put in place? I will ask Mayors to tell us what we can do to become meaningful members of our communities and cities. I'll ask them to ask pastors to help us. I'll then turn around and ask Pastors to ask Mayors to help us. And we will have to have town hall meetings etc. I'll bring our "*Joseph* Project" and *HEART* (Helping

Educate At Risk Teens) together. And perhaps *NAPS* (National Association for Public Safety) can ask Senator Cory Booker and even Rand Paul to meet with us. I don't mind some politicians getting photo-ops etc. But we need a sustained effort to revitalize the No J's... I will literally do seminars on the *No J Factor*. And I will take pains to explain how and why O.J. went to prison as soon as the "no" (no money) went before the "J." And there will be times when I won't be exciting, entertaining or enthusiastic. Sometimes I'll have to have candid, almost 'clinical' conversations with gangs, ex-gangsters and with wannabe gangsters. But my efforts will not start or stop just because a camera is rolling. I might even "ban" the media from every event. Prison has given me a long, tiring, painful and stressful lesson on how to keep working even with the media acting like you don't exist. Don't mind the media just mind the work. It's hard but I learned this lesson in Hades. I've been through the story and now I do see the glory. All I have to do is "show" people my wounds. My spiritual and psychological battle scars will speak volumes...

My clinical approach to crime and punishment will be based upon studies I've conducted and been a part of for over a decade. I conducted one such study which assembled a Dream Team of Corrections experts, psychological and criminal experts. I worked with my team (via teleconferencing and in writing) in Switzerland. And we worked with Warden Jimbo Walker, Patricia Kennedy, Captain Steve Vance, Captain Fred Schroeder, Captain Rhonda Carter and Associate Warden Lisa Johnson-Dovey. We also worked with psychiatrists like Dr. Jennifer Heitkamp, Carlos Solis, Franklin Curren (of Harvard Medical School) etc. We held meetings with these Wardens, Doctors as well as psychologists (i.e. Dr. A. Duran, Dr. Gregg, Dr. Jarman, Dr. T. Friedman, Dr. Jeff S. Kaye and Dr. Gonzales etc.) and prison staff. I held conferences with Daniel Bugriyev (a great man that we need to reach again), Mark Kashirets (where is Mark?), Dustin Nicolodi, Adam Lane and Chairman John Burton etc. And I conferred with my lovely cohorts (partners in crime). And in spite of all the bullcrap I learned a lot. And...

I learned very quickly that (by and large) white people (who are 50 years old and older. And especially those without a college degree) do not believe that the prison and judicial system are racist. You can't convince Steve Vance that the system is racist. Ipso Facto, blacks and whites see things very differently. The good news is that is not true with younger white people. So... Many white people saw Trayvon and they watched Garner get murdered on camera by a cop; using an illegal choke hold. And his "crime" was "selling cigarettes?" And 75-80 percent of whites 45 years old and older saw nothing wrong. "He shouldn't have been selling cigarettes" one prison guard told me. And... C.O. M. Austin and C.O. Orozco clearly saw nothing wrong with the killings...

I wish I had the skills of Dr. Martin Luther King Jr. But I do not. I'm not Malcolm X. But I did learn a lot when Ambassador Andrew Young was nice enough to take me under his wings and mentor me. And I also learned a lot when Rev. Hosea Williams mentored me. But I'm not going to be trying to recreate the 60's in 2016. I won't be trying to convince white people to love me. I'll love them because Christ says so. I'll never be a racist. But if you don't want to talk to me I'll return the favor. But I will have to look black boys in the face and tell them the (cold, calculated and clinical) truth: "Youngster there are tens of thousands of prison guards (i.e. Joseph Stratton, Ryan Couch, Ryan Wenker and Breckenridge etc.) who can't wait to meet you. They want you to go to prison. They feed their families, educate their kids and buy houses off of you and me going to prison. If just 30 percent (just 30) of the young people who committed crimes last year did not offend this year, they would have to lay off prison guards. There are a lot of people who want you to rape, rob and murder. You are job security for them. And that includes these fake-ass judges too. They get to posture for the cameras and look humane etc. But Gerry Spence says those judges are "dead"…"

And I'll continue telling the youngsters that "but let's be honest; Hands Up: Don't Shoot? We not only have to say that to rogue, evil and oppressive cops. But sadly (can we be real?) I as a black man must tell black gangbangers "Hands Up: Don't Shoot." Let's be authentic… So I'll stand with you and tell every rogue cop and prison guard "Don't Shoot." But… In Chicago, in Detroit and all over America I'll have to tell non-cop black men "Don't Shoot." How many more mothers have to bury their babies just because you got mad at them about a ballgame? How many more funerals? Hell: I've seen them kill a guy and then go shoot up the damn funeral. We have some internal work and "therapy" that we need to do. We must do it in groups, in churches, with books and in prayer. We have got to figure out why we wanna kill, rape and maim each other. They don't care about you. They (Allison Claire, Kelli Hammond, John Q. Prison Guard) don't give a damn about your black ass." I'll tell youngsters that "my favorite part of a movie called "Boys in the Hood" was when Ice Cube's brother was murdered in the street. The following morning he said… "I watched the news last night right. And they was (sic) talking about stuff going on in other countries and all that. But they didn't say nuthin (sic) bout my brutha. I said you know why? Either they don't *know*, don't *show* or just don't *care* about what's going on in the hood." And…

I will tell youngsters that "there are many people who don't give a damn about your black (or poor white) ass. They make money off of prisons. Somebody has got to fill 'em up. Who builds prisons? It's a $ trillion industry. Who makes and sells handcuffs, leg irons, tasers and guns? Hell – Vice President Dick Cheney owns some prisons. But… Readers and writers are not allowed in prisons. If you don't want prison go to school. Over 70 percent of us prisoners can barely read. Only 12 percent of U.S. (2.7 million inmates) can read at above the $8^{th}$ grade level. So if you stay in school and graduate. If you get your diploma. You are not welcomed in a prison." I'll tell them "not everybody is out to get you… I.E. look at my checkered past. And after all the bad things they say about me look at *John L. Burton*. I call him Uncle John… Why would a brilliant lawyer who is the most powerful man in California endorse a person convicted of "rape?" He's the chairman of the Democratic Party! But he supports me. Why? God! That's first and that is foremost. And… If the former President of the California State Senate thought I raped that man he would not give me the time of day. Burton despises rapists. But read what he writes about me. And let this be an example that no matter how bad "it" looks for you; if you will study, read, write, think, pray and hold your head up, God will send you an angel. Out of nowhere you'll have to say here comes God via Chairman Burton. Here comes God on September 6, 2014 through Bishop Morton. If you don't faint. I would have fainted if I had not believed that I would see the goodness of the Lord in the land of the living."…

I will send out a nationwide call to youngsters asking them to tell us what they think needs to be done to ameliorate high school dropouts. I want to be interactive and ask good students, fair students, students who have recently graduated as well as student dropouts etc. what they think we can do to catch dropouts and save their lives. We take dropping out of school too casually in America. We've removed the stigma and the shame. How can that be okay? So I want to sound an alarm in Zion. I want to mobilize a desperate campaign against illiteracy. Because if you are a good reader you're more likely to finish school. Finish school and you'll never be a cellmate. We need a war on illiteracy. We need more than words. We need words, money, enthusiasm, town hall meetings and clinics. Hell I might go to Arne Duncan and tell Duncan let's make history together. Never in the history of this great nation has an ex-con gotten out and went on a speaking tour with the Education Secretary. "Arne lets make history. Why can't we make history? Let's you and me go to 10 high schools (in ten days) across the country. You speak and you give me 15 minutes. And I will argue that education prevents *incarceration*. We can do this together Mr. Duncan." If he says no I'll ask the Attorney General. Let's do one event together. This would be unprecedented. I wanna have a Sunday (i.e. the first Sunday in July, 2016) where every American pastor spends at least five minutes urging congregants to find a dropout and encourage them to go back to school. It's critical and it's crucial. This is a life and death matter. We can't let dropping out be "just another day at the park!!" What the hell's going on?

I have a 23-year old (Jacob Paske) who runs *GBG* – youth operations. And I intend to work closely with Jacob on some strategies to promote reading and school campaigns. I will let Jacob Paske and other youngsters (Timothy Hill, Kory Carico, Jacob Faulkender, Tylor Murray-Clark and Cody Baetge) decide what strategies we should execute. But we're going on a national tour whether you attend or not. And if I enter into a place that does not receive me, I shall take the same advice which Jesus gave His disciples. I'll shake the dust off of my feet and leave. Call me a disciple of education. Call me a reading lover… My dad woke me up at 7:00 a.m. on a Saturday. I was only 13 and going to sleep in. He gave me an autobiography and said wake up and read it because "how can a black man stay in the bed on a Saturday morning when men run the world?" He told me that "they're playing golf right now trying to figure out new strategies to cause you to continue to sleep." I got up and I read the book.

Andy Young told me that "only 3 percent of the world populations are the movers and shakers. Three percent of the humans on the planet run the world. And what do they each have in common?" he asked me. I said, "They're all rich." He said, "What else?" I didn't know, I was only 13. He said, "They all *read* several books per month. They read newspapers every day. And they subscribe to publications like "The Economist." Shortly thereafter Andy Young got me a subscription to "The Economist."… Andy Young, Hosea Williams, Rev. Moses Lee Raglin and now Chairman John Burton have all been angels and mentors. God is an awesome God…

I want to talk to Cory Booker (I repeat), Rand Paul, Michael Nutter and to Kasim Reed. I want to talk to pastors (i.e. Bishop Paul Morton, Pastor Debra Morton, Rev. Timothy Flemming etc.) about inviting us to do a "*Joseph* Project" crusade at their church(es)… It will take pastors, professors, prisoners and parishioners etc. working together to heal people... Our young men running around in these neighborhoods are just modeling anger, poverty and crime. Hanging around crippled people makes not walking look normal. We have high school dropouts reaffirming each other and reinforcing one another... And after they run together on the streets, then they come to prison and do it too. And prison is a melting pot of emerging thugs and killers. I need Paul Morton, Otis Moss and Greg Boyle etc. to help to break that curse. I'll be calling for dramatic actions to change these schools and to recruit dropouts back to schools... *Hands Up: Don't Shoot!* I think we must also tell Bloods and Crips "*Hands Down: Don't Shoot.*" Chicago has 100,000 documented gang members. The police must be held accountable for abuse. But with over 20,000 murders last year it's not the police alone who are killing us... *Hands Down: Pick-up-a-book.* Being or feeling stupid is extremely humiliating. And humiliated people often snap. Illiteracy is humiliating... Readers are leaders and Reading makes you powerful. Reading gives you swag. What is a lawyer? Lawyers go to law school and they become lawyers because of what they *read*. Doctors enter into medical school as Misters and Miss. But they become doctors because of what they *read*. So I can go in as Mister. And if I *read* enough I can exit as *Dr.* Manning...

I need you to help us get this book to Todd Dressler, Hugh Michael Hughes, Christopher Eavey (Richmond, LA), Keith Habersberger, Jesus Ayala (and his sister Viola), Tyler Yagley, Collins Key, DJ Carpenter, Forrest Farjadian, *Blair Casey*, Peter Knegt, Kaleb Leeper, Teddy Coffey, Ben Jeske, Luke Kelly, Brooks Buffington, Daniil Turitsyn, Dominic Burrows, PJ Vogt, Jamieson Knopf, William Haskell, Andy Hinds, Hasib Habibi, Paul Tassi and Joel Northrup etc. tell them to get this book...

If you are hurt and broke you need help. You need to learn what to do with that pain... At conferences I'll tell kids that when you drop out of school you play into the system. They want you to be stupid so you can go fill up their prison system. When you fall asleep in school or refuse to read or think, you volunteer to be a slave. Once a kid has been suspended from school he's 60 percent more likely to go to prison. All the signals which lead to prison are visible. Just look. And we must transform this from the bottom to the top. They bring drugs to Chicago from Mexico. And an army of gang members distribute more drugs. I want an army of young people selling books and reading. I call for reading groups, think tanks and classes. Let's become a real education nation...

I was able to set up a telephone call (monitored) with O.J. Simpson in late 2013. We talked for 30 minutes. Certainly O.J. spoke highly of Bob (Blasier). But he denied the murders etc. And he made himself a "victim." O.J. is now No J Simpson. But O.J. can still serve as a powerful example of how not to live life. O.J. can be a role model for how not to become so arrogant and misguided... I can serve as an example of how you can be gifted but conflicted. I was gifted but messed up. And what can you do when your gift will get you to the palace but your discipline won't keep you in the palace?... Did y'all see Mr. Rice (O.J. Simpson, Jr.) knock his fiancée out in that elevator? I can take that one elevator travesty and combine that with the way O.J. used to beat Nicole. And I can lecture on that for the next 30 years. Rice? Simpson? = both black. Both talented. Both in the NFL. Both slick, engaging and affable. One of the things Bob Blasier always told me is how nice and how engaging O.J. is. Bob says he and O.J. once watched a "touching" movie together. And both he and O.J. were crying. I can only imagine the Harvard trained lawyer and the pro football player bawling because of a movie. But in all seriousness I recall thinking "O.J.? Nice?" I always thought him to be narcissistic and as arrogant as hell. But when I thought about how nice Bob says O.J. is it now helps me to understand Rice. There are these people who can play football, paint, draw or whatever. And they can smile and disarm or charm. But they are "evil" on the inside. They have repressed rage and they remind me of two people whom I've studied religiously.

I was housed with the infamous *Eric Menendez* for seven years. We worked together (as porters) for five years. I was then (you can't make this stuff up) housed with Lyle Menendez (at MCSP) for 2 years. I refused to speak to Eric when I first met him. I saw guards like *Joseph Stratton* etc. who were in-love with Eric. And I saw guards (literally) like Ralls, Stratton, Wenker etc. ask him for his autograph. And I kept thinking to myself this man blew the head of his mother off. And you want his autograph? I saw the president of the CCPOA and *Joseph* on the SHU yard having sex with Eric. I could not believe my eyes (but read my books "*Why They Hate Obama,*" "*America's Richest Pedophiles*" and "*Why Republicans Go to Hell*")… But prison is full of perverts (both inmate and guard alike). One was giving Eric fellatio and one was screwing him (read my book "*Kids Killing Kids*")… Candidly? Donald Trump reminds me of Eric *Menendez*.

And as I studied Eric Menendez I learned more about evil, fraud and "predators" than a course at Harvard (or Morehouse) could have taught me. Eric Menendez taught me how authentic the cliché "smiling faces sometimes tell lies" can be. He completely loves himself. He is completely okay sleeping at night. And he walked around here at New Folsom as if he had done the nation a favor by assassinating his parents. I didn't read about Eric or hear about him. I was housed with him. I worked with him and even loaned him money. And… He told me that his father and Lyle were molesting him. I asked why he still writes Lyle if Lyle was molesting him and… Then I see guards (Stratton, Wenker, Mike Jiminez, Mike Martel etc.) smuggling food, computers etc. in to Eric. And…one of the reasons they (George Stratton and Mike Martel) transferred me out of Folsom was because I'd spotted Eric and the guards and they thought I was going to write about it… I arrived at MCSP and Lyle was inquiring about Eric as he had a man-crush on his own brother. But… They're both psychopaths and they smile (Simpson, Rice = nice), nod and wink. And if you piss them off they will cut your head off…

I will take what I've learned (up close and personally) from living with murderers, rapists and molesters. I will take what I've learned… Daniel Henson? He was my next door (cell) neighbor. Daniel was one of the nicest dudes I've ever met in prison. But he was an "Eric" (aka "Rice = nice," aka "okay O.J."). Daniel was 16 years old when his parents tried to break up him and his girlfriend. Daniel killed his stepmom, dad, siblings and the dog. And… What also fascinated me was how badly Stratton, Wenker, Ralls and Martel etc. would treat me because they "thought" (erroneously) that I "raped" a man. But how they were simply "fascinated" with killers? I used to wonder how can killing your parents be okay? It's sick…

But it took me a very long time to learn the dynamics of the prison "subculture." And it is that deep understanding of a dark place such as prison which I will utilize to give lectures and seminars etc. across the country. I have studied these guys and learned what makes them tick. The defining question of my life (while incarcerated on a wrongful conviction) has been "how can Eric Menendez stand here and talk Tony Robbins, politics, sports and spirituality with me and… How can he laugh and smile and go *sleep like a baby* knowing that he blew his mother's head off?" And… "How can Ryan Wenker and Joseph Stratton etc. kiss the asses of killers and cater to people whom they know committed murder and…drive home and sleep like a baby?" I understand (clearly) now. And my job (at home) will be to interpret, translate and convey what I've learned while being *embedded* in my studies (hell) to students, professors and to leaders. It has been a long, tedious, painful, fascinating and a complicated study. And I've had the wise counsel of some brilliant psychiatrists (Dr. Franklin Curren, Dr. Carlos Solis, Dr. Jennifer Heitkamp) and psychologists (Dr. Jarman, Dr. Davidson, Dr. Duran etc.) while I was learning.

    I have walked "through the valley of the *shadow* of *death*" with known murderers. And… (again this stuff is fascinating) some of these psychopaths (i.e. Eric Menendez etc.) had convinced themselves that they were better than me. Because they believed (erroneously) that I had "raped" a man (and yes I do believe people who actually do commit rape are sick and wicked!). But "all I did was kill my dad and blow my mom's head off. Then I opened my dad's chest, bought a Ferrari and went out and partied and"… Guards treated Menendez like a king and *Sherman* like a killer… I can not wait to come and explain to you (at Yale, Stanford, Harvard, Emory University etc.) what I have learned about why, how and when people kill… I can actually (O.J.) teach students "*How to get away with murder.*" And… "How to" understand a "murderer." And… I'll tell you (at Stanford, Morehouse, Clark Atlanta) all about what the *Menendez* brothers, Daniel Henson and a garden variety of other murderers taught me. And I'll share with you what all psychopaths have in common…

    I want readers to find Adam Knox, Gabriel D. Anderson, Cody and Hayden etc. Help us to find AJ Ali, Matthew Tankleff, Justin Brewer, Joe Briggs, Kyle Pratt, Cody Baetge, Eddie Cannon and James Nesmith etc… And… I want to work with Christopher Bird, Brian Banks and Ryan Ferguson. I want to work with Zack Everhart, Alex King, Daniel Kovarbasich and Lucas Nelson. And I want to share what I've learned with you… "He maketh me to lie 'down in green pastures.'" Prison makes you "lie down in the presence of evil." Prisons are houses of hell. Prison is a place that the wicked will come "against" you to "eat up my flesh" (Psalm 27:2). In prisons you find people who "*breathe* out violence." You find workers (Stratton, Martel etc.) of iniquity (Psalm 28:3) "who speak *peace* to their neighbors, but *evil* is in their *hearts*."

    Eric Menendez, Daniel Henson and Lyle etc. have taught me to understand why Blasier thinks O.J. is so affable. And why Ray Rice was so nice when he apologized for assaulting his wife etc. They *speak* peace… But evil (they will cut your head off and shove it up your anus) is in their hearts… Pray for me please… God can turn it around. I hope to see you (at Grinnell College, Emory University etc.) on the lecture circuit…

*Sherman D. Manning*

The guard in underwear is C.O. *Colby Compton*. I've decided to reveal his name. Wonder what his dad and his wife will think when they see his photos? We also have *handwritten* letters by Colby…!

## **Long Walk To Freedom**

That is the title of President Mandela's celebrated book. And... I never thought I would have such a *long* walk to freedom. And I'm supposed to tell everybody that I'm not angry. And I'm supposed to be "politically" correct and talk about a lack of anger, etc. But I would be lying. I am indeed angry that I was tried without a lawyer and convicted by an all-white jury. I'm as angry as hell. But I'm not bitter. The Lord says to be "angry and sin not." Bitterness destroys the vessel that it consumes. My anger is channeled and directed...

After I argued with *Charles Manson* I met his neighbor R. Alcala (Google Rod Alcala). Alcala raped and photographed many women and now he is playing crazy. I never thought I'd get to know celebrated *sickos* like Alcala, Manson and Menendez. But Dr. Burkhart (chief of mental health) told me maybe God wanted me to meet these folks and study them. And to use what I've learned to help others. I was blessed by my meeting with Dr. Burkhart. She is awesome! I plan to use what I've learned from sociopaths etc. to help psychologists and criminologists. I want to also help everyday people (like Jason, Jonathon and Jace from *Big Brother* 2015) to lead better lives. What if we could identify, understand and *prevent* the next *Manson, Menendez or Alcala*. I think my personal contact with these sociopaths (and psychopaths etc.) qualifies me to (at least) "talk" about what I've learned...

There is a strong need in this country for somebody to go through what I've gone through, *survive* it and—then—*succeed*; and show others how to do it too. We have tens of millions of ex-cons (800,000 new ones every year) in this country. If I can exit prison and "*register*" for a crime I did *not* commit, and overcome it etc. there is no excuse for John Q. Ex-con to say, "I can't make it due to my criminal record." It will be extremely difficult for me. I may have to call Dr. Burkhart, Carlos Solis and Dr. Jarman etc. and seek pro bono intervention. And I'll have to lay on my face before God. But I will tell the world that my *past* is not what my *future holds*. I am not *who* they say I am. I will not live *down* to their expectations of me... There is a "promise" (a prophecy) over my life. But "promise" does not abort *process*. And *process* (walking in the wilderness) is painful. But the *wilderness* (prisons, wilderness and trials etc.) will make you strong. I'm tougher than I used to be. You can't come through the mess and trials that I've come through without getting stronger...

T.D. Jakes once said that he spent ten years begging people to come hear him preach. And if he had 20 people it was a good day. But that was "process." And it was *rehearsal* for the *recital*. And rehearsals are boring. And some people give up during rehearsals. And now they come to auditoriums, coliseums, the Georgia Dome and to Phillips Arena to hear Jakes preach the gospel. The wilderness is God's way of *pruning* you... Destiny is inside of you. And God had to *push* you out of your mother's womb. And God will *push* you out of that storm... And... God will *orchestrate* events to get you ready for your *destiny*...

*When* I *rise* I won't be able to say that my friends, my *connections* or pedigree got me to "where I am." But I'll have to say that if I can go from "*registering*" as a "*sex offender*" for a crime I did *not* commit etc. and survive it, overcome it and thrive etc. they can't bring me any excuses for failure. I *will* overcome this lie! I will live my dreams. I want Dalton

Thompson, *Levi Sparks*, T (a 21-year old CALPIA worker. T calls himself a "stud muffin"), McCrae Olson, Franklin McCallie, Luke Johnson (in Richmond, VA), Nurse Ben (used to be a lab tech at Sierra Vista Medical Center), Casey, Mario Herrera, Ryan Fehr and Brandon Hughes etc. to help me tell the poor, the tired and huddled masses etc. that they can "breathe *free*." Google Richard Gellner. I'm the only author in America to have interviewed Richard in the Dekalb County jail. And in retrospect is it mere coincidence that the universe *ordered* my steps to make me meet Eric and Lyle Menendez, Manson Alcala and Gellner? God wanted me to be able to tell Alec Loorz, Brandon Hughes, Jeff Gerber, Michael Dennis and Kevin Droniak etc. what I've learned from these "monsters." I will tell M. Hiscel, Justin Tankersaey, Alex Hayes, Caleb Lamb, Barbara Becnel, Max Wiseltier, Alex Bernhart (UC Berkeley grad) and Travis Shaw etc. what I learned from these people. I want readers to Google the people I name and tell them to get this book. And let's get together. I do not want "everybody" reading this book. I am *not* writing to *every*body. I'm writing Shaun Rushforth, Kory Carico, Timothy Hill, Chris Bird, Ryan Ferguson and Daniil Turistyn etc. I will go to Tavis Smiley, Harvey Levin and Mike Teselle etc. and I'll tell them what I've *experienced*. And…

    I've spent over a decade unwilling to talk about my *conviction*. I used to tell reporters (i.e. Mike Doyle etc.) that I'd only do an interview if they did not mention that I was *wrongly* convicted of "rape." I guess I thought I was better than Joseph, Brian Banks, Ronald Cotton, Rolando Cruz and Pete Rose etc. But now? Hell, call me Tupac Shakur. I'll *rap*, lecture and orate about my wrongful conviction. And if "you" don't believe me? I'll shake the dust off my feet and walk the other way… If I have to make a sign (sign spinner) and stand on a street corner…with a sign that says "Read my book: I was wrongly convicted" I will. I am (literally) willing to get my sign and stand outside the CNN studios (Anderson Cooper), the Tyler Perry studios and bookstores etc. I will do that. But I refuse to be marginalized by a wrongful conviction. And if God be "for me" (I won't need Andy Young or Jesse Jackson etc.) He is more than the whole world against me…

    I want to tell Joseph Latham, Brent (at Sierra Medical Center…and Mason), Roger Peck. Carol Leonard, Roberta Franklin, Austyn Whaley, Austin Prentice, Sam Pritchard, Kyle Gordy, Marty Tankleff and Tim McBride etc. that if I can 'make it' anybody can. I will tell Stuart Watkins, David House, Matt Stern, Zach Friesen, Alex Blench and Trevor Day etc. I'll stand and proclaim to (Oliver Stone, A. Pommerish, V. Cruz etc.) that if I can *rise* ("Still I Rise") again then the 800,000 ex-cons who get out of prison in 2016, 2017 and 2018 etc. can make it too. I want Jacob Gabriel, Max Wiseitier and Nick Boddington to join me on this *crusade*. I will wage a holy-*war* against the illiteracy, *low* self-esteem and the classicism etc. which leads to the *celling* of Americans. I'll ask Marcus Dixon, Betty Anne Waters and Mario Herrera etc. to join me. I will begin the crusade, the *holy-war* (aka campaign) etc.in the "country."

    I'll go to those churches where I preached as a kid (i.e. Antioch Baptist in McDonough, GA, County Line Baptist Church, Tannon's Bridge Baptist Church etc.) and I'll raise up *Gang Bangers* for *God* etc. in the country. If I need to join *Toastmasters* International, The National Speaker's Association etc. I'll join. But I will live my *destiny*. I will make my *mark* in the earth. And my kids will know that God was *with* me when I passed through this earth. And

I'm a survivor. "I'm not gon' (sic) give up!" I live in the greatest country on earth. I live in the land of *second chances*. If Mike Tyson can go to prison for *"rape"* and use drugs etc. and make a comeback etc. and end up lecturing in colleges etc. with his "limited" vocabulary and education, I can make it too. I'll face criticism and opposition. But no weapon that is *formed* against me shall *prosper*. They will come against me but they won't *prosper*. And corrupted prison guards like Joseph Stratton, Ryan Cough and R. Vogel etc. have made me *tough*. I've had to live in prisons with these corrupted guards orchestrating a whispering campaign where they tell other inmates that "he's in here for *rape* and…"

Still I survived it. And I didn't quit. And I kept on *writing*. I kept on *rehearsing*. I kept on believing. I had more *revelation* than I had *situation* but I stayed in the *process*. And I lost a lot of support because (as God told Gideon) there were too *many* me "with" me. And when I stand inside bookstores etc. and promote this book I'll know it was God. And… *If* a bookstore won't let me come *inside* — I'll stand *outside* and promote my books. After living in the most *negative* and deadly place on the planet I'm used to being "hated." But I'll present dynamic seminars and deliver keynote speeches on "haters." They (haters) are the largest unorganized group in the world. If they were to organize they would have $billions of dollars. I'm accustomed to hate. Calling me a "rapist" is like calling me a "Nig—r." It is not true. It does not surprise me. It won't stop me. All the while guard Jimmy McCartney, Adam Hinds and Jeb James (an inmate) were lying behind my back ("he molested a *kid*") etc. I kept on getting out of my bed and playing the "scales." I was *rehearsing* for this *recital* God is bringing me into. I don't need *everybody.* And if I had "fit-in" (with Hinds, Rick Butler, Richard Ford etc.) in the prison I'd be *out*-of-place at home. Still I rise! And I don't hate (Ford, Hinds, Butler etc.) the prisoners who lied on me. To them I say, "Picture me *rolling*."

God is gonna use my life and make it a blueprint. God does the almighty through the least likely. I'll ask Lane Garrison, Nick Prugo and Vincent Thomas etc. to help me tell this story. But if they don't wanna go don't hinder me. I'll go to Winder, GA, to Monroe, GA, Griffin, GA and McDonough, GA etc. And I'll find "a *few* good men" to help me. I'm so excited I can't see straight. It is difficult for me to sleep sometimes. God is getting ready to do something through me… I won't be marginalized… I can speak (on YouTube etc.) about racist politicians like Donald Trump. I can talk politics, business and education etc. I'm not limited to discussing psychopaths etc…

I watched California prison guards (led by Sgt. Vogel) *cell-extract* inmate Farley (in late 2015) and *murder* him. I watched the biggest *gang* in California (not the Bloods or Crips or Nuestra Familia) plot against me. They are the *CCPOA*. And they can kill with impunity. I've seen guards (like McCartney, Wenker etc.) tell prison gangsters that "Mike is a pedophile: rape him." Most prison rapes and murders are set up by prison guards… I just got out of *Hades*… I've just lived to see freedom! I must *testify* about what I saw, heard and experienced in this *living hell*. I will be a *"witness"* against the *monster* factory." I just left a fiery furnace. And I don't even smell like smoke… I pray for *Bryson Cole*, Brandon Gene Martinez and many inmates but my "assignment" is over! It's time to do what He anointed me to do… My book *"Left For Dead"* shall publish soon… *"Left For Dead"* will feature great lawyers like

*Ian Wallach, Jason Feldman, Ed Higginbotham* etc. and I shall talk about walking through the *"valley of the shadow of death…"*

**The Color of Justice?**

The color of justice is *green*. The rich get richer (*justice*) but the *poor* get *prison*. This book has been more about the *No J's* than about O.J… Dr. Martin Luther King Jr. once said that *"Justice* is what *love* looks like in *public."* I could take that one sentence and teach a seminar at Harvard. *"Justice* is what *love* looks like in public." How deep is that? SO jurisprudence falls very short… I intend to get small groups of brothers together (in Monroe, GA, Winder, GA, in Atlanta, GA and in other cities) and organize think tanks; to talk about justice. We need to have a *shift* in our thinking. Not only black folks but all poor folks. The white folks on Jerry Springer are (literally) too poor to be racist. But every group of people (no matter how broke or uneducated) will find a way (and a reason) to discriminate against others.

If you study the *politics* in prisons you'll find a caste system in jail. How can a person who is locked-up for life (i.e. Richard Ford and Rick Butler etc.) have the nerve to look down on anyone? At New Folsom State Prison the guys locked up in A-section (with wax on the floor) had the nerve to look down on the guys living in C-section. And even the guards called A-section Beverly Hills and C-Section Watts. Now I had a lot of money for a guy in jail. But yet I refused to live in "A" section. It (to me) was delusional thinking to be locked up and determine my "status" by the amount of wax on a concrete canvas. I saw where Tookie Williams said he never painted his cell because he didn't consider it home. I refused to paint a cell because it was not my home either… I want to bring small groups of brothers (white, black and Mexican) together and organize "*think* tanks" and "book clubs." We have got to find a way to bring people together other than to watch basketball and football (as I wrote earlier) games. Let's get together and figure out how to transform our minds and to "seek justice." If we can organize just 10 percent of the ex-cons in this country, (that would be 80,000 per year! I'll take half of half of that. I can do this with 20,000 men) and teach them discipline, reading, writing and imaging etc. we will change the world. We must Tell-a-*vision*. We must teach visualizing. If I can teach you to *see* the *invisible* you can do the *impossible*. But as long as I keep you thinking like a slave you'll settle for an outhouse. My daddy woke me up at 7:00 one Saturday morning and made me read "Think and Grow Rich/A Black Choice." I said, "It's Saturday morning and I want to sleep in." He said, "How can a black man lay in the bed on a Saturday when white people run the world?" I got up and started reading…

We need a radical shift in our thinking… A prison guard named Barrazus (at Corcoran) was telling Nurse Brett (a white nurse) that Mr. Obama is a Muslim and he is this and that. And Nurse Brett said that, "Mr. Obama will go down in history as a great President." It busted Barrazus' bubble. But guys like Barrazus Jimmy McCartney and Ross Meiers etc. can't help themselves. They don't understand how this black man got into the *White* House… Mr.

Obama helped me to shift my thinking. You must think outside the box if you want to live your dream. And if you have no dream you need not read this book. This book is *not* for everybody. I'm writing to Jai Breisch, Daniel Malinovsky, Daniel Bugriyev, Mario Herrera and Andy Alexander. I'm writing to Bruce Kroll (and "Cole" at Culver's), Nick Topete, Sam Voss, Hayden (and brother "*Cody*") Voss, Professor Edward Moore and *Austin Haughwout*. I'm writing to Kyle Herrera, Chris Vargas, Hunter Johansson and Tyler Sadler.

…Donald Trump is a political *twerker*. And he is a racist! And he is a pedophile. But he does think outside of the box… After studying Mr. Obama, Dr. King, Joseph (in Genesis), Marcus Dixon and Brian Banks etc. I decided to be radical. I will no longer "hide." I told my team in Switzerland to design a t-shirt that says "*Sherman D. Manning* was wrongly convicted of *rap*e." And I will wear it to the malls. I'll wear it at South Dekalb Mall in Decatur, Lenox Square and at Cumberland Mall in Atlanta. I will be an "original." And… "Here's my book if you want to *read* about it"…

I told you I'm not writing for *everybody*. If I only reach Lucas Knepper, Gary Silvi, Kai Newkirk, Caleb Lamb and Jakob Karr etc. it's all good. There will be *haters*. Jesus Christ (who was perfect) had haters. If they hated a perfect man then what the hell can I expect? Some people will see my t-shirt and be repulsed. Some will smirk. But even the haters will recognize my audacity. I'm just a nobody, trying to tell everybody, about somebody (Jesus) who can save anybody… God won't have to tell me that "there are too many men with you (Sherm)." But I am a survivor and I'm not gonna give up. Prison pulled me back but it couldn't contain my thoughts. I transcended the prisons that held me. When you pull an arrow back it is used to propel it forward. I will move forward. I've been down on the ground and in purgatory. I've been in a virtual *Hades*. I can't go any lower. When you're at the bottom the only way you can go is up. When they're gonna build a building real high they dig the foundation real low. I will go at least as *high up* as I went *low down*. If I don't believe that the God of Abraham, Isaac and Jacob can orchestrate the events of my life and use me. Then I need to stop reading the Bible and quit believing in God. I am like Gideon. I am the *least* in my clan. But if God be for me who can be against me.

I had to be *broken* by the *process*. Every time God used a man in a major way He had to be *small* in his own eyes. Saul started out small in his own mirror. When he got beside himself God got angry. David was small in his own eyes. Gideon, Jeremiah and Moses were reluctant and "small" in their own eyes. I started believing my own press. And God decided to break me back down. And I sat in that prison cell (like Joseph with that "*R*" in his jacket) and started doubting myself. "How am I gonna preach with this wrongful conviction in my background," I cried out to God. And I was scared. And I didn't think I could do it. I became *small* in my sight. And I *lost* a lot of friends while I was in prison. And I lost a lot of money. I lost a lot of my family. But I kept *believing* God! And He said, "Now I can use you. Now I can *bless* you." I felt like Paul. I could not get God to remove my thorn. Paul could preach and teach and could heal others. But he could not get God to remove his thorn. I had to struggle with the *contradiction* of being powerful on the outside but *conflicted* on the inside. And God wouldn't let me quit. I had to *rise above* the whispering campaigns, the plots, the schemes and the *hatred* of *murderers*. And God let me know if I could navigate my way through a cold prison system. If I could rise above the cold and *deadly* politics of the *prison* then I can survive anything civilians throw my way. I'm in a place where even *nurses* are demonic. I watched Corcoran guards violently cell-extract inmate Farley in July of 2015 twice within 4 days. And they killed him on the second extraction. And nurses and Dr. Wang would not even give him CPR. And I heard a nurse say that, "Oh well we got rid of another piece of sh-t!"…

My entire *perspective* on a real "fight" was transmogrified in the prison. I was in a place where guards thought nothing of *retaliating* against inmates by putting a young (i.e. Michael Gorman) white inmate in the cell with "Booty Bandit" and saying, "*Rape* this piece of crap." What kind of human (Stratton, Wenker, Couch etc.) gets pleasure out of seeing a man rape a man? How sick, retarded and demonic must you be to work in a prison? If you can survive a battle, a war and a campaign in a prison you can survive anything. And I'm *tougher*, stronger and more humble than I used to be. If I could navigate in Hades where I had guards (McCartney, Stratton etc.) lying on me and saying, "He's a *molester*." And I was able to survive, maintain and overcome those *deadly* rumors in a house of *stone*. I'll be darn if I can't survive "some" of you all believing that I actually (I did *not*) raped Calvario. I only made it by God's grace. I survived hell because God rules and reigns. And if He does reign I will get to my *destiny*. Prison pulled me way (far) back. But I'll be propelled into my destiny and I will share my testimony…

All I need are a few brothers. I want brothers who are broken by wrongful convictions, babies out of wedlock or whatever. I want to get these brothers (just a few) together and teach them how to *trust God*… I need *you* (who are reading) to tell just a *few* of your friends about this book. Don't tell everybody. Too many people will introduce "mess," doubt and fear. Just find one or two of your friends and tell them to *read this book*… Email the folks I've named (i.e. Austin Prentice, James Merryman, Michael Dennis, Scott Czeda and Kaleb Leeper…Travis Ulerick and Trevor Loflin) and tell them "I saw your name in a book and you need to read it." I want to bring Levi Sparks, Daniel Job and Jerry Wines etc. together. And we can put on clinics.

…If a black man called a terrorist, a "Muslim" and a Kenyan etc. can become the *President* of the *USA*. I can be the President of *Gang Bangers* For *God*. I will seek out Sam Fuick, David Joiner (and Joyner in Georgia), Curtis Sykes, James Nesmith, Sam Pritchard, Jai Breisch and Joshua Scannell. I'll look for Greg Scannel, Matt Stern, Marty Tankleff and James Merryman. And we will work on self-esteem, thinking skills and dreaming skills. Every time I become nervous and think I can't do it I look at the *White* House. Mr. Obama; his grandfather was a domestic servant to the British. His father left his mother when Obama was only 2 years old. Mr. Obama last saw his father when he was 10. And "still I *rise*" sayeth Obama. "Call me a terrorist and anything else you want to call me… Say that my first election was a fluke… But *picture* me *rolling* in the beast!" He rose to the highest office on earth. And Mitch McConnell, Ted Cruz, Dumb Donald Trump and others are still *shell-shocked*… Schwarzenegger said Mr. Obama had skinny legs. President Obama said, "I might be skinny but I know how to *fight*"…

And in prison I've had to learn how to *fight*... So you came from a fatherless home? *Rise above it*! You are an ex-con with a rap sheet? Rise above it... You were *wrongly* convicted (Joseph, Brian, Marcus, *Sherman* and...) of rape *rise above it*. You did not get justice? Testify about it... "*Justice* is what *love* looks like in *public*." And "justice too long delayed is justice denied." I will tell my story at Harvard, Howard, at Yale and at the jail. I'll call *Narcisco* Morales, Attorney Michael Bien and Lauren Vandemortel etc. And we will tell this story. I won't quit until I see *justice* roll down like waters and righteousness like a mighty stream... Even if you are a *No J*... *Rise above it*! And... *Picture me rolling*...

On 7/25/15 C.O. Worth told me that "President Obama is the worst president in history and *we* won't stop until we murder that bastard." I said, "Do you really think some bumbling Klansman will get close enough to take a shot at the president?" He said, "A guy shot the White House... A guy got inside of the White House. Do you think a guy would have gotten inside the White House if we had elected Romney? I know for a fact that *we* will murder Obama." This is the fifth prison guard I've heard threaten the life of Mr. Obama. It is chilling to hear this crap. And sadly, guys like C.O. Wooden, Worth, Lambert, Sgt. Burns and Sgt. Vogel etc. would (literally) murder him if they could... I will try to work with Mayor Bloomberg etc. and help stop gun violence when I get home. I believe that I can speak to gang bangers' kids in the suburbs etc. about sensible gun laws. And I intend to make a difference... I want my readers to help us... I need you (all) to send emails to Attorney John Phillips (in Baker County), Daniel Malinovsky, Shane Bruce, Scott Dangerfield, Joseph Latham, Will Niespodzinski, Brian Zimmerman, Scott Macbeth, Moi Navarro, Brian Glasscock and Austin Ho.

This book is *not* for everybody. I want to reach a targeted (special) group of folks. Email Jordan Ghawa, Jacob Faulkender (Carmichael, CA), Kevin Sullivan (in Isla Vista, CA), Cody Lloyd, Guy Turner, John Toraker, Josh Thibodeaux, Spencer Perry, *Logan Paul*, Ju Hong, Stuart Edge, Kyle day, Tyler Kolb, Derrick Sweeney, Greg Porter, Luke Gates, Jaron Brandon, Jace Lankow, Blake White, Ben Johns, *Cody Hassler*, Chris Hues, Connor Rhea, Tim Sobolenko, Jeff Wozniak, Peter Kneght, *Tommy Beard*, *Matthew Scheidt*, Joey DeFranchesca, Nate Waleseski, *Justin Hempfling*, Paul Jolley, Alex Sutaru, Clayton Burnham, Matt Kwiatkowski, *Robert Mitchell Jr.* (Lowell, MA), Matt Fender, Austin Sisneros, C.J. Sheron, Robert Borrelle, Alexander Adame, Will Haskell, Albert Thompson, David Pate, Brendan Martello, Caleb Butler and Michael Castro. Tell them "you are in this book." Tell them to get it. I will have my team to send them gratis E-copies (if they can't buy it). This is a special book for a select group... We will pay persons to wear a t-shirt (which says "*Sherman D. Manning* was wrongly convicted of rape") to shopping malls etc. If you want a free t-shirt (plus $20.00 to wear it to the mall or football game etc.) send us an email. We will use guerilla warfare tactics to get this book to "our" people. We don't want Trump, Mitt Romney (*Romnesia*), Ted Cruz etc. reading this book. I'm looking for *quality* not quantity... If you have access to reaching the persons I've named tell them to get this book... "*Justice* is what *love* looks like in *public*"...

...Racism is injustice! And racism is raw in this country. Some polls claim race relations are worse in America during President Obama's presidency. That is absolutely not true. We couldn't elect and reelect a president whose father is from Kenya if most of us were racist. Most Americans are not racist. President Obama's election sent *shockwaves* to (the *minority*) racists in this country. And those of us who get along, love each other and celebrate diversity etc. are not newsworthy. Mr. Obama's election(s) exacerbated the racists of America. And…some of them will never change. They'll just have to *die*. I've been in a system (the prison industrial complex) which is run by racists. Every California warden is white. Most of them are racist. I've *studied* "institutional" racism for over a decade. And… I hope to talk about what I've seen (and learned) at Harvard, Howard, Grambling, Hampton and at clubs etc… I will never miss the chance to *elucidate* the mind(s) of Manson, Alcala, Menendez and…California prison guards etc. and to explain how a Vogel, a Stratton, a Wenker etc. these *guards* are really *Mansons* in green!... The president (Mike Jiminez) of the CCPOA is the Osama Bin Laden of Corrections!...

    I will bring Roger Peck, "T" (of CALPIA), Mario Herrera, Davey Blackburn, Kyle Foletta, Frank McCallie, Keith Russo, Justin Brewer, Ian Weller and Max Hodges etc. together. And we will "find a way to *get in the way*" of injustice. "Injustice anywhere is a threat to justice everywhere."… "Prisons are houses of *hatred*. American jurisprudence hates the *poor*… I'll ask *Floyd Mayweather* (Mr. Perry etc.) to help underwrite a *crusade* to get men off the streets, out gangs and back in school. "Tomorrow belongs to the people who prepare for it today."… "Education is a passport to the future."… If I need to use Toastmasters International etc. to teach self-esteem and "confidence speaking" etc. I will. I was taught by *Rev. Hosea Williams* and *Ambassador Andrew Young* to find a way to get in the way!

    Sherman D. Manning
    Follow me on Twitter

# The Sherman D. Manning Speaker's Bureau:

*Sherman* is an oratorical giant, motivational speaker and a prolific author. Prior to his *wrongful* incarceration he was an ordained minister who preached in some of America's largest churches. His preaching "style" was influenced by Rev. C.L. Franklin, Bishop T.D. Jakes and Bishop Noel Jones. *Sherman* has authored more books than any incarcerated author in the United States. He transformed his prison cell into a classroom. He studied criminology, psychology, the science of success, unequal justice, gangs, violence and police brutality. He is an expert on the causes of crime and could lecture seasoned criminologists on criminology.

Dr. Yablonsky calls *Sherman* an "Experience Therapist." Late civil rights legend Rev. Hosea Williams called him "The *Martin Luther King*, Jr. of the pulpit… Microphones seem to explode in Rev. Manning's hand." O.J. Simpson "*Dream Team*" lawyer Robert Blasier calls him a "*Master Writer*." Democratic Party Chairman John L. Burton calls him a "*Literary Warrior*." Rubin Hurricane Carter would be proud of *Sherman*…

Beginning February 19, 2016 *Sherman D. Manning* will be available for classroom lectures, keynote speaking engagements, The *Full Gospel Business Men's Fellowship International*, university seminars, conferences, consultations and associations. His group "*Gang Bangers For God*" will take their campaigns (aka holy crusade) to colleges, academies, institutions and churches across this country. Pastors and businesses as far away as Switzerland began attempting to book *Sherman* as early as June 2015. *Sherman* states that "I can't accept international engagements just yet. I'll be on parole. And…due to my wrongful conviction the only institutions I'm willing to speak at are colleges. Although the *wrongful conviction* does *not* involve a child I just want to be safe. The only way I'm willing to speak at a high school is if my parole officer (or a cop) goes with me." *Sherman* will concentrate his efforts on preventing incarceration. He states "If I focus half of the energy on developing curriculums to keep folks out of jail — that I used to devote to unethical manipulation etc. it will be great! I was *wrongly convicted*. I did *not* do what they said I did. But I did some bad stuff. I scammed some people. I crooked some folks. And God was not pleased with me…

I'm a sports fan. I love basketball! But I'm sick of seeing men who are as broke as a joke; sitting around for hours watching basketball (football and baseball). And every man on the court is a millionaire. If we (men) cut the time we spend fooling around (watching Lebron and Kobé) in half and began to spend that time wisely (studying, reading, brainstorming, creating, inventing and writing etc.), we would become millionaires. I'm not going to just preach and shout anymore. We've designed some specific steps that men can take to stay out of prisons. And…every professor or college student etc. knows someone who is in the joint or has been there. And they most certainly know people who are headed to prison (if they don't turn around now). Our programs will intervene and show folks how to turn around…

I also want to talk to criminology students and"… *Sherman* states that he is so excited about sharing his ideas that 'I'll speak for free (to nonprofits) if people can't afford our fee. I'm actually willing to go to Morehouse, Spelman, Howard University, Hampton University, Harvard, Stanford, Duke and Yale to speak for free… I'll bring my newest book "*The Truth*

*About O.J. Simpson*" and speak for free if that's what it takes.'" (*Agent's* Note: We strongly oppose the idea of Sherman giving free speeches at colleges that can afford to pay!)...

*Sherman* was felled and nearly killed by disseminated Valley Fever. He was the longest hospitalized (14 months) Valley Fever patient in America. For ten months prison officials would not even tell his family where he was. Some thought he was dead. But a white respiratory therapist (Mary Bell) began to pray for *Sherman*. And *Sherman* signed himself out of the hospital and went back to the prison (near death) for a night demanding the prison contact his mother (*Dollie Mae Manning*). She told Maureen Mahony Healthcare Director that she didn't know whether he was dead or alive but to "tell him I'm gonna pray for him and God can heal him." At 96 pounds Dr. Paul Griffin thought Sherman would die. But Dollie and family were praying in Atlanta. Mary Bell and a group of women were praying in Fresno, California. Peter Andrist and family were praying in Switzerland. And God turned it around. *Sherman* was watching T.D. Jakes on T.V. one Sunday and God moved him. "You can't die now because what I spoke over your life and what I anointed you to do has not yet come to pass."

Sherman now admits that sometimes he was in so much pain he wanted God to let him die. He says that on his deathbed he could hear T.D. Jakes and Noel Jones saying "Don't die yet." He says, "I could hear them in my spirit! That is why I know the importance of preaching the word of God." He also saw Rev. Michael Pfleger on T.V. one Sunday and felt God moving through the pastor. And God brought him back from "the valley of the shadow of *death*." And Sherman says "I can never be racist because 98 percent of the physicians who saved my life were white"...

When I left Coalinga Regional Medical Center the nurses (Nurse Norma, Linda Lihong, Susan, Jemma, Jessica, Arianna and Julie etc.) were lined up giving me hugs and handshakes. We wept...many of them thought I would leave that hospital in a body bag. But God allowed prison to punish me because He said (in 2 Samuel 7:14) "...when he does wrong I will *punish* him...but my love will never be taken away from him..." And now I can tell guys in prison and guys in gangs etc. that He may punish them but He still loves them. I thought I would die but I asked God like David "Who am I lord that *you have brought me this far*?" Through the storm, through the rain and off of my deathbed. And (verses 20 & 21) "What more can your servant (*Sherman*) David say to you? For *you know your* servant (you know my weaknesses and my sins etc.), sovereign Lord." And here's why He could *not* let me die! "For the *sake* of *your Word* and *according to your will*, *you have done* this *great thing* (raised me up off of my deathbed)"...and all I can think to say is '*How Great* Thou (Almighty God) are'"...

Sherman says that he was very worried about how he would be received and which churches would actually invite him to preach when he got out of prison because church folk can be unforgiving and judgmental. And he said to God, "How will an ex-con preach? Who am I Lord?" And God showed him Gideon's dilemma: (Judges 6:15-16) "...Gideon replied, 'but how can I save Israel? (How can I still preach the gospel? Go on radio and T.V. shows? Lecture?...) My clan is the weakest in Manasseh, and I am the *least* (least amongst ex-cons; wrongly convicted of a *bad* crime; smut and dirt on my name!) in my family.'" The Lord answered, "I will *be with you*..."

And, *Sherman* knew that he *might* not get support from famous pastors etc. And "I love T.D. Jakes because God has used him to mentor me from a distance. But the bottom line is T.D. might not be with me. I may never get to tell my testimony to Noel Jones. I might not ever get a chance to tell TBN (Trinity Broadcasting Network) how important their programming was to keeping me alive and sane. But God will be with me." *Sherman* admits that like Gideon he argued with the Lord: (verse 13 and 14) "…but *if* the Lord is with us, why has all this *happened* to us?" He wondered why God allowed the wrongful conviction in the first place. And why would God allow him to be convicted of 'that' crime. God spoke and said, "*Sherman*, are you better than my servant *Joseph*? What crime did I allow him to be wrongly convicted of? And unlike you — I was not punishing Joseph. He spent 13½ years in prison wrongly convicted of attempted *rape*. But when *I* got him out I made him a prince!" *Sherman* felt weak and unprepared and he has battle scars and (verse 14) God told him (as He did Gideon) "Go in the strength you have and save …(your brothers) am I (God; not Jakes, Jones or Billy Graham) not sending you?"

    *Sherman* thought "How will I get men to follow me and work with me?" And God let him know he doesn't need 'too many' men. He only needs a 'few good men.'" God led him to Judges 7:2 where He told Gideon "You have *too many men.* I cannot deliver Midian into their hands, or Israel would boast against me, 'my own strength has saved me.'" God let *Sherman* know that he will not be able to think himself responsible. But just as God raised him up off of his deathbed in His timing, God will give *Sherman* a "few good men." And He will "order" his steps. And when God is ready He will allow *Sherman's* gifts (not a con, not manipulation or impersonation) to bring him before great men and women…

    We invite *you* to share this site with others. We want Daniel Jennings (in Tiburon, CA), Daniel Jensen, Daniil Turitsyn (in Succasuna, NJ), David Holycross, Tony Dungy, Abe Brown, A.J. Ali, Austin Prentice (or Prentiss), Joseph Breen, Chris Bird (and Tammie Counts), Mario Herrera, Chris Vargas, Nurse Ben (Sierra Vista Hospital), Casey, Nathan Langley, Jakob Karr, Jacob Goodin, Maxwell Hanger, T.J. Toraker, T.J. Foraker, Timothy Hill, Kory Carico, Daniel Job, Kyle Gordy, Michael Dennis (Grapevine, TX), Alex Hayes, Jimbo Spalding, Angus T. Jones, Mark Ridley-Thomas, Andy C. Alexander, Sam Voss, Hayden Voss, Sean Farmer, Sebastian Demers, Jacob Gabriel, Dakota Sotto, Scott Czeda, Vincent Thomas, Adam Glyn and Max Hodges etc. to see this site. We want *Nick Prugo*, Van Hansis and Nick Topete etc. (a few "good" men) to see this site…

    And we highly recommend that your association, organization, book club, book store etc. schedule *Sherman* for a free book signing and/or reading at your location. Schedule him to give talks, lectures or seminars etc. before your audience(s). View http://GBgod.blogspot.com, www.cafepress.com/Manning, www.NAPSUSA.org or www.ShermanDManning.com... Read his blogs and view his podcasts (coming in March, 2016)… Sherman concludes: "So if I'm able to succeed everybody will know that it has to be God! You can't come from where I must come from and be over 40 years old and succeed; in your own strength. But as Bishop Jakes says 'God can do the almighty through the *least* likely.' I'm certainly the *least* likely. But He will order my steps"… Contact speaker *Sherman D. Manning* today! Hallopeter@sunrise.ch

# **Never Quit**

      I read in my Bible that "The Lord was with Joseph" even though He allowed Joseph to be wrongly convicted of a *sex* crime… And I can't get Judges 6:12 – 16 out of my spirit. Like Gideon I kept wondering "Why has all this happened to me?" I knew He let Joseph (too) get wrongly convicted of a sex crime but even in the prison He was "with Joseph." And I thought He had *abandoned* me. And He showed me (as He showed Gideon) that He was *with* me. And I wondered how am I gonna make it on parole and where can I preach and… He told me (Judges 6:14) to "Go in the *strength* you *have*." Not in the strength you can *see*, touch, taste, smell or feel. But if "you're gonna walk with me you've gotta *walk* by *faith* and not by *sight*." He said… "in the strength *you have*." And my message to the people will be "You have the power"… But I still struggled with why did my support group abandon me? I used to be able to call Ambassador Andrew Young at home. I knew Jesse Jackson, Jasper Williams etc. and Rev. Hosea Williams. I could call him at 2:00 in the morning.

      Why did God allow me to be *alone*? God said (Judges 7:2-4) you have "too many men *with* you." And if I allow you to reach T.D. Jakes, Noel Jones or Tony Dungy while you are in prison etc. when you make it you'll think it was your connections. But I said, "But God you were with Joseph even in jail." And He said, "But did I not *isolate* Joseph by letting him go to prison? I caused Joseph's own brothers to *abandon* him because of their jealousy. I isolated Joseph from his own mother and father by letting him go to prison. Joseph never got a visit from his family. I allowed him to go to prison to teach him to trust *me* and not *men*. I didn't let him get 'too many men' around him. Even when he interpreted a dream for Pharaoh's servants and said, 'remember me.' I caused them to *forget* Joseph… If Joseph hadn't gone to prison before I made him a prince he could say it was his connections, associations or education that brought him to a palace. But when I raised up an ex-felon who had no voting rights; when I took a *registered sex* offender and made him a prince, he could not boast against *me*." God said, "I cannot allow you to have too many men with you. I've *caused* people to abandon you so that *when* I *raise you* (an ex-felon) up you'll know it was *me*"…

      I wept! I cried out to God! "How great thou art! Holy, holy is the Lord God Almighty!" So He (and Him alone) will *orchestrate* the events of my life and *He* will…to every prisoner, gangster or bad boy reading this. *You* have the *power*! Go in the strength you *have*. Get right with God and He will bring you out. He may *cause* folks to leave you to teach you to trust Him. And… I'll *see* you in February 2016!...

## **The Killers Amongst Us:**

    I'm probably the only author in the nation who knows Eric and Lyle Menendez personally. And who has also stood face-to-face with *Charles Manson*. And as a journalist who is embedded in 'his' story I can report that the common thread I witnessed in Eric, Lyle and in Charles is this: they are all in love with themselves. You can't convince them that they are infamous. What is frightening about Lyle, Eric and Charles is how 'boy next door' they can appear. The same is true of O.J. Simpson. Simpson is described by Bob Blasier as a gregarious, charming and "just a great guy." But O.J. Simpson (like Lyle and Eric) is a *stone cold killer*. But what should really alarm Americans is the fact that we have 33 terrorist training camps in California. And there are thousands of U.S. training camps across this country. These terrorist camps are called prisons. I'm not reporting something I've only read about in a tome. This is not some theoretical assumption. I am in the prison as I pen this tome. And as I prepare to be released from prison I can truly state emphatically that U.S. prisons are (indeed) terrorist training camps.

    I spoke with a guy (today) who actually has a plan to get out of prison and go and attempt to assassinate President Barack Obama. He was a borderline racist when he entered the prison. And he has mental issues. And when he sees guys like Donald Trump and Ted Cruz on TV they reinforce and exacerbate his hate. He is a human powder keg. He is a ticking time bomb. And the prison serves as an incubator for hatred and anger and for racism. The U.S. prison system is built upon hatred, separation, segregation and on racism. Judge Joe Brown spent only 5 days in prison and called it a *slave warehouse*. What troubles me is that I have met *Christopher Harper Mercer*. And I have met *Dylan Roof*. When I say I've met them I mean I've met their kind. I know white guys right here in prison (who have parole dates) who believe that black men and Hispanics are "taking over." I've met guys here who are "mad with the world" just like Mercer. And just like Roof. And I would bet my head on a silver platter that I will one day read where some of these guys went into black and Hispanic churches and tried to kill people. I will read about these guys molesting babies, maiming and killing people. And instead of prisons rehabilitating them and getting them ready to assimilate and to reintegrate back into society, our prisons are getting them ready to join ISIS. I've literally conversed with guys who plan to try to join ISIS when they get out of prison. It is absolutely scary and it is absolutely true.

    Today (as you read these words) there are men sitting in juveniles, jails and prisons who are being taught, trained and bred to become terrorists. Google Brian Nichols from Atlanta, GA. Ask yourself where did he learn to kill and why was he that angry? Most of the guys that we see who maim, rape or murder without blinking an eye were "bred" to kill inside of prisons. And upon close scrutiny and analysis we'll find that the guys who did not learn it (directly) from inside a prison, they very often learned to murder (indirectly) from the guys who had been in prisons. One of the reasons gangs are so successful and powerful is because of the power of "mentoring." We have perhaps the most successful "Big Brother" mentorship and internship programs inside these gangs (Bloods, A B, Crips and Nuestra Familia etc.). I have meticulously and methodically studied gangs in prison (while in prison) for over a decade. My initial thinking was that my studies would center around gangs which consisted of prisoners. Yet the more I studied the more I learned that members of law enforcement (i.e. The Thin Blue Line etc.) also have gangs.

I was introduced to the most powerful gang in the California prison system which is "The Green Wall" aka 723 (Seven represents the numerical equivalent of the letter G and twenty-three represents the letter W for Green Wall). Every prison guard in the state of California is a member of The Green Wall. The Green Wall's cover is the CCPOA (California Correctional Peace Officers Association); which is led by Mike Jiminez. The CCPOA is extremely powerful and well connected. They have the Governor of the State (Jerry Brown) in their back pocket. They gave Brown's campaign $2 million. Prison *guard* gangs smuggle in the cell phones, drugs and weapons to the inmate gangs. And when—or—if a guard gets caught smuggling the Governor (routinely) turns a blind eye. What should concern John Q. Citizen (you) is the fact that these guards consistently, routinely and deliberately wreak havoc in prisons. They foment racism violence and a culture of division. And from sunrise til sunset almost 2.7 million men and boys are literally "studying evil" (shameless plug but read my books "*Kids Killing Kids*," "*Creating Monsters*," and "*American Dream – A Search For Justice*").

…When I first wrote about how prisons were breeding murderers and "monsters" I sent my book "*Creating Monsters*" to Professor Dylan Rodriguez. At that juncture he was at UC Irvine. And he told me that he used my book "*Creating Monsters*" to teach his sociology class. And he wished I could come and speak to his class at UC Irvine (full disclosure; it may have been UC Riverside). Well I guess I should look Professor Rodriguez up because I can actually "speak" to Professor Rodriguez's class now (in February 2016). And I quite frankly, have a lot to say. We need to sound an alarm in this nation. We need to capture the attention of our citizens. And someone needs to let them know that our prisons (right here on U.S. American soil) are pre-training for future ISIS terrorists. We have nearly 800,000 prisoners being released from prisons every year. And a large number of them are a threat to the safety and security of American citizens. Many of them will not get on the plane and go to Syria and fight. But they will get instead on the bus or train and blow up the neighborhoods and our churches.

My fellow Americans: Listen to me; I'm not a politician. I'm not running for office so I don't need your vote. I'm not the pastor of some large church so I don't need you to believe in me. I'm not raising an offering or seeking a donation. If you choose to believe (erroneously) I'm a "rapist," "thug" or a "murderer" it is actually okay. I have studied violence, criminality and human nature at its very worst; from the inside out. I know what makes molesters, rapists and murderers "tick." Put me in a room with 100 convicts and I can tell you (in ten minutes) which 80 – 85 inmates are actually predators, rapists, molesters and murderers. I can identify the psychopaths as well as the sociopaths. I can also identify the 10 – 15 so-called molesters, rapists and murderers who are actually innocent and/or not guilty. I can also tell you (with 90 percent accuracy) which 82 prisoners will reoffend within one year. I'll also identify the 15 –

25 who will graduate to more vicious and violate crimes. I will also identify the 5 – 10 who are actual "domestic terrorists"…

When I was at Folsom State Prison working with Eric Menendez 8 hours per day, while guards (i.e. Mansky, Stratton and Mike Todd etc.) were kissing his behind and treating him like a celebrity. I was studying him like a science project. I conducted the same type of detailed studies on Lyle Menendez when I was housed at Mule Creek State Prison. I also studied Charles Manson (although not as closely as I was able to study the Menendez murderers) while I was housed at Corcoran. And when I was still naïve regarding politics (and I love politics) I used to think I could testify before Congress about what I'd learned when I get home. But I've come to understand that well over 60 percent of our Representatives (including the recently retired John Boehner) are alcoholics and prescription drug addicts. And most of them are stuntsmen. It is all a game to them. They're not genuine. Ipso Facto, they are not my "audience." Prison (as President Mandela famously told Oprah) gives you the time to sit down and "think."

I also studied the media. And some of my favorite media personalities (i.e. Chuck Todd etc.) actually let me down. But I grew up and learned to understand the media. By the time you're reading this I suspect Trump will have already dropped out of the presidential race. But what fascinated me was how Chuck, George Stephanopoulos and even Scott Pelley bowed down and kissed Trump's behind just to get interviews with him. They knew that if they made him look "bad" he would refuse to appear on their shows. And they would lose ratings. Trump would not have given Tim Russert an interview because Russert was a real journalist and a numbers man… In July of 2015 I saw Trump announce that "I make (earn) $400 million per year." In October George (on "This Week") told Trump that "Forbes estimates that you earn $250 million per year." Trump interrupted, "I earn $605 million per year." So Trump was well over double the Forbes estimate. And he'd inflated his own figure ($400 million) by $205 million in just three months and George did not push back on it. There was even a report Trump was paying people $50.00 each to show up at his events so he'd have "crowds." But neither Todd, nor George or Scott ever asked him about "paying attendees."

I received a real life lesson of the corporate owned media in which Dr. Cornel West so often speaks of. I still watch Meet the Press, This Week and 60 Minutes. But I watch with a critical eye. I now know the media is all about "money." They will overlook obvious blemishes, potential scandals and gigantic inconsistencies *if* they can achieve "ratings" by "overlooking" them. This is why Tim Mak's story (about Trump "raping" his ex-wife) got so little traction. "If we expose Trump as a rapist or as a toe-tapping imbecile whose heart pumps only defecation — we won't be able to interview him and get the ratings." Our media personalities have all had to join the "Trump" fan club just to land an interview. They've sacrificed the truth for ratings. And I was appalled by that circus. But watching it educated me. I'll never be on "Meet the Press or "This Week" because a Todd or a George would say, "Who is *Sherman D. Manning*?" And I'm okay with that. Todd, George and 60 Minutes 'taught' me that media attention per se means nothing. They can be bought. And before I get back to the "killers amongst" you let me say: Many of the people you see on the so-called "panels" on the political shows are "paid" by the politicians. I. E. Trump *paid* Matt Dowd to sing his praises and to try to convince Americans that Trump could be the Republican nominee. I consider it sinful, a fraud and a shame for a person to masquerade as a neutral "panelist" while he's being paid to promote a candidate on a news show. That turns my stomach. But such is the state of our politricks amidst this "super PAC" political climate. It's all very dirty.

Likewise our "criminal justice" system is also dirty, corrupted and biased. Consider Dr. Jeffrey Abrams in El Cajon, CA. The criminal justice system treated him like the media treated Trump. Dr. Abrams molested an 8-year old girl. He raped disabled women etc. And… His probation report recommended 21 years in prison. Yet, in September 2015 he received 1 year "probation." And Deputy District Attorney Kerry Conway (we'll never know how much she was paid) expressed "satisfaction" with his sentence. I'd stake my life on the fact that Dr. Abrams (who is a $ multi-millionaire) bought and bribed the judge and Conway. He is a sadistic pedophile and a 'real rapist'. And he will not spend one day in prison because he's rich. Our entire judicial system (from the U.S. Supreme Court on down) has been compromised at the feet of money…

But for the guys who are actually in prison it is a "war zone." It is a "breeding ground." I often announce that I attended UCHU (i.e. UCLA); The University of California at "*Hate*" University. And I graduated with a Ph.D. My 600 page tome "*Kids Killing Kids*" was my dissertation. In prison "They do not sleep unless they have *done evil*; and their sleep is taken away unless they make someone fall. For they eat the bread (*bred*) of wickedness. And drink the wine of violence." That is Proverbs 4:16 and 17. And it is also the U.S. prison system per se. In prison I saw guys (similar to Trump) who flattered themselves in their own eyes. And "the words of" their "mouth are wickedness and deceit… He devises wickedness on his bed" (Psalm 36:2-4). Guys sit around in prison and literally devise "wickedness," violence and stabbings "on" their "beds." And…

When I think about the so-called justice Kerry Conway got for the victims of Dr. Jeffrey Abrams. And as I closely scrutinize the judicial system I'm reminded of Isaiah 10:1-2 "Woe to those who decree unrighteous decrees, who *write* misfortune, which they have *prescribed* to rob the needy (i.e. Abrams' victims) of justice, and to take what is right from the poor (98 percent of U.S. prisoners are poor. And… Abrams' victims were poor) of my people"... But I think verse 4 is also for Kerry Conway, Dr. Jeffrey Abrams and the judge they may have bribed: "…they shall bow down among the *prisoners*…" Psalm 27 talks about people who "breathe out *violence*." In order to breathe out violence you must be rotten to the core. But also in order to 'breathe' violence it must be in the air. And unfortunately in a prison both the guard (keeper) and the prisoner (kept) have to "breathe" the same "violence" which is in the air. And I used to try to understand what Rubin "Hurricane" Carter was talking about when he'd state that prisons destroy anybody and everyone who comes in contact with them. But after I studied a while and watched a while, Rubin's words were elucidated for me by a host of witnesses. I've watched prison "destroy," "break down," "radicalize" and "*wickedize*" (my word) guards and inmates. We are now breeding a group of "super *predators*" in juveniles, jails and prisons.

And the problem with our current politicians is that they are not willing to think long-term. We have knee-jerk, reactionary and run-of-the-mill politicians running this great country. And they don't think that all of these folks we locked up two-and-three decades ago will come home. They are coming back to our communities and neighborhoods. And they'll bring the residue of the violence, hatred and the ignorance of the prison with them. And what I'd like to know is what do we expect them to do? Are you willing to hire an ex-con who was in prison for ten years? Who do you know that will hire an ex-con on parole for 'rape'? Do you even want him to cut your grass? Are you willing to allow him to wash your car? You don't even want him living in your community. So since you don't want him to live near you or work for you and since "most" people do not want to hire some 'rapo' etc. my question is what shall we do with the 94,000 'sex' offenders who are paroled every year? My goal is not to attempt to get you to be sympathetic. I just want you to be intelligent. And let us decide what we as a society are going to do with ex-cons. And if we do not decide to become concerned with 'how' they are treated while they are supposed to be getting rehabilitated — we will continue to be plagued by '*Killers Amongst Us*'.

We ought to be asking Hillary Clinton, Bernie Sanders, Rubio and Carson what they will do about Corrections, criminal justice, guard abuse and police brutality etc. if they are elected (I didn't mention Carly because she has proven to be a blatant liar already. And I expect Trump to be out of the race by February or March 2016). We have to make the "celling" of America a part of the political discussion(s) and debate… "*Black lives matter?*" I agree; and "*Ex-cons lives matter.*" It is time for the body politic to discontinue evading and disregarding the fact that we have a U.S. prison system which is run like something out of the 1950's. And our prisons are preparing men to join ISIS…

Guns? A white prison Sergeant pointed out to me that the NRA is "actually racist and classist." I asked how so and he explained it to me. He said, "The only people the NRA don't want to have guns are black men." He stated, "Almost 70 percent of the black men in this country cannot ever own a gun. Because once you've been convicted of a felony you lose your right to own a gun or vote. And even when you complete parole you can't get a gun. Have you ever seen the NRA fighting to get gun rights for ex-cons? How many black members does the NRA have? They want you (blacks) unarmed and unable to vote." I thought "wow." This came from the mouth of a white Sergeant. I wish I could ask Hillary, Bernie, Biden or Ben Carson about that…

If I do a 'Vine' it will be about politics. I plan to do a press conference my first or second day home. My press conference may air on the internet. But the day I get home I intend to gather a couple (maybe 3 or 4) "*Gang Bangers* For *God*" (*G.B.G.*) supporters and we will do a press conference. And from that day forward I'll be blogging, doing podcasts and tweeting etc. regarding the presidential race, criminal justice, The Thin-Blue-Line, The Green Wall and America's "*terrorist* training camps." I might look up Logan Paul and have him teach me how to use Vine etc. I'll use modern technology to tell the world how we're producing killers, terrorists, rapists and molesters…

I was in Los Angeles County Jail. It is actually the largest and most abusive jail system in the world…not in the nation; but the biggest and the worst in the world. The L.A. County Jail has been sued hundreds of times. It has spent $ hundreds of millions of dollars settling law suits. But it is still the most deadly jail in the country. I would pay John McCain, Hillary,

Bernie Sanders or Rubio etc. to walk with me through L.A. County Jail. I'd pay either of them to walk with me through Atlanta's Fulton County Jail. These are cesspools of violence. And I want anybody (any politician, criminologist, sociologist or psychologist) to tour L.A. County or Fulton County Jails with me — and then tell me how anyone can come out of that hell sane. As I write these words I hear a white inmate yelling "Don't rape me man! Pleeease!"… He's yelling this in a cell down the hall. And the prison guards are ignoring him. Their attitude is "You shouldn't have come to prison." And with all the wrongful convictions we have in America? Maybe he very well shouldn't have 'come' to prison.

…My fellow Americans: This young white inmate was (indeed) *raped* at R.J. Donovan State Prison in 2015. And I'd guestimate that he will be paroled by 2017. So what kind of man will he be when he gets out? When you sit in prison and you are afraid all the time it damages your psychological apparatus. Dr. Terry Kupers has done studies on what fear, noise and depression does to the mind(s) of prisoners. When you spend 5 – 10 years afraid and you are forced into a gang and forcefully raped etc. And… White inmates are even disallowed to take psychotropic meds in California prisons. White gangs do not allow white guys to take meds. So if you have a mental problem; oh well. And the guards won't intervene. When you live in fear, without your meds etc. and when you become *prey* for prison predators etc. live like that for a decade and what else can you be but a predator or a terrorist?...

Just between you and I let me tell you that *Orenthal James Simpson* probably did murder (in cold blood) Nicole and Ron. And I believe someone was with O.J. and helped him. It could have been his son, his friend (A.C.) or even Cato (his houseboy). But I don't believe O.J. did this alone. And I'll admit that for years I actually believed he did 'not' do it. *Johnnie Cochran* (Barry Scheck, Peter Neufeld, F. Lee Bailey and *Bob Blasier* etc.) was just that good. A great trial lawyer will make you believe a man with blood on his hands is just using ketchup. And Johnnie and his "*Dream Team*" made a believer out of me. And…eventually I came to understand (clearly) that O.J. did it and he got away: "*How To Get Away With Murder.*" And it was not his court trial that convinced me either. It was *something* else…

But we are breeding O.J.'s, Erics (Menendez), Charlies (Manson) and other predators every day in prisons. I remember a guy named Ed Stokes. He was a child molester. In 2003 I told the warden that I'd talked to Stokes and that he planned to molest a child as soon as he got out. "Warden: I'm willing to wear a wire and record this pedophile talking about what he's gonna do to kids if it will keep him in prison," I said. The warden dismissed me out of hand. Two months after Ed got out of prison I saw him on Inside Edition. He had bought an old ambulance. He lured a young boy into an ambulance and he viciously molested this boy. I think the kid may have been 8 years old. And there are more (many more) Eds who are getting out of prison tomorrow, next week and next month. We need to assemble a panel of experts to figure out who is likely to become a "monster," a "pedophile," a "terrorist" and a "murderer" etc. And we need to begin to address it now…

We ("G.B.G.") at *Gang Bangers* For *God* intend to stop by TMZ-Live in February 2016. We actually owe Harvey Levin (Max Hodges and Dax Holt) a huge thank you. TMZ was the first national TV show to say ("say my name, say my name") the name "*Gang Bangers For God*" on the air. We owe TMZ for exposing *G.B.G.* (*Gang Bangers* For *God*) to America.

We will tell Harvey, Dax and Max (although Max is no longer with TMZ) thank you. And — as we launch this campaign to expose America's "terrorist training camps" etc. we will take it to the politicians. We wrote hundreds of politicians when I was in prison. Hundreds! And I can name (on one hand) the ones who wrote back: Congresswoman Karen Bass, Congresswoman Barbara Lee, Senator Dianne Feinstein and *Democratic Chairman John Burton*; period. I probably wrote all 535 House of Representatives at least once. But they think prisoners don't matter. But as I'm coming home we will demonstrate that they do. We have family members and friends who vote. Some of us are on Twitter and on Facebook. Some of us are articulate enough to put two sentences together. And some of us can *write* and organize…

I've read at least fifty books about 'the media' in the past 3 years. I've read perhaps a hundred books about politicians. And I've watched every "Meet the Press," "This Week" and "Face the Nation" over the past 12 years. And I studied these "political" leaders. I know these guys. I can tell you how many times Donald Trump (or Rubio, Bush or Clinton etc.) blinks his eyes per minute. I know their breathing patterns. I know when they are reciting, memorizing, lying or evading etc. And I know when the media has been "bought off." And we intend to get with Tim Mak, Ari Shapiro and Dylan Marron etc. and we will 'discuss' these things. I'm passionate about telling professors and college students etc. what I've learned about the power, the hype and the *hoax* of the American media…

Donald Trump was a "media hoax." He was built, fed and fueled by the media. The media who understood (clearly) two things: A. Having him on your show is a ratings bonanza! B. If he does not like your questions he won't go on your show! And they (all of them) compromised their own integrity just to get him on their show. It turned my stomach watching those guys allow Donald to testify (aka testa*lie*) about *not* accepting any money. Yet his website clearly asked for (and receives) donations. And he clearly sold his books, caps and t-shirts at rallies. Trump did not 'self-fund' his campaign. He *earned* money by running for president. If you look at the amount of books, caps and t-shirts he sold while running for president (he sold more books in one month in 2015 than he did for the entire year of 2014) etc. he's earned $ tens of millions by running for president. The same thing with Ben Carson. These guys write a book (at the height of their campaigns) and sell them all during the campaign. And keep in mind that both Ben and Donald use *ghostwriters*!! So they are not really "writers" or "authors"…

"*Gang Bangers* For *God*" will talk to the American public about the Simpsons, Menendezs and the Mansons Amongst us! And we don't expect the corporate owned media to help us. So (with the power of the internet) we will build our own bonfires on the web…

## **How You Can Help:**

    We want Michael McCracken (in Lincoln, CA) to join us as a G.B.G. ambassador. Help us to reach Michael. We want Tim Mainella (in Dover, NH) to join us as an ambassador etc. (we pay small stipends to some of our ambassadors. Contact us to inquire). We want Eddie Olsen (Chula Vista, CA) to join us. We want Tanner Franklin (at San Diego State University) to join our ambassadorial team. We want Quinn Halleck (at UCLA) to join us. We want *Cedric Gregory* (in Nashville, TN) to join us. Cedric is also nominated for a *G.B.G.* leadership award. We want Professor Edith Lester on our advisory board. And we hope to present one of Professor Lester's classes with a *G.B.G.* lecture. We want Jacob Lescenske (Las Vegas) to join us. We want Malcolm Salvoora and Henry Kremer on our team. We want to work with Matthew Todd Miller and Derrik Sweeney. We want Levi Pettit and Landon Barabas on our team. We'd like to have *Hill Harper* on our advisory board. We hope Lila Perry (at Hillsborough) will work with us. We want Sheldon Ruby (Franklin and Marshall) on the team. We want Caleb Phillips, David Jeremiah and Nick Sexton (Christian High School in San Diego) on our team. We want Jack Roccato (San Diego State) and Alec Hartman on our team. Both Jack and Alec are concerned with helping via Catholic social programs. We need them. Jackson Long is a guy we need. We need *Jordan Goodin* on our team. We'd like Jack Baddour (in Chapel Hill, NC) to join our team. We'd like to have Professor Edward Moore as an advisor. And we'd like to have Austin Haugwout (at Central Connecticut State University) on our team.

    We need a digital street team and we hope Thomas Greely (Tracy, CA), Brooks Randolph and Joshua Taylor (University of Toledo) will work with us. We'd like to work with Jordan Maguire and Dr. Johnny McGuire. We want to work with Steve Moses. We need Kale Trimble (Daytona Beach) on our team. We want Noah Hayden, Christian Michaels (Dallas) and Evan McKeel (Richmond, VA) on our team. We want Trent Dorsey, Dave Franco and Aaron Smyth on our team. We need Professor Paul Butler as an advisor. We want Daniel Kitchen (a videographer at Christian High in El Cajon, CA) on our team. We want Garrett, Nick and Noah (all in the drama club at Christian High School) on our team. We want Alex Bernhart (a graduate from UC Berkeley) and Shawn Lewis on our team. We want Gunter McCourt (Delta State University) and Derek Piquette on our team. We want Neil Davidson (Sacto, CA) on our team. We want Jake Exkorn, Collin Stark and Collin Finnerty on our team. We want to work with Chance Doyle (Café Hope), Dr. Charles Stanley (in my hometown) and maybe Bishop Vaughn McLaughlin. We want *John Furnari* (Hacienda Heights, CA) on our team…

    America's criminal justice system is actually playing "*Correctional Roulette*™" with people's lives. And in the process "creating" stone cold killers. We want to speak to criminal justice and sociology students about this "correctional roulette." And *G.B.G.* is ready to offer a "Correctional *Heimlich* Maneuver™." Judges are using prisons as a (*man care*) "day care" for men. But the care is not there. And in the process we are threatening public safety. We want Matthew Bailey (Pensacola), Marcos Munoz (Serra High School) and Tony Goldwyn on our team…

Mary gave birth to Jesus and she'd never had sex with Joseph. For the rest of Mary's life there were people who suspected she'd lied. Some of them never did believe that the Holy Spirit impregnated her. And the Lord reminded me that just like some of them never believed Mary's story, some of them will never believe me. But no matter how many people thought Mary was lying, Jesus still came out of her body. And Jesus still did exactly what God wanted Him to do. "Everybody" did not believe Mary! And "everybody" will not believe *Sherman D. Manning*. Some of them will be "suspicious" til the day I die. Some of them will be suspicious after I'm in heaven. More than 2000 years later I can still find some folks who don't believe that "a *virgin*" Mary gave birth to Jesus. But I know that Mary was not lying. And…even in the midst of those who will suspect that I'm "lying." My job is to continue to strengthen "*Gang Bangers* For *God*" and to continue to *write*.

We want Riley (aka Sixth Man) on our team. We want Aspen Manning and Julian Gonzalez. We want Melinda Hunt (in Birmingham, AL) and her brother Christopher. We want Dr. Kyle Turner as an advisor. We want Shaun White, Adam Melcher, Nash Grier and Cole Wilkinson on the team. We want Matthew Lowe (at Duke) and Evan Spiegel. We want Michael Powers and David Horner (Evansville, IN) on our team. We want Christopher Vargas, "T" (T works at Corcoran State Prison) and *Mario Herrera* on our team. We want Curren Caples and Daniel Horton. We want Richard James Carlson, Tyler Grindstaff and James David Larson on our team. We want Professor Jeremy Barr and Dan Childs as advisors. We want *Joel Carpenter* (In Portland, ME) on our team. We want Hugh Murphy and Steve Murphy. We want Trevor Leja on our team. We want Brandon Marshall on our advisory board. Professor Anita Elberse invited Brandon to speak to her Harvard business class. We hope she'll invite *G.B.G.* also. We want Jeff Deskovich as an advisor.

…Black men and crime are linked (by the media) like peanut butter and jelly. In spite of Columbine, Chris Harper-Mercer, Dylan Roof and T.J. Lane etc. when the media says "crime" or "poor" they immediately show you file footage of black people. They've never associated poverty and the *white* citizens you see on the Jerry Springer show. The media has an unwritten rule wherein they hide white trailer parks. You don't see them on TV and it affects the psyche of the nation. It is *media bigotry*… We want G.B.G. "think tanks" to discuss these things. We also want Michael Giles, Luke Sears, Kyle Love, Nick Topete, Stephen Karr and *Brandon Urbas* on our team. We want Steven Evenhouse and Willie Steed. We want Benjamin Schlappig, Jack Dale (N. Richland Hills, TX) and James Wood (San Diego State freshman) on our team. We want Sam Ray (Vanderbilt, TN) and Francisco Sousa. We need Zach Seabaugh (Atlanta, GA), Tim Franzen, Noah Jackson and Blake Shankle. We need Stone Martin (in South Carolina) on our team. We need James Larude and Joshua Leonard (in Newborn, GA) on our team. We want Max Marmer as an advisor. We want Alex Pourazari and Austin R. Moore on our team. We want Scott Kelly (Middletown, CA), Chef Flynn (at Eureka), Clint Barbour and Beshara Mashney (Anaheim) on our team. We want Brandon Kuehl, Beau Sorenson, Blake Jones and Alan Fox (in NY) on our team.

We want J.T. Mora, Trevor Douglas, Clayton Beckham, Cody Fry, Alex Shier, Zach Kaltenbach and *Kevin Mayberry* on our team. We want Alex Sheets, Brady Olson, Scott Wiener, Harrison Schrock (UCLA), Alec Hersh (Franklin C. Marshall), Reid Blake (George Washington University), *Colin Yost* (at Princeton), Jacob Zuniga (San Diego City College), Cameron Didion, Michael James Williams (Hemet, CA), Felix K Jellberg, Jack Bartlett and Anthony Patera. We want *Cameron Dallas* on our team. We want Doug Dodd and Brian Flores on our team…

    As I pastor Ex-con Baptist (LOL) Church: We all fall down but we can get up. We don't fall *from* grace we fall *to* grace. And we need the "grace" to get up. And it is what I've *learned* in the *fall* that qualifies me to "strengthen the brothers"… I will call Rev. Shane Harris (in San Diego) and Jonathan McCrae (St. Cloud, MN) and ask them to join our campaign… I learned a lot in this "fall" and my message to every man is that no matter how low we fall we can get back up again. I told them at Folsom State Prison that, "I'll rise again! Can't no prison cell hold my body down." I had to learn how to transcend the *metal* bars and the *mental* bars. But the chains on any of my people are the chains on me. And as long as we are bound by psychological bars and chained I can never be free…

*Sherman D. Manning*

*G.B.G.* (*Gang Bangers* For *God*)…

## **Empire Mass Incarceration:**

    We were ecstatic to see Lee Daniels (a very brilliant man) mention "mass incarceration" on his hit show "*Empire*." My friend in Switzerland told me, "We must try to get Mr. Daniels to have you on Empire with your books; like he had Al Sharpton." I wish "Scandal," "How To Get Away With Murder" and "The Good Wife" would all also write "mass incarceration" into their shows…

    Recently the federal government decided to release 6,000 inmates (drug addicts) early. Senator Cory Booker and Rand Paul have passed some bipartisan legislation. It is well intentioned but (potentially) wrong-headed. 70 percent of the inmates who came to prison as addicts remain addicts. I can attest to this experientially because I'm "embedded" in the prison (my story). I know where the bodies are buried (so to speak). I know who smuggles drugs into prison. I know how they smuggle drugs in. I know who has cell phones and how they order the drugs etc. So 70 percent of the 6,000 inmates being released are still addicts. Prisons do not "treat" drug addictions. Most prisons don't even pretend to; they're mere warehouses. The few prisons with programs are underfunded and understaffed. We do have too many people in prisons. And a lot of "us" should not have been sent to prison. But if you "break it you own it." And prison breaks men and boys. And it destroys our lives. So if the State decided to release ten thousand of "us" tomorrow, 8,200 would return within a year. Who is going to *hire* us? Who will 'house' us? And what do we do about our diseases (alcoholism and drug addictions)? A woman is abused (or assaulted) by a man every 12 seconds in this country. One person is killed with a firearm every 16 minutes in America. 92 people are killed daily with guns. And drug addicted ex-cons do a lot of the beatings and the killings. The *mass incarceration* is a major *crisis* in America. But simply "mass" releasing people is like someone being willing to *comfort* you in your crisis. But although they comfort (release) you they are unwilling to *carry* you to your *deliverance*. When you've been locked up in a violent prison ("monster factory") for several years while addicted you are thereby afflicted. And you don't merely need someone to acknowledge you with rhetoric or to comfort you with a release. You need to be transported to your deliverance.

    In Mark Chapter 2 the Bible says, "Then they came to Him, bringing a paralytic who was *carried* by four men. And when they could not come near Him (Jesus) because of the crowd, they uncovered the roof where he was. So when they had broken through they let down the bed on which the paralytic was lying." They *carried* this man to Jesus. They could have just felt sorry for him like a rich man passing a beggar. But they decided to pick him up and carry him to the help that he needed to get out of the bed. I really (really) doubt (very seriously) that Senator Booker is going to be able to get Republicans to agree to "carry" ex-cons to the jobs, programs and the housing that they need to "get out of that prison bed." I personally believe many people like recidivism. They have to see it coming. How could they not? And 'when' the parolee reoffends they can say, "We need to lock him back up." These "sympathy releases" are a recipe for disaster.

And I hope I can talk to Mike Slater, Tom Joyner and Steve Harvey etc. about this. I hope we can inspire Chance Pena (in Tyler, TX), Cole Criske (Temecula, CA), Adam Stuart (Irving, TX) and Patrick Carroll (Collinsworth, TX) to work with us on exposing the need for "deliverance." We want Anthony Patera, *Jared Goodman*, *Jordan Robbins* and Sam Peeples to work with us. We want to contact the president of San Diego City College (Anthony Beebe) and try to speak to his sociology and criminal justice students. We will hire "*method* actors" etc. (like *Vincent Thomas* in L.A.) and even dancers (Derek Piquette, Kent Boyd and Jakob Karr etc.) to help us use "entertainment" to shine a light on "mass incarceration," the lack of "rehabilitation" and…

The U.S. terrorist training camps which are "*Creating Monsters*™". (Read my *book Creating Monsters*). Without light there is darkness. And in darkness evil can hide. And all that it takes for evil to rage is for good men to remain silent! We (G.B.G.) won't be quiet. …Look for my book "*Left For Dead*" in March of 2016…

# **Mass Incarceration: 2016**

"The *grave* waits," states Ta-Nehisi Coates. And the grave is the prison system. He calls it a grave. Judge Joe Brown calls it a slave warehouse. And I call it Hades (hell). I believe President Barack Obama is our nation's greatest President. And I credit his Administration for at least addressing mass incarceration. But they did not go far enough. And if Hillary wins she owes it to poor whites, blacks and Hispanics to finish what President Obama started. And she should reverse the harm done (via AEDPA and PLRA) by President Bill Clinton.

And John Q. Citizen must continue to pressure politicians to stop this "lock-em-up and throw away the key" policy. I wish that "mass releasing" inmates would solve the problem. It will not! I've stated that a part of me believes that the only reason 'some' Republicans supported Senator Cory Booker's Bill to release 6,000 federal prisoners is because they know it may fail. When you spend 'time' in prison it destroys your mind. And when you are released you'll probably reoffend. And the moment 'they' reoffend then Ted Cruz and Mitch McConnell etc. can say, "See I told you they should be locked up." Mass incarceration may not be a 'conspiracy'. But mass incarceration may as well 'be' a conspiracy due its effects. The people must rise and change this. And don't depend on our spineless politicians to do it. These guys (in Congress) are bought, paid for and they are *owned* by the NRA. And a politician who is unwilling to standup to the NRA is a coward. And he ought to be run out of office with all deliberate speed.

We're talking about non-violent offenders who are drug addicts. That is only a start. We need to have a conversation about hundreds of thousands of men (many black and most poor) who are incarcerated on trumped up rape allegations. A real rapist ought to be in prison — period. But people have been lying about rape since the beginning of time. That started in Genesis with Joseph. And no one wants to consider the fact that some of these guys who have "done it before" did *not* do "it" the first time. But they plead guilty because "if you plead you get probation. But if you go to trial you'll probably get an all-white jury. And although I do *not* think you did this they may convict you," sayeth their lawyer. "And if you get convicted you will get 20 years in prison." So you actually plead guilty to a crime you did not commit. And now you are "convicted of a *sex* crime." And if a man or woman ever gets angry at you all they have to do is say, "He raped me." And candidly they can just say, "He hit me." And when the cops pull the record and see where you were "convicted of a *sexual* battery out in Virginia." They will (literally) talk the person into accusing you of rape! "So we can get this scumbag off the streets for good."

This happens every day in America. But white wealthy child molesters (like Dr. Jeff Abrams in San Diego) get probation and house arrest (because he can bribe D.A. Kerry Conway and the judge). We all want to talk about how Johnnie Cochran, Scheck, Lee Bailey and *Bob Blasier* etc. got O.J. "off on two counts of murder." But nobody raises hell about serial pedophiles getting "off" every day. Why? Ask Kerry Conway! Because most convicted pedophiles are white and wealthy! We have a "war" on drugs and a "war" on gangs. But you don't see a "war" on pedophiles! Because if you had a "war" on pedophiles half of Wall Street would go to prison! But...

They will lock me up for over a decade because a grown ass man (Mr. Calvario) says he was walking at 2:40 a.m. and a strange black guy offered him a ride. And he did not like the black guy but he got in the car to get a ride to "get rid of the guy." And Calvario testified (under oath) that the minute he got in my car (to get rid of me) I pulled a gun on him. And after he says I pulled a gun he says he decided to "put on my seatbelt." Asked why? He replied, "Because I always put on my seatbelt whether a gun is drawn on me or not" (I repeat). The case is a shining example of "wrongful convictions" being used to incarcerate tens of thousands of us. A prison counselor told me that she read my entire case. And "it's a bullshit case," she said. "It proves they wanted to silence you. They figured they would destroy you with a rape conviction. And they figured you'd be embarrassed to talk about it. Most guys convicted of rape crawl into a hole and hide," she said. "If I were you I'd talk about it! Talk to Lisa Ling, Anderson Cooper and Tom Joyner etc. Talk to anybody who will listen. That is the only f-cking way a change will come," she told me. So I am talking and writing! I am wrongly convicted of rape! And I am "actually innocent." And I'm not the only one. There are many more... I want readers to Google Glenn Ford! And Google Dale Cox. Find the 60 Minutes interview that aired 10/12/15. Watch Mr. Ford and Dale Cox. And then tell me how much you believe in our criminal justice system. It is absolutely rigged and flawed. Call Attorney Gerry Spence and ask him how many men are in prisons on "trumped-up" rape convictions. All I need to do is 'say' you raped me. And you go to jail!...

The photos of the man in underwear in this book is prison guard *Colby Compton*. He gave them to an inmate he had sex with (I repeat). An inmate cannot consent — so it was "rape." I published them to prove a point. Inmates (male and female) are raped every day in prisons (by guards, civilians and by other prisoners). I saw Matt Doran interview a former guard (on Crime Watch) regarding "sex" with inmates. I wish he'd called me. This book is probably the first (and only) book published (in the world) by a prisoner with photos of a current guard in underwear! Colby Compton is working at Salinas Valley State Prison right now.

Prison *rape* is an everyday part of "mass incarceration" and "Hades." I can name 20 male (married) guards at Folsom State Prison who rape male inmates. And guards routinely smuggle cell phones, Oxycontin and cigarettes in for "sex." It is Guards Gone Gay (G.G.G.) and Guards Gone Wild... Associate Warden Ross Meirs convinced Jeff Macomber to sweep Colby's rapes under the rug due to civil liability!... I could write a dissertation on "sex" in prison involving "guards" and inmates. I tell mothers (all the time) who have 17 and 18-year old sons in trouble to do anything they can to prevent them from ever entering prison because guards will rape them! And if the guards don't rape them their cell partners will. This is a discussion we need to have. And I am ready and willing to have this discussion. I want readers to tell Mike Walters, Lisa Ling and any talk show host you can.

I want to talk about how the "*grave*" waits. I am an expert on "the grave." Susan Sarandon said, "I'm heartbroken for the state of our judicial system." I hope we can work with Mrs. Sarandon to elucidate this "rigged" judicial system. I want *Colin Yost* and a couple of his friends at Princeton to work with us. Some people say "*Gang Bangers* For *God*" is like a secret society because it's so hard to join. We handpick a select group! We want Jack Baddour in Chapel Hill, NC to work with us. We want Anthony Patera and Zachary Nathaniel Anderson. Zach was wrongly convicted of statutory rape. We want to reach Jared Goodman and Sam Peeples…

Joseph was convicted (in Genesis) of a sex crime. Tupac Shakur was convicted of a sex crime. Rolando Cruz, Brian Banks, Ronald Cotton and Marcus Dixon etc. Ask Jeff Deskovich how easy it is to be deemed a "rapist" and a "predator." And then they expect you to roll over and die. I will not die! Not yet!... We want to work with Dylan Marron, C.J. Sheron and Lila Perry. We want Lila to get a few friends at Hillsborough to help us. And we want Michael McCracken in Lincoln. We want *Emma Weinman* (in San Diego) to work on our team. We want Tony Sosa (San Diego) and Jack McCain on our team. Jack McCain is a Christian student in San Diego. He slept outside in October 2015 to "experience" homelessness. We need people like Jack on our team. We want to talk to L.Z. Granderson about our work. God allowed me to be "isolated" for my development. I'm ready now.

I want to find Danny Mackey and Councilman Jonathan Miller. We want *Nick Prato* (a college student in Arizona) on our team. Nick has been through hell and high water. He is battle-tested. We want Lance Corporal Jeremy Benton (and Lance Corporal *Jacob* who was with Benton when they met President Obama) on our team. We want Mark Caparelli and Trenton Hunt (Hunt is a student in San Diego) on our team. We want to reach *Douglas Dodd* and Lance Barabas. We want Jake O'Donoghue, Harley Litzelman, Brendan Martello, Ryan Fitzgerald and Ryan Hulselbus on our team. I want to work with Riley (the Sixth Man) and with Nic Carlson. We want *Ricky Manning*, Trey Enloe, Jason Stevens (Carlsbad), Joshua Stipp and Alex Weinberg. I'd like to find *Max Marmer* and Lasse Herrmann and get their input. We need people like Derek Sweeney (at Georgetown University), Luke Gates and Greg Porter on our team. We want Rocco Gogllotti, Zac Sunderland, Jai Breisch and Jack dale. We want Michael Dennis in Grapevine, TX and Tanner Franklin.

We will change the game. We will elevate the debate. We need to shine a bright light on wrongful convictions. There is a reason Barry Scheck and Peter Neufeld decided to start the Innocence Project. And *Bob Blasier* told me that Barry and Peter are "saints." I want to see college students (in their criminal justice and sociology classes) having discussions and debates about "mass incarceration" and about how "wrongful convictions" contribute to "mass incarceration." We cannot have this discussion without input from prisoners and ex-cons. This debate is actually past due. And I want every youngster reading this book to debate it. Don't wait on the Congress. I'm telling you (with the exception of Karen Bass, Barbara Lee, Diane Feinstein and a few others) most of these guys warming the seats in our House of Representatives are absolute "crooks." They can be bought by the Koch brothers or the NRA etc. or whoever. We have judges and prosecutors (i.e. Kerry Conway) who are for *sale*. And the rich get richer but the poor get prison. And the beat goes on…

I want Christian students like *Jack McCain* (the San Diego student) to *pray* about this book. Pray about "*Gang Bangers* For *God*." And then join us in dealing with the words of Jesus (Lord and Savior) in St. Matthew Chapter 25. With God all things are possible. So it is "possible" that we can inspire a few (i.e. 100) students (i.e. Jack McCain, Jordan Goodin and Brandon Urbas etc.) from diverse backgrounds etc. to join our team. We'll use method acting, docudramas, performance arts, clinics, seminars and workshops etc. to dramatize the issues which we want to transform. I need Jack McCain, Leo Goldsmith and Alec Hartman etc. to *pray* for "*Gang Bangers* For *God*." God does answer prayer. Read "*Left For Dead*!"…

# The President Barack Obama Project:

*NAPS*, *G.B.G.* (*Gang Bangers* For *God*) and a small group of Swiss (and American) entrepreneurs etc. will form this project in concert with *Sherman's* other seminars. We will use the powerful, awesome and miraculous story of President Obama's life in churches, colleges, clubs and groups. "I feel like nobody has really captured the awesomeness of the Obama story in a national movement. And his chilling story is a testament to the power of the *American Dream*" states *Sherman*. "How unlikely that a black guy who has a white mother from Kansas and a black father from Kenya; a community organizer — could become a United States Commander-in-Chief. He had no family money. He was not Barack "*Kennedy*" Obama. He wasn't Barack "*Rockefeller*" Obama. But he's Barack "*Hussein*" Obama. And he defeated and conquered a long list of challengers (including *billionaire* Mitt Romney) and rose to become the first black man to darken (no pun intended) the Whitehouse."

And he continues, "I wanna use the President's fascinating story to motivate youngsters (and even the elderly) to know that if you wish upon a star your dreams can come true. I wanna even motivate ex-cons and ex-gangsters to know that they are not what they (haters) call them. You can't allow what the police/prosecutors or prison guards call you to define who you are. They called Obama a terrorist, a Muslim (as if that would've been negative), and even Hitler. They called him Kenyan etc. But now they call him *Mr. President*. And I want to use this tremendous story to empower people."

*Sherman* concludes, "Historians will write about President Obama a hundred years from now. They'll talk about how his presidency ushered in a woman (Clinton) and Latinos etc. But we (*NAPS*, *G.B.G.* and *B.O.P.*) will write, speak and teach in (real time) the now!"… If you would like to schedule a B.O.P. conference, seminar, clinic or workshop at your school, group, club or business etc. contact us today… Sherman says, "I would be remiss if I did not thank *Peter Andrist* for all he's done. Peter is a Swiss businessman who has been my best friend for 24 years. He never turned on me. He never believed what 'they' said about me. And I love Peter as if he was my own brother. I thank his beautiful wife Katrin for allowing him to help me. Peter told me that, 'You have some Rubin Carter, some Martin Luther King, Jr. etc. in *you*. When people hear you speak they'll know you are *not* who they *say* you are…'"

Sherman salutes his team in Switzerland (led by *Peter Andrist*). And he says: "I can't wait to *speak* and to preach and tell this story. I am excited! I need to reach Travis Ulerick, John Mandern, C.J. Sheron, Daniel Bugriyev and Brian Banks etc. And…let's get it started. Maybe Floyd Mayweather, Tyler Perry or even Steve Harvey will help us kick this off!"

© Sherman D. Manning — December — 2015

# **American Crime Stories:**

Somebody asked me if I'm friends with Malcolm Jamal Warner, Cuba Gooding or John Travolta. "Because it's very ironic that *American Crime Stories* (with Malcolm, Cuba and John etc.) starts in February 2016; right after your O.J. book publishes. And they just so happen to be doing the O.J. Simpson series — in February! Were you tipped off?" a guy inquired. I do not know either Malcolm, Cuba or John. But I feel like I do know O.J. Simpson. And we are building, creating and making more O.J. Simpsons in prison every day. During O.J.'s trial for double homicide he was able to afford justice. The rich get justice and the poor get jail. Robert Blake was able to afford (the great Tom Mesereau whom I almost hired for my trial. Tom was a lot less expensive when I knew him) justice. And don't forget (as I wrote earlier) about Ethan Couch. He killed 4 people and received probation. I'm certain his dad bribed Judge Jean Boyd (who just so happened to retire the next year). And the child molester/rapist Dr. Jeffrey Abrams? He too got probation. Will we ever know how much he paid Deputy D.A. Kerry Conway and his judge?...

Ethan Couch claimed to be suffering from "affluenza." Translation? Too rich to jail! Billionaires buy elections and millionaires buy justice. It all comes back to money. I'm reminded that Sheldon Adelson stated (in 2011) he was willing to personally spend $100 million to defeat President Obama. The Koch brothers spent $200 million trying to unseat him. And the Romney campaign spent $900 million. One Democratic consultant states that more than $2.1 billion was spent trying to defeat Mr. Obama. But the Obama machine defeated Koch, Romney, Adelson and all other machines. And the same machine(s) which tried to buy the last election have a vested interest in prisons. America had 500,000 people in prison in 1980. Just 35 years later we have over 2.2 million (one estimate says 2.7 million) in prison. We spend $81 billion per year on prisons. And police, prosecutors and corrupted judges routinely play chicken with justice. I believe that at least 10 percent of all prisoners are wrongly convicted. That would be almost 250,000 people. No human being is perfect. Anyone who thinks that juries get it right 100 percent of the time is naïve. Any system that gets anything right 90 percent of the time is a great system. So if judges and/or juries render the right verdict 90 percent of the time (and that is a high estimate) we'd still have over 200,000 people who shouldn't be in jail. Hell — even if they got it right 95 percent of the time we'd have 125,000 folks in prison wrongly convicted.

And when it comes to trials and prisons I am an "authentic source." And I can tell you that some judges (i.e. Robert Altman) and prosecutors (i.e. Mary Hanlon) are corrupted. They will do anything to convict… When Hanlon discovered I had a witness to verify that there was "no rape" she played dirty. My witness was in jail and his testimony was solid. He *lived* with the alleged "victim." Hanlon had him (Brett Nelson) released from jail, and had his charges dismissed. And they (the prosecutor's office) sent Brett to Oregon a day before my trial (I repeat). It's pretty sick but prosecutors (ask *Gerry Spence*) play chicken with justice; daily. And then we all play *"correctional roulette"*… What turns my stomach is seeing courts send 17, 18 and 19-year olds to prison. And once they serve 4 or 5 years in here they are ruined for life. Putting youngsters in prison and expecting them to get *rehabilitated* is like telling a person with an *infection* to lock up in a room and get better. But you refuse to give them any antibiotics. It's like locking a man in a room with 4 or 5 rattle snakes. If they bite him and inject their venom he's doomed. If he's lucky enough to fight them and to kill them he becomes dangerous and deadly in the process. Living in prison is a dangerous endeavor. And you have to become hyper-vigilant in order to survive. You'll become a lone wolf, violent extremist or a domestic terrorist before you leave "here." If I told you some of the stuff I've seen men do to other men (in prison) *you* would *not sleep for a week*! I've seen bone-chilling violence and murders. I hope I can talk to Tom Joyner, Mike Slater and Sally Sears etc. about these things. Sally (at WGCL in my hometown) did a story on cell phones in prisons. They showed how "we" get them in. But… They never explained that 80 percent of our phones are brought in by prison guard staff.

…I am praying that I can find Narcisco Morales, Jonas Maines (in Maine), Officer Kenneth Casey (with the D.C. Police Department), John Mimbela, Eric Valdez (Houston, TX), Anthony Padilla, Jeff Deskovich, Daniel Villegas, *Douglas Dodd*, Hill Harper, Andrew Thompson, *Kale Trimble*, *Max Marmer*, Lasse Harmann, Aaron Quinn (Vallejo), Brooks Randolph, *Nick Prato* (No. Arizona University), Jake Zoard and Barrett Foa. And I hope to convince them to help us to proclaim justice.

Prisons would not be a part of the dialogue were it not for Bernie Sanders. As a graduate of "*Hate* University" I'll join the conversation. We want fellows from Sigma Alpha Epsilon to join the discussion. We want politically active students (i.e. at San Diego State University, Georgetown University and at Emory University etc.) to join the discussion on "*correctional roulette*." I believe (deeply) that people like Tanner Franklin, Jack Roccato, Malcolm Salvoora and Jacob Lescenske etc. can help us devise strategies and policies that correct Corrections. I think they can move the country away from hyper-incarceration and toward hyper-education… I wish Bernie Sanders would win. But… If Sanders inspires thousands of students (i.e. Derrik Sweeney, Jacob Saxe and Nick Stoeberl etc.) to join the dialogue regarding "prisons." And if they then join a conversation about "wrongful convictions," "false accusation," pseudo-rehabilitation and "*reintegration*" etc. this will all help create a "*more perfect union*"…

Perhaps (?) "we" can get this book to Lee Daniels, Cuba or to Malcolm etc. and they can use it on their set(s). And this book will help "spark" the conversation (on campuses across our great nation)… I will remind you that "*Left For Dead*" publishes in February 2016. And it is a must-read…

I'll see you on Periscope, YouTube, Facebook and on Twitter@ShermanD.Manning…

## **Epilogue:**

    I actually (I repeat) *write* my books. I used to wonder what Dr. Cornel West meant by the term "corporate owned media." And I used to wonder why Rev. Hosea Williams always taught me that many "systems" in the United Sates are "rigged." But I've learned a lot watching *Donald* Chump. This buffoon publishes a book-in-November in which he admits that he "manipulates the media." And yet reporters still kiss-up to him while "knowing" he's playing them. But… I noticed how "well" and how "much" CBS covers Mr. Chump and lo and behold; come to find out that CBS *published* his book. So at the end of the day the joke is on the poor, working and middleclass. So the media builds Donald up and covers his every word. They (the media) cover everything "Donald." And… *Donald* is a coward!...

    They (the media) make him relevant and newsworthy. And then they (the same media which are promoting him and claiming to wonder why he's being covered) publish (and promote) his book. So CBS gets "ratings" (= money) by having Major Garrett to sit down and interview Donald. And then CBS gets more money by "publishing" a book Donald did not even write. It's a 193 page portrait of an egomaniac. And yet Tim Mak will not get any coverage because he interrupts Donald's narrative. Mak believes (as do I) Donald raped his ex-wife. And Michael Cohen (Donald's "mob" lawyer) paid her to change her story. Cohen had the audacity to say a woman could not be raped by her husband. And Donald claimed to disagree but he did not fire Cohen. The media are in cahoots with Donald. I had to stop watching "Extra" because they (Mario Lopez and Ajay etc.) seem to be Donald's personal cheerleaders…

    I'm afraid that just as Donald has hoodwinked us while being aided and abetted by the U.S. media, we have also been hoodwinked, bamboozled and suckered by America's *criminal justice system*. It is an $80 billion fraud! Our criminal justice system may as well be a "debtor" prison system. You pay to play. And if you can pay like Ethan Couch and like physicians in San Diego etc. who *molest* disabled children, you will not ever see the inside of a prison. It is an abomination. We have a prison system which is built on the backs of blacks, Hispanics and poor whites. The system is designed to destroy "black" (and poor) men. The same media (which will *not* cover this book like they will a book by Donald)… The same media which has built up a racist, lying, bigoted clown like Donald; this same media has built a deep, dark and entrenched bias against blacks in this country. Thanks to the "media" (I repeat) black men and crime go together like peanut butter and jelly. When your local media mentions gangs, drugs or violence they show black people. Yet, even though most *pedophiles* are white you don't see a linkage (in the media) between older white men (i.e. Jerry Sandusky, Dennis Hastert, Dr. Mike Melcher etc.) and pedophilia. For every black or Hispanic man you show me who is a pedophile I'll show you 20 Jared Fogels!

    Who owns CBS, NBC and ABC? Who runs them? All you have to do is watch "Big Brother" (on CBS) and you'll see that somebody (at CBS) does not like too many Black people. Especially intelligent black people. I guess there goes my dream of being interviewed by *Gayle King* (a *queen*), Nora and Charlie Rose. I guess I shall never sit at the table and have "The

Talk" with… But maybe Whoopi (and Joy) will have me on "The View"… This is not a very racist country. And the country has definitely not become more racist because of President Obama. The racists (who are in the minority) have simply become more enraged because this great country elected President Obama…

Back to the criminal justice system: Because of the empirical data I gathered while trapped in prison I developed "the view" that (requires authentic thinking) many judges and prosecutors may as well be viewed as the mafia. They are involved (literally) in "*organized crime.*" They (these stone-cold judges and conservative prosecutors) decide "who" goes to prison!... If you look at the case of Dr. Jeffrey Abrams (in El Cajon, CA) he should be *under* the prison. And Deputy District Attorney Kerry Conway (I repeat) looked straight into the camera and "justified" (justilied) why Abrams (who is very wealthy) was okay "not" going to prison…

I'm a forgiving person and I'm not one to become "bitter." I'd gotten over my anger at the system for wrongly convicting me. But in retrospect it is absolutely unspeakable. I was put in prison for allegedly "raping" a man. And… I was tried without a lawyer by an all-white jury… When Attorney Murray J. Janus (famed trial lawyer) read the testimony of Ricardo Calvario Janus said, "A first-year law student could have shredded this false testimony"… I.E. Calvario said I was "following" him. And he simply got in my car "to get rid" of me because he was "tired" of me following him. He said as soon as he sat in my car I pulled a pistol on him. He claimed I pointed it at his head. And then "I put on my seatbelt," he said. "Calvario, why would you put on a seatbelt with a gun to your head?" He said, "Because I always put on my seatbelt whether a gun is pointed at my head or not." …And this paragon of integrity sent me to prison on this utter fabrication. But…

I forgive Calvario. He was a tool. I will spend my life exposing the corruption of the system. It was Detective Dave Winkler, Prosecutor Mary Hanlon and *Judge Robert Altman* who "rigged" the trial (charade) against me. I can handle a jury getting it "wrong." Juries are humans. And people are not "perfect." But lawyers? Detectives and judges? I *passed* a polygraph test! And… I am convinced (deep down in the city of my *soul*) that Winkler, Hanlon and Altman "knew" that I was *not guilty*. But… "So what; he probably got away with something he *did* do. So let's send him to *prison*!"... There are tens of thousands of people in prison who did not do it. And this threatens public safety. The system is "rigged." And our *media* have "blood" on their hands…

I want readers to please help me to contact Ashby Sorenson, Spencer (from "Survivor" 2015), Tyler *Grosso*… I want Grosso on our team. We can pay him for his help. We want Zak Williams (to help us teach financial literacy) and Lance Bass. We want Michael Bass (Richmond, VA) and *Eric Look* (Eric is in Park City, UT). We want *Kai* Kloepfer (Kai is a brilliant guy in Boulder, CO) and PFC Bryce Keller. *Nathan Brown* (Serra Mesa) is an awesome guy. We need Nathan! We want Ronald Keith Dunn and Brian Graham in Richmond, VA. We need *Zachary Ivey* (an awesome dude in Texas), Jordan Robbins, Alan Fox and Sam Ray. John Bono (in O'Fallon, MO) is a guy we need. *Colin Yost* is a brilliant Princeton student. We need Yost, *Joshua Stipp* (Temecula, CA), *Kale Trimble*, Moi Navarro, Bradley Scott Montgomery, Benjamin Golden and Joseph Latham on our team… What CBS has done with "Donald" is like setting a fire and then pretending to be the hero by alerting people to the fire, and then "publishing" a book "about" the fire. Donald is a "media" hoax. And much of our *criminal justice* system is also an $80 billion "hoax." Maybe I'll get a YouTube channel to discuss it since CBS won't cover me…

…In October of 2015 'Donald' requested Secret Service protection. It should have been denied since he brags that he has so much money. And he claimed to be self-funding his campaign. Then he admits that he has not spent a dime "because the media covers me for free." So Donald should have taken all the money he should have spent on his campaign and hired his own security. We've been had and hoodwinked again. And… Many of these so-called commentators (who don't disclose it) go on 'Meet the Press' and other shows. And they'll talk up a certain candidate. But they don't reveal that they are paid (by the campaign) to talk them up!...

What I love about President Obama is how brilliant he and his team were. They knew that many of these media personalities were being 'paid' to convince Americans that he could not win. Remember the Rev. Jeremiah Wright tapes?... Remember the *Mark Fuhrman* tapes? Same strategy!! Johnnie Cochran and his "*Dream Team*" already (well before they disclosed them to the prosecution team) had the Fuhrman tapes (tapes of Detective Fuhrman calling blacks the "N" word etc.). But in a stroke of genius they saved them and used them to convince the jury that Detective Fuhrman was "a lying genocidal racist." And since he's a racist "you must acquit O.J." And the media had the Rev. Wright tapes (by the way I love Rev. Wright and I think he's a brilliant preacher) for a long time. And they withheld them until the last minute to take him down. Many black candidates would have attacked the media (as I'm doing but I'm not running for office). And that would have been a big mistake. Senator Obama knew that would be viewed like "crying racism." So instead he gave a masterful speech and the rest is history. One of my friends estimates that well over $3 billion was spent by power brokers who did not want him to win. $3 billion!...

And a lot of those power brokers (including Donald) earn a lot of their money off of our $80 billion "*criminal* justice" system. They don't want crime to go down. They make too much damn money off of crime. Rev. Hosea Williams taught me that "crime *pays* as long as you're the one administering justice." The justice system is just like a prison system. It is biased, racist and it is for sale. How can we allow wardens (with high school diplomas) to run a prison with 4,000 inmates and 900 employees? And they (hillbilly wardens) control $100 million budgets… Just as guards smuggle drugs and cellphones into prisons (I've personally watched it) and then complain about contraband. Judges accept bribes every day. And even if they don't accept bribes they come to the bench with an inherent bias and prejudice against the poor. And they send the poor and downtrodden to prison every day. But Ethan Couch (for example) never saw the inside of a prison. I could lecture (for weeks) about the "Ethan" effect on "justice." This blatant judicial bias, judicial bigotry and judicial injustice runs rampant in American courtrooms. A court reminds me of a prison. You see tons of blacks and Hispanics in court. But they are the defendants. And most of the folks with the power (the judges, the prosecutors and police) are white. In the prisons the inmates are all of color. The administrators are mostly white. Ask Governor Jerry Brown how many of his 33 wardens are black? None! Zero!... So I must "pastor" Ex-Con Baptist (LOL) Church. And the message is clear: I will tell black (white and Hispanic) men that we must get ourselves "*educated*." How many 20-year old boys have never *read* a book? Readers are leaders. We must get it together. Jesse Jackson used to say "true power is not in the State House or the White House. But it's in your house and in my house."

    I want to *hire* Zachary Ivey, Chance Pena, Anthony Patera, Eddie Olsen (in Chula Vista), John Bono, Justin Frazier, Scott Czeda, Jacob Goodin and *Alec Knudsen* to work with "us"! And I hope that *Nathan Brown* (Serra Mesa, CA), Nick Dannenberger, Noah Hayden, *Kai Kloepfler*, Benjamin Golden and *Tyler Grosso* will hear about our team and be inclined to join us. I hope we can find Jason Kaseman, *Joshua Scannell*, Greg Scannel (in Dallas), Tyler Grindstaff, *Jack Dale*, *Matt Scheidt*, Mario Herrera (in Sacramento), Mark Kashirets (nurse) and "T" etc. and get them on board. We need a national campaign to educate and activate people. We must take back our "criminal justice" system from bigots like Donald, Ben Carson (a master Uncle Tom) and other plutocrats. Donald, Ted Cruz and many other Republicans "bank" on crime and ignorance. They have "*Romnesia*" (aka amnesia) regarding St. Matthew Chapter 25. "I was in prison and you *visited* me not." That word "visit" (translated) meant to "restore." Nearly 800,000 inmates will get out of prison this year. Who will help "restore" them? If it's up to Donald, Ben Carson and other *banksters* etc. they'll just reoffend (because no one will hire them) and go "back to prison where they belong." And *Donald* will go buy him some *new hair* from his profits off of crime...

    ...*Ben Carson* is the third worst thing to happen to black Americans. It turns out that he's a sneaky liar with an ego almost as large as Donald's. Ben just hides his narcissism behind a mask of alleged Christianity. This dude has a portrait of himself with Jesus. He insinuates that he (Ben) himself is a black Jesus. Ben's house is said to be a "temple" unto himself. His home looks like Donald's office. All you see on the walls is Ben.

    ...I'm a Saturday Night Live fan but I refused to watch it on 11/7/15 because of the racist host. Yet, I woke up on 11/8/15 and was floored to see GMA lead their newscast with Donald and SNL. A Texas judge was gunned down the night before. Russia asked the FBI to join their investigation of the downed plane in Egypt. Two Louisiana cops were arrested (11/7/15) for murdering a 6-year old boy and wounding his father. But in light of all of that ABC decided that an *ugly* old white man hosting SNL was their top story. I nearly (literally) vomited. I indict the American media on fraud, monopoly and duplicity. "They" have built Donald up although they know his platform is a complete deception. Ben lies and claims he hid some white students during a riot in 1968. He tells this lie to try to win white votes. But it will be a cold day in hell before the Republican Party nominates a black man for U.S. President. Donald is as fake as his (hair growth) hair. But the Republicans are willing to nominate him over "Ben-Jesus"...

    "*Gang Bangers For God*" is recruiting "a few good men" to join us in a *crusade* that encourages "football and politics." The football part is easy because we love sports. But we've got to get men to start loving politics... Republicans do not want black people to vote. They've erected barriers nationwide that prevent blacks (Hispanics and poor whites) from voting! Dr. King, Ambassador Young, Rev. Hosea Williams etc. etc. fought and bled for the right to vote.

And the American criminal justice system is now one of those barriers used to prevent blacks (Hispanics and poor whites) from voting. As a convicted felon you can't vote. This is exactly what Ted Cruz, Donald, Mitch McConnell and many others want. White people have lost their majority. So now they must manipulate a monopoly. They do so by locking out millions of voters. Otherwise how will the ever get another ole, stale, white, male president?...

...My fellow Americans; the criminal justice system (via *thousands* of juveniles, jails and prisons) is a threat to national security. When nearly 2.7 million men are in prison that is a problem. And these are vicious and violent prisons. I just left an extremely violent prison. I was awestruck by the torture which I witnessed in the U.S. prison system. And I kept reminding myself that 90 percent of these guys (in prison) are "coming home." Because abuse, dehumanization and evil are practiced in prisons etc. the prisons are a direct threat to our nation's security. There are guys in prison (in America) who have parole dates and they are planning to blow up planes and kill judges when they get out. And they can't get a job and don't have a place to stay when they get out. So they "study evil!"

...Oprah says that God sometimes allows horrible things to happen to you so that "you will *never* let it happen to somebody else." There was a reason He allowed Joseph to get locked up in prison on a sex crime that that he did *not* commit. God had a plan for Joseph's life. And He has a plan for my life. I will shine a light and people will find their own way. I will ask Narcisco Morales, Ryan Ferguson, Brian Banks, Daniel Kovarbasich and Alex King etc. to join me on this crusade. I will call *Jeff Deskovich* and even Angus T. Jones etc. I'll ask Lane Garrison to join the crusade. We have been through it. We need to be the new Rubin "Hurricane" Carters. We need to explain (over and over) to every day citizens "why" what goes on in prisons "must" be important to them. I want a *dynamic* (not the usual co-opted politics) team to help us do it.

I want to talk to Juan Escalante, Steve Wilheim, Raymond Flores (Citrus Heights), Tyler Grady, Callahan Walsh, *Mark Kersey* (in San Diego) and Tadd Carr. *Matthew McCormick* Jr. (in Chula Vista) was beat down (when he was only 16) by a San Diego police officer. And the cop got only a slap on the wrist. Matthew is somebody I want to work with. We want Tom Schaar, Benjamin Golden, Scott McCreery, Brandon Urbas, Joel Carpenter, Riley (the sixth man), Anthony Patera, Dr. Kyle Turner, Ricky Manning, Jordan Robbins, Jared Goodman, Nick Prato, Dylan Marron, Congressman Scott Peters, Hairo Torres, *Trenton Dorsey*, Kevin Lockhart, Mike Mowry, *Matt Fender*, Justin Styron, Charlie Puthi and *Reoh*. *Reoh* is a UC Berkeley student runner who is not defined by his disease — I won't even name his disease. But I want *Reoh* on our team. If you are reading I need you to email Reoh, Alex Bernhart and Eric Look etc. and tell 'em to get this book. And we need them...

What do we do to help men coming out of prisons? The answer is in St. Mark 6:34... Politics? Ben Carson says he is a devout Christian. And 'Donald' also claims (now) to be a Christian. Donald and Ben are summed up in St. Mark 7:6 – 7. I repeat: *Ben Carson is the third worst thing* (person) *to happen to black people*. And... The media buried *Tim Mak's* "rape" story on Donald... *Ben* and *Donald* ought to trade places with *O.J. Simpson*!...

The Republican Party is more afraid of the NRA than they are of ISIL (ask Paul Ryan or Ted Cruz). Even Donald is afraid of the NRA. Donald is a *coward* and this coward may be

a *rapist*. What kind of man says "my *daughter* is so sexy that if I were not married I'd *screw* my daughter?" Donald said that! He is a sick man… *O.J. Simpson* needs a cellmate…
www.NAPSUSA.org
ShermanDManning@Gmail.com
www.CafePress.com/Manning

www.ingramcontent.com/pod-product-compliance
Lightning Source LLC
Chambersburg PA
CBHW080339170426
43194CB00014B/2616